# THE POETIC CHARACTER OF HENRY REED

James S. Beggs

UNIVERSITY OF HULL PRESS

THE
UNIVERSITY
OF HULL
PRESS
Cottingham Road
Hull
HU6 7RX

A CIP catalogue record for this book is available from the British Library.



Published 1999

Paperback ISBN 0 85958 671 5



Printed by
LSL Press, Bedford, England

# ACKNOWLEDGMENTS

Many thanks are due my professors at the University of Tennessee: Dr Marilyn Kallet, Dr Allison Ensor, and especially Dr B. J. Leggett. I appreciate, too, the indulgences of my department chairpersons, Dr Steven Tabachnick, Dr Betty Inclan, and Mr Paul Neumann.

Thanks also go to Dr Robert Heilman and Mr Wesley Wehr, who consented to giving two interviews apiece and offered me the best insights into Henry Reed the man. The Cal-Berkeley library and vending machines gave me much-needed intellectual and physical sustenance.

My wife's parents, aunt, and uncle offered much tangible support (library runs to Berkeley, for example) and emotional support.

My students nobly studied 'Movement of Bodies', which may not be quite as good as I think it is.

My parents gave me a love of learning, a passion for words, and, most importantly, humility (I still can't beat the old guy in Scrabble).

I especially thank my wife Leslie for tolerating my workaholic tendencies and surviving many nights when I was out of town on research missions, or at home but not at home.

*DEDICATION*

*For my grandmother Irene Mable Holland Coats*

## NAMING OF PARTS

# A VERY GOOD MAN OF LETTERS, INDEED: APPRENTICESHIP AND CAREER

> "... the generous host, the often amiable, the oftener witty, the gaily ironic, the languidly pedagogical, the urbane censor morum, the gentle shepherd of his flocks and colleagues, Henry the tuneful Reed."
>
> *Robert B. Heilman*, memorandum to Henry Reed

'The man who wrote 'Naming of Parts'. Perhaps that is how most American students of literature would expect the Englishman Henry Reed to have filled in the 'Present title and position' space in 1963 when he applied for a Visiting Professorship at the University of Washington in Seattle. 'Independent writer' is what Reed actually wrote on his Washington biography sheet, which, looking at his fifty professional years, turns out to be a fair assessment. Except for an early one-year stint as a schoolmaster at King Edward VI School in Birmingham, which he had attended as a boy, Reed had been able to make a living entirely from his own ink. After working as a journalist for a time in his early twenties, he began to forge his literary career. It was a working life so diverse that one might muse, as Roger Savage has, 'Could there be two Henry Reeds perhaps, or even three?' (158)

There were actually four Henry Reeds: Reed the poet, Reed the radio playwright, Reed the translator, and Reed the critic. The latter two roles brought him the least renown and the least financial reward but consumed a large share of his energies for over half his life. His busiest work as a critic–of novels, radio programmes, and poetry for elite British periodicals–came in the five years after World War II, while in the next decade his opinions reached English audiences over the airwaves of the British Broadcasting Company. His translations and adaptations for stage and radio, of French and Italian drama primarily, were seen, read, and heard in the fifties, sixties, and seventies. The greatest legacy he left to his native literature was a large body of radio drama, both witty comedies set at home and more serious pieces, typically about young writers and artistic personalities, set in Italy. A half-dozen of these twenty-odd plays, if we include also his 1947 adaptation of *Moby Dick*, are artistic triumphs. The critics favoured his studies of Italian figures like the Duke of Gonzaga Vincenzo I or the poet Giacomo Leopardi, but English audiences may have appreciated most his recurring comic characters, notably the twelve-tone 'composeress' Hilda Tablet. As a poet, Reed is known by some for 'Chard Whitlow' (a parody of T. S. Eliot), but 'Naming of Parts', one of his *Lessons of the War*, remains his work best known to English and American readers. The publication of his *Collected Poems* in 1991 should expand his modest trans-atlantic reputation as the man who happened to write one of the Second World War's most celebrated poems.

Partly upon that reputation, no doubt, Reed was hired for the position in Seattle. The school terms he spent there in the mid-sixties are a blip on Henry Reed's screen. For the first and only extended period of his life, he was not earning his living by writing, and he seemed comfortable and happy. But when he was being considered for a full-time position, what must have seemed like sheer perversity led him to alienate his colleagues and department chairman in Seattle, and he was not offered a new contract.

Something nagged at Henry Reed. Many students at Washington did view him merely as the man who wrote 'Naming of Parts', and his friend Wesley Wehr had the sense that 'life was something that *used* to happen to Henry'. He had cultivated himself as a poet, had begun his career as a poet, and made his early name as a poet. What he had always admired most in other writers, of all genres, was their lyrical quality. And though whatever was pragmatic in him would not allow him to list his profession as 'Poet,' I believe he always perceived himself as a poet. At some point in his mostly sad and unfulfilled life, Reed discovered that his grooming for poetry had become an end in itself. He was a cultivated man, indeed an immaculately groomed man of letters, but he lacked the vigor and originality to be a great poet. Poetry, poets, and poetic personalities had infused nearly all his work, and he did make in his final years a noble return to some uncompleted lyrics from the 1950s. Henry Reed was a votary, a lifelong worshiper of poetry. He should be remembered also as a good man, a very good man of letters, and a good poet who wrote some great poems.

---

Inauspiciously, Henry Reed's life began, in Birmingham, England, on 22 February 1914.[1] The circumstances of Reed's birth on that chill day in no way seemed to point toward a fertile life of letters. His mother, Mary Ann Ball, was illiterate. His father, Henry Reed, though a lover of reading, was a very physical, hard-working man, a skilled bricklayer and foreman at Nocks' Brickworks. He was also a hard-playing man, a heavy drinker and womanizer who fathered, along with Henry and his older sister Gladys, an illegitimate son who died in the Second World War. The elder Reed's vocation and avocations were not likely to have helped cultivate the poetic sensibilities of his namesake. Moreover, in 1914 at least, the brawny west-midlands region of England suffered from a great intellectual identity crisis, with a wide gap perceived between London–Oxford–Cambridge and the rest of England's cultural and academic life.

The young poet-to-be had some advantages. Jon Stallworthy speculates that, ironically, some of Reed's literary proclivities may have come from his mother, with her 'remarkable memory' and her 'well-stocked repertoire of fairy-stories–told with great verve–and songs to enchant her children and grandchild' (Introduction to *Collected Poems* xi). At Birmingham University, he enjoyed the tutelage of men like E. R. Dodds and Louis MacNeice, and intellectual give-and-take from classmates who went on to accomplished careers in letters and the arts: George Painter, Walter Allen, Robert Melville, the sculptor Gordon

Herrick, and the painter John Melville. To be sure, he also received some financial support. The young writer's first trip to Italy in 1934, celebrated along with four later visits in Reed's 'wholly autobiographical' radio play *Return to Naples*, was financed by his father.

Still, Henry Reed made his ascent toward high culture and a life of poesy largely on his own. He earned a scholarship in 1931 for study at Birmingham and sped through his education with ardour and honours. His University of Washington biography sheet reports that he was awarded the Churton Collins Prize in English literature as an eighteen-year-old undergraduate, and he garnered the coveted Charles Grant Robertson Scholarship for graduate study in 1934. When he completed his thesis, *The Early Work of Thomas Hardy*, in 1936, he took first-class honours as Birmingham's youngest M.A.

Perhaps around this time, Reed made a vow similar to that of the young hero of *Leopardi*, his dramatic study of the great Italian poet: 'I am going to know/ All the books in the world and all the languages!' (23) One of the books for Reed was *Remembrances of Things Past*, into which he made vigorous youthful excursions with his classmate, Painter, who later dedicated the first volume of his Proust biography to Reed. His zest for reading, so finely cultivated early in his life, would later serve him well in his book-reviewing days in the late forties, when he would sometimes have to read and respond to three long novels in three weeks. He remained a hungry reader all his life: in a 1967 letter he remarks (matter-of-factly, in a post-postscript) that in '[t]hese last months' he had read *The Warden*, *Great Expectations*, the complete Carson McCullers and, for the second time, seventeen novels of Georges Simenon, most likely in the original.

Such fluency in French is evidence of the virtuosity Reed achieved in foreign tongues. Part of this accomplishment was sheer gift. But part was hard-won, gained through independent study, and clearly a conscious facet of his apprenticeship towards a grand literary career. He studied Classics in his adolescence and acquired Greek and Latin early on. The former was not taught at King Edward School, so he taught himself and had gained enough proficiency by 1951 to write a free adaptation of a Theocritus poem for Sir Arthur Bliss to set to music, as well as later earning a commission to translate Sophocles' *Ajax*. His Latin was good enough to win him the Temperley Latin Prize and his initial scholarship to Birmingham.

His Italian, honed by a second and third visit to Italy in 1936 and 1939, helped gain him a transfer from the Royal Army Ordnance Corps to the Italian section of the Government Code and Cypher School in 1942. For all the ineptness of the Army's way of doing things satirized by Reed in his war poems, his military superiors at least were perceptive enough to recognize his greater aptitude for languages than for learning 'to manage a bren gun, an anti-tank gun & various other kinds, to use a bayonet, to throw hand-grenades and whatnot and to fire at aircraft' (Letter to Gladys Winfield, in Stallworthy xiii). He was later transferred to the Japanese section, where he taught himself Japanese and worked as a translator. On the Washington biography form he modestly listed Latin as a language 'studied' rather than 'read readily', and, despite his knowledge of these languages, Japanese and Greek received no mention. Though his early delvings into Proust were probably conducted in English, his character in *Return to Naples* speaks French at least 'un peu' by his first Italian visit in 1934.[2] Given his special genius, though, along with his incentive to know the peoples and literature of the continent, we can be sure that fluency in this, the sixth of Reed's languages, followed soon after.

In fact, Reed was producing English adaptations of full-length French plays, as well as of Italian drama by playwrights like Pirandello and Ugo Betti, for the wireless by the early 1950s. Perhaps, though, a short piece he published as 'Imitation' in June 1950 says more about Reed's attitude toward languages: his tag identifying that poem as 'From the French of Arnauld and the Italian of Leopardi' speaks to his sometimes conspicuous erudition. Although they could not have earned him much more than a day's rent money, his sixteen lines indebted to two poets in two languages illustrate vividly another facet of his preparation for the life he would lead, 'often quite aggressively so', says Savage, 'as a Man of Letters, one of the literate intelligentsia' (160).

Languages, then, brought him another step closer to his goal of membership in the intelligentsia. Wide and frequent travel paid still another installment of his 'union dues'. It is significant, in fact, that shortly after Reed took his M.A., his first professional published pieces were travel articles, among his other journalistic duties at the *Birmingham Post* and *Manchester Guardian*. Research junkets, both on assignment for those periodicals and independent efforts to expand the Hardy work he had begun with his Master's thesis, took him to nearly every corner of the Isles, particularly the south and west of England. He travelled extensively on the continent as well, sharpening his language skills, which in turn deepened his European experience. Notable excursions included at least two more visits to Italy, in 1947 and 1950, and an extended holiday in Cyprus in 1948. An appearance in Greece was reported by J. R. Ackerley, Reed's friend and the longtime literary editor of the *Listener*, in 1960. Some of his journeys to Italy and Greece were funded by the BBC, and the research undertaken later helped shape his 'Italian' plays: *Naples*, *The Streets of Pompeii*, *The Great Desire I Had*, *The Unblest*, *The Monument*, and *Vincenzo*. In a life which included only one sustained romantic relationship, with a young writer named Michael Ramsbotham in the late 1940s, Italy was Reed's enduring passion, and these six plays, collected and published in 1971, he said 'constitute memorials, however ephemeral, to the love I have always felt for her' (Foreword to *The Streets of Pompeii*).

His frequent travel in Europe also further stoked his interest in painting, sculpture, and music (particularly opera); after all, a man of letters must be a man of all the arts.[3] *The Streets of Pompeii* and *Vincenzo*, particularly, include many loving meditations upon wonders of European art and architecture, including a Rubens nude, Giulio Romano's depiction of Troy, and the exedra of the Priestess of Mamia in Pompeii. Ten years after his graduation from Birmingham he was steeped enough too in contemporary art to report with elegant ease, in his Radio Notes column in the *New Statesman and Nation*, his praise for Robert Melville's radio elucidation of 'cross-breedings of cubism and fauvism' (25 October 1947, 329).[4]

In a *New Statesman* review of 1946, Reed comes just short of saying that the Mediterranean experience is necessary to 'an Englishman's education' (31 August; in Savage 176). In that review he implies the same about the Englishman's 'sensibility'. The reserved and flusterable '*H.*', as the cast list designates the autobiographical hero of *Return to Naples*,[5] is forced to reevaluate his English sensibility when confronted by the frankness and uninhibited sensuality of the Neapolitan family that more or less adopts him. When the family's matriarch asks him, 'Have you sweated?', just minutes after they have first met, he can only stammer: 'I ... I don't think I have swe ... psp ... persp ...' (180). He is further taken aback when she feels his chest and back to determine that he has indeed 'sweated'. Later, one of her sons reports ('*with real off-handedness*') to *H.* that his tryst with an Austrian woman has gone 'Quite well, yes. Twice' (204). During those two hours, *H.* has been at a bookshop, reading *Three Contributions to the Theory of Sex*. It seems clear that Reed found the bluntness and spontaneity of the Italian family (or the Mediterranean personality in general) an important counter to his (or the Englishman's) inclination towards emotional tentativeness and caution, even repression of natural feelings. Though he ultimately concedes that 'experience of the South Seas, China, Russia and India' is also vital, to Reed it is always Italy–the land, its language, art, and people–which exerts 'a strange power of benediction' over the English artist (Savage 176).

At least in these early years, the cosmopolitan Henry Reed was still trying to repudiate the image of Hal (as he was known to his family) the provincial Reed. There is no small embarrassment in *H.*'s tone as he describes to the young Alberto the three 'piazzas' of Birmingham, one named after 'An engineer, I think'. When prompted by the wide-eyed boy, he plays an unconvincing apologist for his birthplace: '(*after thought*) Yes. Yes, Alberto, there is much splendour in Birmingham' (175). A lowbrow stigma still clung to the city, its region, even its university. Reed's friend and classmate Walter Allen, a literary critic, wrote in his memoirs that a 'university man' in the thirties was either an Oxford or a Cambridge graduate, with no other alma mater meriting consideration. In the late twenties and early thirties, the arrival on the literary scene of Auden, born in Birmingham, and then MacNeice, who taught at the University, helped dispel that perception. In time, Allen wrote, 'It became a point of honour to assert that I was a graduate of Birmingham, thank you' (28). Nevertheless, Jon Stallworthy reports, as late as 1943 Reed was renouncing the region of his youth, adopting 'a somewhat Sitwellian manner', having lost (or perhaps affected the loss of) his Birmingham accent (xiv). An 'elegant butterfly', says Stallworthy, was 'struggling to break free from the Brummagem[6] chrysalis' (xii).

Perhaps in compensation for the perceived deficiencies of his upbringing and education, Reed acquired all the manner, and mannerisms, of the standard English intellectual of the 1930s. It is hard to believe that Reed took no license in *Return to Naples* with the facts of his own life, but if we do accept his insistence on the authenticity of the autobiography, we can admit *H.*'s reports (usually elicited by blunt and guileless questions from the Neapolitans) that he was in the thirties both a socialist–with great reservations about the 'Duce' (Mussolini) whom the family so reveres–and a religious sceptic who was raised Protestant but no longer practised the faith. To complement his adopted politics and theology, he took up smoking and began his lifelong relationship with alcohol. The first blush of the affair must have been exciting, and drink no doubt fueled his famous wit at gatherings. And though Reed did not adopt the ultimate mannerism of dying from drink before the age of forty like Dylan Thomas, alcohol certainly hastened the onset of poor health in his later years. Apparently, Reed played a little tennis in the 1930s,[7] and in the 1960s he and Elizabeth Bishop dabbled in some exercises prescribed by the military manual. But robust athlete-intellectuals like Rex Warner were rare, certainly not the norm in Reed's day and in his circle. His was a sedentary life of the mind–strolling through a hall of paintings or standing in front of a sculpture, sitting in a theatre seat or in front of a typewriter or in his heavy armchair, or across two glasses of wine from another intellectual–in which the heaviest task of lifting might be to empty an ashtray or reposition *Ulysses* on one's lap.

Finally, while one cannot quite term homosexuality a mannerism, Reed by the forties certainly had discovered he was attracted to men. Homosexuality was then still a major scandal in the bourgeois world, but in the literary circles of mid-century it might be winked at. Indeed, if an artist's sexual preference were not flaunted in an undignified way, it might even raise his literary stock just a little by focusing more sharply his image as an artist alienated from the common herd. Reed was always discreet, never predatory toward his students, and rarely toward any young boys, as his friend Joe Ackerley was. The homosexuality of many writers in Reed's generation and the one before–Ackerley, Auden, Christopher Isherwood, and E. M. Forster, to name a few–seems not to have affected their careers too adversely. In Reed's case, it may even have offered a greater access to the unfettered minds and hearts of women, resulting in 'an extraordinary sympathy with women's most profound emotions' and the gift for portraying them 'with tenderness and understanding' (Cleverdon, cited in Stallworthy xv-xvi). But Reed's sexual orientation, too, possessed just the slightest hint of pose, a cultivated differentness that made him feel more like an artist.[8]

Of course, Reed was not always consumed with simply behaving somehow like a writer. He was writing. His first publication, apart from his articles in newspapers and contributions to the Birmingham literary magazine, was 'The Captain', which appeared in the *Listener*, titled simply 'Poem', in December 1937. A witty and sometimes uproarious sequence of poems called 'Green, Spleen, & c'. had also been completed by 1940 but remained unpublished in his lifetime. Four other poems saw print by the end of the decade. Surprisingly, Reed's fledgling career was slowed little by the war; one might rather say his conscription into the Royal Army Ordnance Corps in the summer of 1941 merely redirected it. Although his *Lessons of the War* (three of which were composed before he was 'demobbed' on V-J Day) and a later poem called 'Psychological Warfare' satirize the monotony and ineptitude of training methods[9] and convey a keen wistfulness for civilian life, Reed in all truth had a good war. Unlike his own half-brother and fellow British poets Alun Lewis, Keith Douglas and Sidney Keyes, he survived the conflict and in fact never saw action. He wrote to John Lehmann, editor of *New Writing and Daylight*, that his time was mostly consumed by marching, drilling, weapons training, and 'learning to be a clerk' (Lehmann 168). Reed chose to view even these years as part of his apprenticeship. He always insisted that he not so much served as 'rather *studied*' in the Ordnance Corps, and it was there that he entertained his fellows with comic imitations of their military instructors. These impromptu performances were dry runs of sorts for the distinctive sergeant-voice that carries so much impact in his six major war poems. They were further development, too, of the theatrical aspirations that he had shown in his acting and producing forays as an undergraduate and hinted at the dramatic career that awaited him on the other side of the war.

During his year in the RAOC, later while convalescing from pneumonia, and especially while working in the Foreign Office, he was able to work on his radio adaptation of *Moby Dick* and many of the poems which later appeared in *A Map of Verona*.

Lehmann published a few of these poems during the war years as well as an essay, 'The End of an Impulse'. Reed's first major critical piece was a jeremiad on the decline of lyric poetry, victimized, according to Reed, by protégés of Dylan Thomas, whose tendency to 'shout', and of the Auden-Spender-Day Lewis group, whose overuse of near-rhyme and relaxation of an 'already liberal [rhythmic] pulse' were turning verse into merely 'a series of arbitrarily divided prose statements' (121). Lehmann called Reed's own prose statements the kind 'a young poet or critic writes who is preparing to lead a literary revolution' (169).

However, as Lehmann added, 'No vigorous pursuit of the enemy ... took place' (169). Perhaps Reed was too busy having a literary career to lead a literary revolution. Soon after V-J Day, it was clear that Reed was a literary man, fully bonded and insured: the long apprenticeship was over. In only one of his four literary arenas, his translating, had he not yet appeared publicly, though all the groundwork had been done: in just three years would appear *The Monument*, part one of his dramatization of the life of Leopardi, with numerous embedded translations of that poet, and in three more his first translation from the French, a radio adaptation of Henri de Montherlant's *Malatesta*. By war's end his career as a critic, poet, and dramatist was flourishing. In fact, 1946 proved to be Reed's modest *annus mirabilis*. *A Map of Verona*, in its London edition, came out early in the year and was on the whole very well received; a half-again larger edition with expanded notes by the poet was published in New York the next year. Reed's first radio piece, *Noises*, was produced in March,[10] and *Moby Dick* entered rehearsals at the year's end, to be broadcast in January 1947 (with Ralph Richardson as Ahab), just four months before *Pytheas*, Reed's third radio offering. In his novel-reviewing and criticism he had proved himself, as Lehmann put it, to be 'an ungullible critic and no respecter of reputations' (169). In addition to the poets he had chastised in 'The End of an Impulse', respected writers of fiction–Evelyn Waugh, Nabokov, Kafka, and Hemingway among them–also were finding their reputations disdained by the young critic.

Also appearing in 1946 was his longest critical piece, a British Council pamphlet called *The Novel since 1939*, which included many generous assessments of novels and novelists alongside the severe ones. As always, the aggressive erudition seared through his critical work. In *The Novel since 1939*, he dismissed any discussion of 'best-sellers', insisting on discussions only of serious fiction from the viewpoint of 'an intellectual addressing intellectuals' (7). Even more brazenly, he began a review in the *New Statesman* of earlier that year with the words, 'Everybody will remember that encouraging moment on page 108 of *Finnegans Wake* when ...' (2 February, 89).[11]

The last years of the forties brought more reviewing tasks, for the *New Statesman and Nation* and the *Listener* primarily, including the 'Radio Notes' feature in *New Statesman* from late 1947 through early 1948. The next decade was Reed's busiest at the BBC: fourteen of his original plays were broadcast. *The Streets of Pompeii* (1952) won the Italia prize, a prestigious award that was conferred also on MacNeice and on Dylan Thomas (for *Under Milk Wood* in 1954). British radio scholars Savage and David Wade both cite four of these plays as making lasting contributions to radio literature; *The Streets of Pompeii* and *Vincenzo* are at the intersection of their lists.[12] During this period, Reed also became something of a radio personality, giving numerous talks on Eliot, Joyce, Hardy, and literary issues such as the place of verse drama in contemporary literature, and participating in round table discussions with other poets of the day, including Cecil Day Lewis and Laurie Lee.

Reed's radio discussions of literary figures were unfortunately symptomatic of his career's heavy reliance on other writers. If Reed styled himself an 'Independent writer' in 1963, the previous decade, his most productive as a man of letters, showed just what a *dependent* writer he had become. At the peak of that decade, for instance, no fewer than three of Henry Reed's stage plays opened in London during a single season, the fall of 1955; in truth, however, they were his *translations*, of Ugo Betti, the

Italian playwright who had died two years earlier and whose work and reputation Reed promoted throughout the decade. Other of Reed's 'dependent' works of the fifties included published translations of two novels by Balzac and one by the Italian Paride Rombi, as well as adaptations of continental writers for radio broadcast, including Laforgue, de Montherlant, Pirandello, Virginio Puecher, Samy Fayad, Jacques Audiberti, and Silvio Giovaninetti.

All the while, through his radio work and written criticism he was continuing to champion the work of English-speaking giants. His continuing interest in Herman Melville had begun during the war, when he composed much of what became his 'formidable' radio version of *Moby Dick*, written, according to Wade, 'as if its adapter had conceived it all himself' (*British Radio Drama* 226). His advocacy of Melville continued with a highly laudatory and keenly perceptive review of 'Billy Budd' in May of that year and was to reemerge much later in a second *Moby Dick* broadcast (with a revised ending) in 1979. The *raison d'etre* of a critic's trade, of course, is the artists whose work he illuminates, and several of those were even more acknowledged giants than Melville: Joyce, Eliot (Reed was an especial advocate for *The Cocktail Party* and other verse drama) and, most religiously, Thomas Hardy. For twenty years he had been working on a biography of Hardy (it was never completed), and he continued to keep the great poet and novelist in the ears of British listeners through his radio talks and his adaptation of *The Dynasts*, broadcast in six parts in 1951. Reed's print and radio criticism, as well as on-air readings, also promoted the work of other masters, ranging widely from Yeats and Whitman to Daniel Defoe. He also offered qualified praise of the novels of Charles Williams and Robert Penn Warren and was a rather early proponent of Eudora Welty's fiction.[13]

Even the most witty and creative work of Reed relied on the efforts of other, greater artists. His narrative poems and dramatic monologues, for example 'Tristram', 'Chrysothemis',

'Philoctetes', and 'Antigone', of course take as their ultimate source the Greek oral tradition or a Greek artist's rendering of that tradition. In the Foreword to the plays of his *Streets of Pompeii* collection, he offers a sort of blanket disclaimer against plagiarism, conceding that the 'learning' found in *Streets* and the four non-autobiographical plays is

> the learning of others, which I have stolen, adapted, malformed, sometimes inverted, and almost invariably fantasised over ... Readers who know my sources will be able to blame or pardon me accordingly.

But recognizing in these plays, for example, long passages from the Leopardi poems Reed translated as 'To Himself' and 'The Broom', beautiful and usually apt lines, one is inclined to pardon Reed's borrowings.[14]

At times, though, it seems that Reed's wide learning was more of a curse than a boon. It often narrowed his audience, as he testily and unrepentantly acknowledged in 1949: 'Some listeners are fools, and some are not, and we cannot wait for the fools to catch up to their betters' (*BBC Quarterly*, cited in Savage 160). And whenever Reed brought his act to an audience, it was as if he opened a suitcase full of Eliots, Leopardis, Balzacs, and Hardys who might at any time shove him off to the wings and commandeer Reed's show. Indeed, at worst Reed the 'dependent' writer was guilty of unconscious parroting of others, especially Eliot, as numerous critics including John Lehmann and Frank Kermode have observed. Henry Rago, reviewing *A Map of Verona* for The *Commonweal*, found some of the lines in 'Chard Whitlow', Reed's intentional parody of Eliot, to be 'indistinguishable from his more sober efforts' (16 January 1948, 353). But in 'Chard Whitlow' itself the parody is deft and incisive, as even Eliot acknowledged, recognizing Reed as the best parodist of his work that he had encountered (MacDonald 218).[15] And in the plays centring on the biographer Herbert Reeve and the twelve-tone composer Hilda Tablet, part of the reader's pleasure is derived from a knowledge of the words of someone else. In these, Reed wittily parodies many victims, some topical and obscure, but most within the grasp of reasonably educated listeners. The kind of popular music lyrics his young character Brian Shewin pens in *The Primal Scene, As It Were...*, with their hypercorrected grammar and pseudo-urbanity, are recognizable to any generation:

> Yes, something was wrong then,
> Between you and I,
> And oh, I could see
> From the look in your eye,
> That *arrivederci*
> Meant 'good-bye'. (172)

At two other levels of accessibility to listeners are his parodies of the language of many canonical and contemporary novelists –James, Lawrence, and Graham Greene, for example–as well as that of his own BBC's Third Programme (Savage 168-9).

All the radio work of Reed in the fifties (and on through the next two decades) is given much of the blame by several critics for the comparatively sparse poetic output of his later years. John Lehmann lamented that, 'very soon after the war and the publication of his first book, Henry Reed abdicated from poetry' (169). Lehmann and others hint that the abdication may have had some compulsion behind it, and that the usurper was the BBC. Elizabeth Jennings, citing also Terence Tiller, observes that the BBC had a way of inadvertently staunching the flow of poetry from the writers on its staff (1253-4). Savage, too, writes that Reed 'soldiered on' with his radio plays for the BBC, which 'was perhaps too welcoming' of talents like Reed, Louis MacNeice, and Edward Sackville-West at the expense of their employees' other creative aspirations (163). Over a period of nearly twenty years, beginning in the summer of 1950, Reed published only three poems. The third of these, his fine narrative poem 'The Auction Sale', owing much of its dual-voiced manner to Reed's great *Lessons of the War*, appeared in *Encounter* in 1956. 'The Auction Sale' is surely one of the 'hopeful signs'

Lehmann observed in an afternote to his 1960 autobiography that Reed's 'long exile' from poetry might be over (169).

Lehmann's hopes proved to be unfounded, at least for the next decade, during which Reed remained busy for the BBC. The purest of his creative work for British radio, however, was over: he had produced no original plays in a serious vein after the mid-fifties, and the last of his comedies (or radio 'pieces' as he called them) in the Shewin-Tablet series was broadcast in October of 1959. All of his radio work in the sixties was translation and adaptation, of Betti, Dino Buzzati, Romain Weingarten, and Natalia Ginzburg, whose short play *The Advertisement* was broadcast in 1968 and became the last of Reed's published translations.

Along with Reed's angst over the drying-up of his poetic well was likely a sense that his personal life was careening. He was drinking more than ever and, after the relative stability of his homosexual relationship twenty years earlier, his graspings at love and sexual fulfillment had taken an air of increasing desperation. Perhaps these factors led to his signing of the document that shaped his life of the mid-sixties: his application for a Visiting Professor position at the University of Washington. The chairman of the English department there was Robert B. Heilman, a Shakespearean scholar who in his earlier years had been associated with Cleanth Brooks, Robert Penn Warren and others in the New Critical movement. In a letter to this writer (9 July 1993), Heilman recalled that he and Reed met during one of Heilman's sabbaticals in London, possibly through their mutual interest in English theatre. When Theodore Roethke died in 1963, the void was filled by Visiting Poets, among them Elizabeth Bishop and Vernon Watkins, and supporting actors like Reed who took Visiting Professorships. Reed's post freed him from the duties of teaching lower-level composition classes or sitting on committees; he was expected, instead, to teach the 'Roethke' courses (in the study of and the writing of poetry) and other upper-level and graduate literature seminars and surveys, as well as deliver lectures or give readings.

Though Stallworthy reports that Reed hated his early year of schoolteaching in the 1930s, at this point in his life he came to appreciate it.[16] According to Heilman's assistant Dorothee Bowie, he enjoyed the opportunity to show his expertise and knowledge because 'he knew he was good'. A tenderer side of Reed the teacher comes through in a handwritten note to Heilman thanking him for his kind attentions to Reed's students at an end-of-term party: 'I know, from repeated telephone calls, that the KIDS were delighted. And that is what we are *here* for' (6 June 1966). Though he found American students a joy, they were also a source of frustration. Especially at this time in the 1960s, in his view they seemed to think that all poetry was haiku or free verse. He and Bishop commiserated over their students' complete lack of understanding of both the poetic tradition and the craft of poetry, of metrics particularly. Still, Reed would have agreed with the appraisal of his Birmingham classmate Walter Allen, who also taught in the United States: 'American students, who are, by and large, considerably less well prepared than their English counterparts, are often because of this more keen and responsive, as if suddenly waking up to the pleasures of learning' (264).

By nearly all accounts, Henry Reed was an excellent teacher.[17] Sandra Kroupa, now a Special Collections librarian at the University, was one student who appreciated the discipline his teaching provided. Admittedly one of the sloppy students who came to his course with the idea that poetry was just emotional gush on paper, she greatly valued the many exercises he gave forcing her and her classmates to set their poetic ideas into shapes and forms. Henry Carlile, a poet now teaching at Portland State University, found Reed to be 'a wonderful teacher, a great reader of poetry' who insisted his students learn to write sestinas, villanelles, and sonnets (Fountain and Brazeau 216). Reed could certainly be sneering toward many on the faculty he considered provincial, and downright uncivil toward others; in the classroom, however, he reined back his notoriously ironic tongue. With his students, said Heilman in a 1993 interview with this writer, he conveyed a 'sense of ease' and 'camaraderie'; 'his wit was not corrosive' toward fledgling writers who had not arrived at the level of smug mediocrity he felt Washington colleagues like Rolfe Humphries and Nelson Bentley had attained.

And, although there must have been painfully lonely times in his sparsely decorated rooms in the Wilsonian Hotel, Reed loved Seattle. That love for Seattle may have been his peace-making with Birmingham. For all its beauty, Seattle offered barely more sunshine than Reed's birthplace, and, although he especially favoured Ballard, a Scandinavian part of town, he also loved the industrial Seattle: the factories, the rugged docks, and the shipping and fishing centres. He celebrated all these elements in what Wesley Wehr, presently a paleobotanist at the Burke Museum in Seattle, calls Reed's 'Northwest' poem, now apparently lost, a long comic piece with all 'the Henry Reed twists and turns to it' which the poet tested before a small audience in his Wilsonian apartment. It prominently featured the words *salmon* and *clam*.[18]

For the most part, Reed seemed indifferent to the Pacific Northwest's natural charms, be they clams, whale migrations, or the great Mt. Rainier. But the city offered Reed plenty of social and intellectual stimulation. Seattle was and is a unique 'college town' which is also a large, vibrant city, so presumably Reed could always find enough of cultural interest between visiting speakers and artists on campus and music and theatre around town. Fortunately for a man who never drove a car, the pocket of town surrounding campus was replete with good bookstores, restaurants, cafes, even pubs in the English style. And Seattle and the University in the late fifties and early sixties formed a yeasty centre for literary and artistic activity to rival Kenyon College, Vanderbilt or Heilman's own Louisiana State of earlier decades. There was of course Roethke, the giant talent and ego who dominated before Reed's arrival in 1964. But in those ten to fifteen years, the list of other poets and writers who came through the University is also impressive: Bishop, Vernon

Watkins, David Gascoyne, Léonie Adams, Carolyn Kizer, James Wright, David Wagoner, Mark Strand, and Richard Eberhart.

Part of Bishop's term as Visiting Poet corresponded with Reed's year as a Lecturer in English, 1965-6. Wehr says that Reed was Bishop's 'grounding wire' when the two were colleagues at Washington. Once, he responded to a last-minute call to 'pinch hit' for Bishop when she became ill on the day of a reading she was to give at Parrington Hall, even though his opening remarks reveal his distaste for the local fashion: 'I share with Miss Bishop a disapproval of poetry readings–but since they are all the go here, I shall read today'. Though Bishop's presence buoyed Reed, made him feel a part of poetry again, their relationship had its unhealthy side. According to Heilman, 'Henry was very much inclined to be ironically condescending to the rest of the ordinary world and he brought out that side in Elizabeth'. Often, when Reed and Bishop were to be picked up by Heilman and his wife for some occasion, 'they took a certain pleasure of making us, as bourgeois, just sit in the car and wait'. Bishop and Reed were brought together by their interest in travel and sense of alienation from their own country and countrymen, and, unfortunately, by their abuse of alcohol. As poets, perhaps they felt further alienated from others, though their homosexuality, like a two-poled magnet, may have exerted the strongest pull away from 'the rest of the ordinary world' and toward each other. The alienation at times metamorphosed into a sense of superiority over the provincials. At times this manifested itself in the harmless diversion of reading bad sentences from student papers to each other over the phone (Millier 377). At other times it showed forth as sniping against fellow poets like Eberhart, in the same way that Reed was always carping at his fellow Hardy scholars like the American R. L. Purdy for any number of crimes in accuracy or interpretation.

Heilman and others speculate that, at least for Reed's part, the snidery was part of a usually reined-in bitterness, or even jealousy, toward other literary people who had 'made it'. Sandra

Kroupa had a sense that Reed felt his best creative work was hopelessly behind him, that, his teaching excellence not withstanding, he was in some ways an ageing, pitiable man hanging on to the withered laurels from his one great poem. His attitude towards other literary people might show itself in good-spirited remarks, as in a letter bemoaning how Purdy was working on Hardy's letters 'with a zest that shames me every time I contemplate it'. Or it might turn much darker, as in the inexcusable cruelty with which Heilman believes Reed and Bishop treated Rolfe Humphries, an elderly colleague with a portfolio of workmanlike poems and respected translations. Humphries was an even older, more pitiable man who would seem to have been beneath Reed's wrath, the kind of soft target, like an obviously weak student whose work would never be held up for derision, at whom Reed was generally classy enough not to aim his scorn. But perhaps in Humphries, Reed saw what he was afraid he himself would soon enough become: an old man with only some workmanlike poems and respected translations to his name.

Wehr speaks of a tendency, even a need, among certain artists on the one hand to create beautiful, crafted things in their art and, on the other, to 'defile' their personal lives in some sort of inarticulate revolt. In the end, Henry Reed defiled the good thing he had in Seattle. To Bishop's dismay, he fell progressively out of touch, as he often had with Bliss and Ackerley before and as he would later with Heilman and Walter Allen. Heilman says that he behaved as a model man and colleague in his Visiting terms, but during his full year, when he was being considered for a permanent position, he became a 'dreadful pest', complaining about his teaching schedule and calling to be driven somewhere at inconvenient times. He was not asked to return.

The last productive decade of his literary life, the 1970s, began on a reinvigorating note. In October 1970 an excellent war poem, 'Returning of Issue', was published in the *Listener* and later that year collected with 'Movement of Bodies' and Reed's original three *Lessons of the War* into a beautiful limited edition. The rest of the decade, though, settled into the same routine as the previous one. His BBC productions again were strictly translations and adaptations, with just one addition to his repertoire (Giuseppe Giacosa) alongside further works by Pirandello and Ginzburg. Reed surely awakened one morning in the early 1970s–if indeed the dawning had not occurred earlier–to the realization that the creative spark for radio was snuffed completely and it would be more and more difficult to kindle his poetic spark into flame. He no longer felt like a poet. He was a Man of Letters.

Perhaps the shame in that appellation was acute only when held up against the great promise of the mid-forties, when 'Naming of Parts' and 'Chard Whitlow' and even *Moby Dick* seemed ready to confer the title of Poet upon Henry Reed. For though Reed was now merely a Literary Man, he was a very good one, embracing all the qualities of such a man beyond those which barely paid his bills. He had remained active on only one of his major writing fronts, that is, his translations and adaptations of continental writers. But he was still a man whose work and opinion were greatly esteemed, if rarely remunerated.

In the last three decades of his professional life, for example, he was widely appreciated and sought as an adapter, critic, and editor of the work of others. Sir Arthur Bliss said that he had really no one else in mind when he looked for a lyricist for two projects: an adaptation of Theocritus and a group of modern madrigals for the coronation of Elizabeth II in 1953.[19] When J. R. Ackerley was shopping a screenwriter for his novel *Hindoo Holiday*, Reed was the man whose gifts he coveted (*Letters* of Ackerley 276).[20] When Walter Allen 'dreamed a poem' one night or rather 'dreamed what [he] thought might become a poem', he diffidently sent the resulting typescript off to Reed for scrutiny (64). Ackerley, himself acknowledged as a gifted editor, once at least was 'taken down a number of pegs' by Reed after innocently sending to his friend a manuscript for a new edition of *Hindoo Holiday*. Reed liked it but returned gently, 'I hope you'll take the opportunity of correcting its grammar' (*Letters* 250). Embarrassed but curious, Ackerley worked with Reed and was 'astounded' yet thankful for the mortifying changes that had to be made on nearly every page before the piece went off to press. Ackerley later wrote that if he 'disappeared', Reed would be his second choice after E. M. Forster to pass on the proofs of a second novel to his publisher (*Letters* 122*n*.).[21]

Reed in fact became something of a curator of the purity of the English language. To some, this insistence on precision in diction, along with his ardent rejection of neologisms, might seem overly fastidious. But Heilman, who shared Reed's love of Latin and 'grammatical, linguistic, and stylistic appropriateness', saw no 'literalness and rigidity' in his friend's strictures. 'What I sensed in Henry', he says, 'was rather what seemed to me good taste' which was 'intolerant of journalistic errors, loosenesses in the use of words'. Reed's passion for correctness in the use of the language shows ironically in his great war poems and his best satirical plays, where his characters misuse the language sometimes blatantly, as well as in more subtle ways which do not escape Reed's ear. But his satire is not strident, as he gently exposes the common speaker's proneness (especially in stressful or on-the-spot situations) to wordiness, vagueness, malapropisms, and pretentious or bureaucratic language. Though not quite possessing Orwell's insight into the dangers of misused language, Reed was on the other hand neither reactionary nor schoolmarmish. He was simply a man of taste. 'I never knew Henry to even come out with something uncouth', says Dorothee Bowie. 'He just didn't–not that he didn't *know* it all'.

Reed was expected by his friends to 'know it all', not just in questions of linguistics, but in matters political, literary, and historical. Kenneth Allott and Stallworthy speak of his prodigious memory, especially for quotations from Shakespeare. Robert Heilman was himself, in Walter Allen's words, a 'redoubtable scholar' (269); in a between-terms letter to Reed in London, Heilman nevertheless seeks his friend's advice on some troubling quotations–none apparently more than a two-word phrase–which he cannot place. That Reed was consulted by one of such erudition bespeaks Henry Reed's reputation as a man of learning who Heilman says had 'a far better knowledge of the history of English than most American Ph.D.s'. Reed's responses, while thin on substance, exhibit his usual wit and a refreshing self-deprecation. 'Agreeable distresses' he suggests may be from 'The Duenna', though he hopes it is a misprint of 'agreeable mistresses'. 'Whenever in doubt', Reed advises, 'attribute to George Sand'. He also had an extraordinary memory for dates–even those 'of not any particular prominence', recalls Heilman–in history and literary history. His delivery of these arcana was more as a 'jest' or 'game', adds Heilman, never in a mode of putdown or showoff.

The game was often played at social gatherings, where Reed would almost always 'perform' and where he would always drink too much. By his later years, many of his mannerisms had congealed into tiresome habit. Indeed, Reed's affectations as a Literary Man began to take on at least a hint of the pathetic. Reed was always a gracious and generous host, but he was also a lingering guest, one who Heilman and Ackerley report was inclined to stay as long as alcohol was available.[22] In London he also did much of his drinking at the Savile Club, with its long tradition as the noted haunt of many literary greats. But even the Savile, from its heady days of Hardy, Yeats, Henry James and Robert Louis Stevenson, had slipped a rung or two by Reed's time and could boast at best Cecil Day Lewis and Stephen Potter among its membership. In these days, too, Reed was a bit too inclined to mention his connections in the theatre world, for example the rising Shakespearean actor Derek Jacobi and the solidly entrenched legend Laurence Olivier. Heilman concedes that Reed probably did have an 'adequate acquaintance' with Olivier, but especially after the 'Sir' had been conferred upon the great actor, 'Henry would say repeatedly, "I, of course, call him *Larry*"'. Reed had attended all rehearsals of his radio plays in the fifties, but likely he was less welcome in the seventies. His life was accelerating towards anti-climax.

In the last decade of his life, too, poor health, poor eyesight, and financial difficulties greatly limited his output. 'Yet prowling round the three or four poems from the 50s I still want to finish', he wrote in a moment of what passed for optimism during those years, 'occasional jerks forward do occur' (in Stallworthy xvii-xviii). Those forward jerks apparently brought closer to completion a fragment, 'The Sound of Horses' Hooves', which Stallworthy includes in *Collected Poems*, along with 'The Vow' and '[*L'Envoi*]', the lovely poem which ends the collection. Reed's notebook entries and a series of letters from Walter Allen to mutual friend Heilman chronicle Reed's physical decline. He had spent some time in hospital in 1980 and complained of arthritis; 'God knows it is very painful to move about', he wrote in a notebook entry of March 1985. Though Allen had remarked in 1973 that Reed seemed to be healthy and drinking less, alcohol and Complan seemed to be his only sustenance near the end.

In 1981 Allen wrote, 'I'm afraid I now think he's unhelpable, though I'm glad he seems always able to get help'. What kind of help Allen means is uncertain, though in his last years Reed needed and received not just medical but also financial help. Reed had set up and then neglected a 'nest-egg' account while in Seattle, into which Dorothee Bowie had periodically deposited her own money to keep the account afloat. His landlady in London apparently forgave him many a non-payment. In his March 1985 notebook entry, he wrote that 'The Income Tax, and [his] all but paralysed will about it', draped a pall over all he did. Perhaps, though, even the British government was charmed by this man as the Navy had been forty years earlier, when he did not report after having been called to service and the 'matter [was] silently dropped' (*Who's Who*). He likewise seemed to have the quality both to endear himself to and to vex those who cared about him despite his failings as a correspondent. Many had no recourse but to lament to others that Reed had not been in touch. Allen's letters to Heilman seem to echo Bishop's plea to Wesley Wehr that 'HR MIGHT write me!!' (26 February 1967). His December 1980 letter seems to sigh: 'I've written to him two or three times and had no reply. Peggy will be dropping a christmas [*sic*] card to him in a day or two, dropping, I don't doubt, into a bottomless void'. In a letter of May 1982, Allen writes that he had sent Reed a copy of his recently published memoirs five months earlier but had received no answer, attributing the non-response to Reed's 'normal pathological indolence'. The references to Reed become shorter and sadder. In 1985: 'Henry has passed out of our life entirely, and as far as I can see everyone else's too'.

Almost all of Reed's friends remembered not just the sad severing of ties but how Reed magically passed *into* their lives or returned to them after long absences. Bliss called him 'the most elusive of my friends ... with the faculty of sudden appearance and sudden disappearance' (191). Ackerley wrote once of how Henry Reed 'suddenly materialised' (*Letters* 165). All of these lives he enriched, though how much joy they were able to bring into his world is less evident. Certainly in his life there were pockets of peace: in his one extended romantic relationship, with Michael Ramsbotham in the forties; in a theatre seat in front of a well-produced opera or play; or, even better, in the euphoric day or two after he would turn in his just-under-the-deadline radio scripts and breathe in the freshness of early rehearsals with the actors he loved. But his life in between welled up with episodes of sharp loneliness: an early 'tormented affair with a boy who developed paranoia' (Stallworthy xii); '[making] himself scarce' so Joe Ackerley can pick up a 'pretty' Turkish boy in Greece, 1960; a scene in London in which a young man, plied all afternoon with Reed's champagne, throws up in a taxi; a hopeless attraction to Derek Jacobi; a cold, bleak day, Thanksgiving 1967, as he pecks out letters to Seattle friends from his moth-eaten flat at 9 Upper Montagu Street in London; or an even colder, bleaker first of December as sleet, rain, and snow fall in London and he stares at nineteen unanswered letters and waits for a man to fix his water heater. In January 1986 Walter Allen, his classmate, longtime friend, and fellow literary man, wrote to Heilman, 'I haven't had a cheep out of Henry for five years'. On another cold day, less than a year later, Henry Reed died.

Three days after Reed's death on 8 December 1986, Douglas Cleverdon, who had published the 1970 edition of Reed's great *Lessons of the War* and produced most of his radio plays, wrote in an obituary for the *Independent*, 'he was not only a poet of *great* sensibility; he also had a lively sense of comedy and of the absurd, and a remarkable gift for dramatic invention' (in Stallworthy xv). His friend's adjectives are rather modest for a eulogy: the one great which Cleverdon dispenses is really just a synonym for *much*, modifying a narrow aspect of Reed's literary gift. In fact, it seems that Reed went directly from apprentice to journeyman, unfortunately bypassing master altogether. Most of Henry Reed's work fell short of the grandly tragic or profoundly lyrical. Perhaps his life did not offer enough materials. He lived through nothing comparable to Melville's 'unimaginable crowded years' of experience aboard trading vessels, whalers, and men-of-war (Preface to *Moby Dick* 5), nor to the contact with lower classes of people experienced by Melville, Joyce, and Hardy. He lacked the high religious impulse of Eliot. There was nothing in Reed's physical ills–arthritis, weak eyesight, liver complications–to rival the sheer romance of Leopardi's hunchback, sustained through years of loveless, punishing study in his father's library.

Many great works have been produced by hardworking, journeyman literary people of no sustaining genius. Significantly, at the end of his introduction to *Collected Poems*, Jon Stallworthy quotes Randall Jarrell's contention that a 'good poet is someone who manages in a lifetime of standing out in thunderstorms to be struck by lightning five or six times: a dozen and he is great' (xxiii). 'By this criterion', says Stallworthy, neglecting to make clear whether he is referring to the criterion for 'goodness' or 'greatness', Stallworthy makes some place for Henry Reed in the poetic pantheon. Jarrell is an interesting authority to cite, since he, along with Ambrose Bierce, is the best example of the 'Reed syndrome' from this side of the ocean. The greatness of their signature war pieces eclipses the frequent excellence of their other work. No one can gainsay, for example, the brilliant wit of Bierce's *The Devil's Dictionary* or the wrenching pathos of Jarrell's 'The Woman at the Washington Zoo'. As we ought not allow the lifetime accomplishment of Jarrell to be overshadowed by the perfection of 'The Death of the Ball Turret Gunner', so let us allow great works like 'The Auction Sale', 'Judging Distances', and *The Streets of Pompeii* to find their rightful places in the sun alongside 'Naming of Parts'.

1 It is ironic that Reed shares a birthday with George Washington (albeit in a different calendar), in nearly every way Reed's antithesis: a very public man, a warrior and statesman of great action, few words, and little sympathy with the aesthetic.

2 *Return to Naples* illustrates the keenness of Reed's ear for nuances of sound and language, as well as his expectations that these finer points could be conveyed over the airwaves and appreciated by his listeners. 'Stage' directions in the play call for the Italian father to speak French with an Italian accent, suggested also by Reed's spellings, of *content* as *containt*, for example, *nouce* for *nous*, and *shinema* for *cinema*.

3 It is probably significant that when Reed reported to Kenneth Allott for a 1950 anthology of verse on the people he felt privileged to know at Birmingham, he included among the seven 'the painter John Melville, the [art] critic Robert Melville and the sculptor Gordon Herrick' (237).

4 Reed's commentary is also disturbing in its way: that he is writing a print column about someone talking on the radio about critical *isms* established to label works of art (which the listener, of course, is not viewing at the time) foreshadows how far from direct creative work his career would later drift.

5 The members of the Italian family call him *Erric'*, a clipped provincial form of *Enrico*.

6 According to *The American Heritage Dictionary*, 'Cheap and showy; meretricious ... [Alteration of *Birmingham*, England (from the counterfeit coins made there in the 17th century).]'. More commonly used as a way of representing a rather disdainful view of a provincial town.

7 Perhaps Reed's dalliance with tennis was on the model of Ugo Betti, his favorite Italian playwright, a robust man who was seen on the courts even in the last months before his death.

8 By his later years, Reed had scaled back his sexual life so markedly that both Robert B. Heilman and Wesley Wehr considered him virtually 'neutral' sexually.

9 'Our departmental training', he wrote to his sister Gladys in July 1941, '...is an official secret, known only to the British & German armies...' (in Stallworthy xiii).

10 A fifteen-minute version, *Noises On*, was followed in the same year by a thirty-minute entry entitled *Noises – Nasty and Nice*.

11 It is possible to read other tones into this statement, of course. It could be written with a narrow scholarly obliviousness or, more likely, with a healthy amount of facetiousness.

12 These assessments are found in *British Radio Drama* (Cambridge, 1981). In separate essays, Savage, Wade, and the editor of the collection, John Drakakis, also remark the merits of Reed's radio adaptation of *Moby Dick*.

13 Reed's sensibility later found an even more suitable match with the melancholy fiction of another woman writing of the American South: Carson McCullers. In a 1967 letter to Robert and Ruth Heilman he wrote, 'MacCullers [*sic*] is wonderful. The Deep South without the glue of Faulkner or the patchouli of Tennessee Whatisit. I do [wonder] why she has never become part of the Courses'.

14 Roger Savage (168) observes also that Reed 'hides' a lengthy Rimbaud quotation in 'A Map of Verona'.

15 Eliot concedes that some of his critics would have ranked Reed second to Eliot himself as a parodist of Eliot.

16 This assumption lies behind Reed's remark in a letter to the Heilmans that Vernon Watkins' wife Gwen 'began to enjoy teaching earlier in her experience than I did'.

17 The only dissenting voice is William Matchett's. Matchett, who now teaches at the University, thought of Reed as 'an absolute charmer' who was nevertheless 'a very lazy teacher' (Fountain and Brazeau 217).

18 Henry Carlile sees the twists and turns as parodic. Reed at least once said in exasperation, 'If I see the word *salmon* in another poem, ...' (Fountain and Brazeau 216).

19 Despite his generally left-leaning politics, Reed harboured, in Stallworthy's words, 'aristocratic fantasies' (xiii). In addition to his work for the coronation in 1953, he had written in his Radio Notes column (29 November, 429) that one would have to be 'a very stony person' not to have been moved by the wedding of Prince Phillip and Princess Elizabeth in 1947.

20 Reed likely would have rejected the offer. Ever distrustful of the visual image and its supposed impoverishment of the imagination, he had taken a BBC-sponsored television writing course in 1952, but never produced any work for that medium.

21 According to Peter Parker, Reed recognized that if Ackerley used his dog's real name 'Queenie' in a reminiscence on his canine friend, 'titters among the literati' might be aroused. Reed's caution led the book to be retitled *My Dog, Tulip* (311).

22 Dorothee Bowie's husband Taylor reports that one evening after he, Reed, and Frank Kermode had drunk too much, Reed tripped on a curb and fell 'like he was on a hinge'. Characteristically, he got up immediately as if he were not troubled by the inconvenience.

# EARLY POETRY: MISUNDERSTOOD GIFTS

Though one of his radio plays takes us inside *The Private Life of Hilda Tablet*, Henry Reed 'never presumed to parade the actualities of his [own] private life before the public' (Savage 189;).[1] He was such an unassuming soul that it is difficult even to trace a narrative in his life. It is just as difficult to trace a narrative in any of his poetic works. Only 'The Auction Sale' (1956) maintains a consistent, unstylized or unrefined storyline of any length. For a man who invested so much of his literary life in the study of long works of fiction, this seems quite an oddity. Moreover, three of the literary precursors he most esteemed—Melville, Hardy and Joyce—were best known as novelists, and two at least were interested in narrative line in their mature work. And if, as the author insists, we regard *Return to Naples* as entirely autobiographical, then Reed himself once had novel-writing ambitions:

> *H.* I shall write a great novel.
> *Bruno* Only one?
> *H.* No, Bruno, a great number. (199)

'*H.*' Reed also read novels ravenously, in at least three languages, translated long novels, and reviewed them at a daunting rate for the *Listener* and the *New Statesman and Nation*.

What Reed always admired most in his novelist-heroes, though, was the poetic quality in their work. As he wrote in *The Novel since 1939*, Hardy 'remains important because of the tragic breadth he brought into the novel, because of his sense of design', but 'above all because of the strong poetic element in his novels' (9). To Reed, despite what he sometimes seemed to regard as the inherent inferiority of Thomas Hardy's first genre,

> Hardy was never less than a poet: and the *lyrical quality* which pervades the atmosphere, the setting and even the character drawing of his novels, is what gives him his particular and original glory. His sense of form and his poetry have greatly affected the English novel. (9)

Similarly, Reed asks us to forgive Melville's overly romantic streak in *Moby Dick* as symptomatic of 'the exuberant manners of a different age' (Preface to *Moby Dick* 5), and to look instead at the 'Melville that matters', the poet-novelist who

> begins his book with the words 'Call me Ishmael'; who speaks of the times 'whenever it is a damp, drizzly November in my soul'; who recalls to us Narcissus and 'the tormenting, mild image he saw in the fountain'. (Preface 5)[2]

Even Reed's alter ego from the radio plays, Herbert Reeve, speaks reverently of Joyce's alter ego, Richard Shewin, as 'the poet's novelist'.[3]

There was always the sense in Reed that his translating and adapting (at least of full-length plays and novels), his radio comedies, and his criticism were as the insurance business was for Wallace Stevens, and that particularly his successful and reasonably lucrative radio plays were mercenary endeavours, mere hackwork which he hoped might one day free him to be what he really wanted to be: a poet. Three of his dramatic studies are about young poets, and many of the others portray characters of poetic sensibility, usually butting their poetic heads against a world that has no place for them. As more than one critic has shown, many of his poems can be read as allegories of the predicament of artist-types in a world hostile to lyricism. It is also significant that the 'occasional jerks forward' in the last years of his literary life nudged ahead his work on poems he had abandoned in the fifties—not plays from that era, or a novel from the thirties, or a short story or critical piece from any period in his life. In his self-conception, in fact, he might have taken either

Hardy's or Melville's literary career as a model. As Melville had written saltier and more sensational sea adventures before he wrote the great epic he wanted to (and turned to verse much later yet), so had Hardy abandoned the long-fiction genre that had made his literary fortune to devote the entire twentieth-century portion of his career to poetry, his great love.

There is little doubt that for most of his life Reed conceived of himself as a poet-butterfly striving to burst through the straitening cocoon of genre and unfortunate circumstances. All his plays before 1950 contain substantial verse portions. *Moby Dick* includes verse interludes spoken by Father Mapple and Ishmael, and *The Streets of Pompeii*, à la *Romeo and Juliet*, even embeds dueling sonnets in the dramatic verse of two young lovers. *The Unblest* and *The Monument*, his studies of the Italian poet Giacomo Leopardi, are written entirely in verse. Moreover, Reed continued to champion verse drama even after its brief twentieth-century revival had itself swooned and was in need of reviving. By the most simplistic definition of 'poetry equals verse', as Roger Savage points out, Reed was even a 'poet' in his prose plays, since nearly all of the serious drama and even most of the comedies contain song and verse passages.

With the properly more inclusive definition of poetry which Reed himself applied to the novels of Hardy and Melville, however, he is in many ways as much a poet in the urbane and stately prose of the choric narrators in *Streets*, *Great Desire*, and *Naples* as he is in his first collection of poems. And that is what, ultimately, speaks to the failure of *A Map of Verona*. Reed's first and only volume of poetry is shackled by his overly constraining definition of poetic and a misjudgment of his own poetic gifts. In the souls of all writers reside, in lesser or greater proportions, poetic 'strands'. If we could isolate them in Henry Reed, we might identify five: the Narrative, the Lyrical, the Dramatic, the Comic, and the Aphoristic.[4] As can be seen in the exceptional poems in *A Map of Verona*—'Chard Whitlow' and 'Lessons of the War' (to be discussed, along with two 'Lessons' added for the

1970 edition, in Chapter 4)—and in a sequence of unpublished poems from his early years, Reed's genius for the comic and his dramatic acumen were already highly developed. They would flower in his immaculately constructed radio plays of the next decade. If Reed had been able to step outside himself and, with perspective, honestly assess his poetic make-up, he might have been wise to nurture his gift for dramatic and comic verse. But his grooming as a Man of Letters, his wide reading in the classics, and his reverence for earlier writers—especially for a certain kind of artist symbolized for him by the physically deformed, alienated poet Leopardi—impelled Reed to knead his own poetic personality into the wrong mold. In truth, his poetic gifts were, in order: Dramatic, Comic, Lyric, Narrative, Aphoristic. The Aphoristic manner was absorbed from many of his literary ancestors, distant and near—Leopardi and Melville, Auden and Eliot—but that strand was the most awkwardly woven into Reed's poetic fabric. He detested didacticism in imaginative literature, and his own aphorisms, while prominent and aggressive in his critical writing, mar his poetry: they come off as too obscure, too derivative of Auden and Eliot, or too diluted with his characteristic hesitations and qualifiers. He eschewed the Narrative, as perhaps too prosaic, not unique to poetry, as he undervalued the Comic and Dramatic as simply falling below the lyric in his own scheme of decorum. And he overvalued the Lyrical—both his gift for it and its relative merit among the other strands.

Even his definition of 'lyric' seems far narrower than that of *The American Heritage Dictionary*, which admits any 'poetic literature which is representational of music in its sound patterns and generally characterized by subjectivity and sensuality of expression'. The *American Heritage*'s definition of 'lyrical' brings in an additional criterion of deep 'feeling or emotion', expressed 'in a direct and affecting manner'. In Reed, though, the manner is rarely direct and the emotional and verbal range exceedingly narrow. As his early poetry failed to acknowledge, music has crescendos, rumbling kettledrums, and even cymbal crashes; its variations need not be so subtle as the dynamic difference between *pp* and *ppp* to be worthy of the attention of sophisticated listeners. As to subjectivity, Elizabeth Jennings calls many of the poems in *A Map* 'personal' (1252) and John Carey labelled the collection outside of 'Lessons of the War' and 'Chard Whitlow' 'private' (577); but 'recherché', the adjective Roger Savage applies to some of Reed's radio plays (172), perhaps better fits the near solipsism of some of the poems. There is a huge range of emotions available—not just quiet ones near the centre of the spectrum—which a lyric poet might express 'in a direct and affecting manner' or draw out in even the elite group of readers Reed expected to reach. In *A Map of Verona*, for the most part, these truths seemed to have escaped Reed. The poet who in a sense mentored Reed from a distance of one hundred years, Giacomo Leopardi, wrote poetry in a rueful, melancholy, or even darker vein, and the tortured Italian hunchback was the basis for Reed's concept of what a 'poet' ought to be. Reed's own refined cultivation did the rest: squeezing all passion into wistfulness and longing, all barbaric yawps into mild, stammering protests.

A. T. Tolley saw Reed's misplaced emphasis, too, as partly a function of the age during which Reed was cutting his poetic teeth: '. . . in the forties sensitive observation of the physical or the psychological seemed at once a sufficient and a necessary ingredient for a work of literature' (290). For Reed's part, too often sensitive apprehension of the beautiful was the necessary and sometimes sufficient element. 'Sensitivity', continued Tolley,

> is the badge of the alienated artist from Oscar Wilde to Cyril Connolly. An unattached sensitivity, cultivated for its own sake rather than as a concomitant of the exploration of significant experience, is a feature of much of the bad writing of the forties. (291)

In *A Map of Verona* Reed was all too anxious to wear the badge, leaving much of the collection open to Carey's other adjectives: 'wan' and 'merely sensitive' (577). Though Tolley does not explicitly label any of Reed's *A Map of Verona* 'bad writing' he does call one piece a 'rather precious, literary poem' (25) and levels the 'precious' charge on a number of other passages, not excepting the untouchable 'Naming of Parts'. But even outside of 'Lessons of the War' and 'Chard Whitlow' there are enough 'precious' moments (in the broader, less pejorative sense of the word) to warrant for *A Map* the 'respectful attention' Henry Rago felt was deserved. These are the instances—and we wish there were more—in which Reed strikes out on his own, leaving behind Eliot and his penchant for the Aphoristic; when he allows a Narrative to run free for a stanza; when he seems not ashamed of his Comic and Dramatic strands; in short, when he writes not out of duty to the Muse of Lyric poetry but for Henry Reed.

---

In 1946, *A Map of Verona* appeared first in London, divided into three sections—'Preludes' (ten shorter poems, including 'Lessons of the War'), 'The Desert' (six poems), and 'Tintagel', four poems on the Tristram and Iseult story—plus two longish, semi-dramatic poems featuring figures from classical myth and literature. This little volume was expanded the next year for a 92-page New York edition with an additional sonnet; a new dramatic piece, 'Antigone', to accompany 'Chrysothemis' and 'Philoctetes' in 'Triptych'; and notes by the author. The notices for both editions were almost uniformly favourable. Granted, three of those were from periodicals which had published a number of Reed's poems and which may have felt obliged to promote the work of the local lad. The most gushing appraisal came from *Time and Tide*: 'No better first book of poetry has appeared for many years and it would be foolish to expect another comparable before long'; the volume would reward anyone with 'a regard for writing that combines profound imagination with beauty of expression' (dust jacket of *A Map*). The *New Statesman and Nation* announced that 'all the hints seem to be here of larger work', an assessment based more on the poet's expression than his imagination. 'Already Mr. Reed has a mastery of the blank verse line as extended by Eliot', continued the *New Statesman*, calling Reed's lines 'highly finished and exactly chosen' (jacket). 'His versification is accomplished', contributed the *Listener*, 'full of bold and subtle variation, melodious . . . following the beat of the poetic thought with the fluency of a well-trained orchestra' (690). One independent reviewer, Harvey Breit of *The New York Times*, remarked the 'scrupulous' language of Reed's verse and 'how right its long line strikes us—a line that rises and falls as naturally as the surf's rhythms, and as punctuated with surprises (if one listens carefully) ...'(8). Similar paeans to Reed's adroitness with form in *A Map of Verona* have been sung by later critics such as Frank Kermode, Kenneth Allott, and Elizabeth Jennings.

The coattails of 'Lessons of the War' and 'Chard Whitlow' were long and easy to grasp; surely some of the other poems garnered a disproportionate share of the effusive early praise for *A Map* by tugging those coattails. But there are other possible reasons for its unduly warm reception. Since the poems collected in *A Map* were first published in the period of 1937-46, the volume's overall seriousness (augmented perhaps by the author's notes to the New York edition) must have seemed suitable to an era of Depression, brewing conflict, and the Second World War itself. Critics may also have been attracted by nearly every poem's stance of beauty for beauty's sake against what they viewed as the aggressive materialism and acquisitiveness of the age. However hyperrefined and enervatingly aesthetic (sometimes anaesthetic) the poets' counterreaction to the mood of the era, critics might have found the retreat preferable. Most significant, as at least two commentators suggest, was that Reed's verse was a welcome relief from the rantings of the self-described New Apocalypse, a group of writers that flourished for a time in the late thirties and early forties. They were unabashedly anti-intellectual, and their loosely controlled, turbulent imagery is the kind Breit applauds Reed for shunning: in *A Map*, he says, there is none of the frenzy 'that has been gaining momentum among our poets'; there is 'no rhetoric', no 'demagogic extra appeal to the senses'. Similarly, the *Listener* reviewer congratulates *A Map* for refraining from 'uneasy exhibitionism, … verbal blushings and eruptions, … ham-handedness and tripping over [one's] own feet' (8).

From one quarter, at least, the backlash was quick and severe. This devastating response to the 'exceptional unanimity of praise accorded to Mr Reed's volume' came from G. D. Klingopulos, writing in *Scrutiny*[5] barely half a year after the London publication of *A Map*. Klingopulos's scythe swept through all but four of the twenty-four poems in the collection and managed to cut all to stubble of various heights—even 'Lessons of the War'. His second reading of the book, elicited by the favourable reviews, confirmed his initial sense that many of Reed's poems 'seemed wordy failures, and several unambiguously bad' (141). Klingopulos savages Reed's lack of content especially, seeing most of the poems as exercises all the more empty when their stylistic echoes of Sassoon, Marvell, Auden, and Eliot set the poems unconsciously next to those of the greater writers. And although Klingopulos is unkind even toward much of the sheerly literary in Reed—his allegory and symbols, his rhymes, metres, and 'spurious rhythms'—he still implies that other critics have been blinded by Reed's verbal polish into failing to perceive the poems' lack of substance, real episode or real emotion. The longer poems, he maintains, 'contain a great deal of worked-up feeling', that is, artificial feeling tricked out by glib sleight-of-word; nearly all of these poems Klingopulos describes as 'entirely verbal'. Perhaps more stinging than his vitriol is Klingopulos's subtler contention that without a foundation of grander figures, truer emotions, more concrete happenings—in short, 'a more impressive content'—Reed's verse, despite its variety of forms, is 'only fluency at low pressure' (144).

Klingopulos's grievances are legitimate. Part of the failure of the majority of the poems in *A Map*, particularly in 'Preludes' and 'The Desert', is that they announce themselves as dramatic or narrative poems in their first few lines, then fail to honour that implicit contract with the reader. The dramatic and narrative frameworks are rickety structures. In a dramatic poem, readers expect 'drama', as it might be defined in one of two ways. First, we hope the poem will be 'play-like', in that we can envision a fully imagined scene as backdrop to the words; that there might be at least one implied listener whose character traits we may infer as fully as those of the sharply drawn speaker or speakers; that there will be implied actions or at least gestures which help the reader come to know the characters; that these characters might even have names, as we expect of dramatis personae, names like Ed or Etta, perhaps even evocative names like Fra Lippo Lippi or Eben Flood. Secondly, the poems will be spoken at some exciting, 'dramatic' time in the lives of the characters; the reader will thus sense tension, intensity, or at least anxiety. These are rigorous standards, to be sure, but criteria most of which are met by the great practitioners of the dramatic poem: Browning, Tennyson, and Reed's own venerated Thomas Hardy and T. S. Eliot in poems such as 'Ah, Are You Digging on My Grave?' and even 'The Love Song of J. Alfred Prufrock'.

From narrative poems we anticipate all the above elements, along with actions, events, or at least incidents recounted in such a way as to make a reader feel suspense, to heighten his or her heart rate for a time. This is not to say that narrative poems demand lovers' quarrels, fistfights, or protracted car chases,[6] though readers of *A Map of Verona* would welcome even a character snapping a pencil in frustration. But Reed had no interest in narrative for its own sake. The few 'dramatic' events or bold physical gestures which appear in his poems tend to be enacted through a scrim of vision, dream, memory, or imagination, as for example when Chrysothemis, who has not witnessed the episode, envisions the violent death throes of her father Agamemnon. More characteristically, Reed's narrative and dramatic poems are evidence of his misproportioning of his poetic strands. The comic strand makes almost no appearances in the fabric whatsoever, and the narrative and dramatic pretences of most of *A Map* serve only as perfunctory vehicles for his often obscure allegories and unprofound aphoristic pronouncements and usually unaffecting essays at lyricism.

'The Captain' and 'Hiding Beneath the Furze' are somewhat exceptional in that each maintains a brief narrative of some independent interest. There is genuine action, viewed directly.[7] 'The Captain,' Reed's first published poem, describes a shipwreck:

> The sides burst in, and the masts
> Broke, and one huge white sail
> Flowed beautiful over the sea,
> Till the suck drew it under.[8]

The last of the three five-line stanzas speaks of the captain's 'great remorse' as he watches his men '[s]wimming to the dreadful mouths/ Of the sharks for plunder'. The storyline is thin, though it may loosely attach to 'Sailors' Harbour', the previous poem of the group of six Reed called 'The Desert'. That poem warns of deceptive winds which may blow the sailors' craft '[t]o shipwreck and ruin'; 'The Captain' begins, 'It was shipwreck, after all'.[9] Despite the atypically action-packed narrative, Reed may still be more interested in writing just enough story to 'earn' the captain's aphorism of the second stanza: 'Oh God, how man/ Makes his own thunder'. He also seems to enjoy manoeuvring his poem through a lyrical progression of widely spaced, stanza-locking rhymes: 'under', 'thunder', and 'plunder'.[10]

'Hiding Beneath the Furze' is a longer narrative, which builds some suspense as the reader follows a man who escapes his pursuers by hiding in thick brush, then finds asylum in the cottage of an old woman who lies to protect him when the would-be captors question her. But the tight, alternating rhymes in the last stanza, two of which provide a faint, delayed echo of words which have appeared in the earlier five stanzas, along with the refrain 'And this can never happen, ever again', suggest Reed's desire to give the poem the sensuous musical quality of lyric. The refrain, also, and the broadly sketched, almost cliched characterizations of the unnamed protagonist, the motherly old peasant woman, and the 'evil captain' are Reed's attempts to universalize the poem's events,[11] though, as in the case of many poems in the collection, the meaning of the allegory remains opaque. Perhaps the poem depicts, more globally, an unwarranted sense of security: Neville Chamberlain's appeasement had as much as promised that aggression such as Germany's would 'never happen, ever again'. But as prospects for peace in our time were abruptly dashed by Hitler's invasion of Poland in 'Autumn 1939' (the parenthetical subtitle of the poem), so do we find the friends of the man in the poem, who are awaiting his safe return in stanza five, unceremoniously dead in stanza six.

'The Forest', a sonnet of 1946 which made its way into the New York edition of *A Map of Verona*, provides a more typical narrative—less physical, less 'dramatic'. After the inauspicious ugliness of line 4— '...we along the darkness crept and kissed'—Reed maintains an affecting narrative, perhaps surprising in such a short, tightly structured piece, through the poem's last ten lines:

> The great ice closed upon each beast and bird,[12]
> And we lay mute and warm in its embrace,
> The soft disturbances of night we heard
> Seemed only shadows rustling to their place.
>
> They found their place, lay quiet, and were still.
> Momentously the night reigned; phantomwise
> The hours progressed upon their way; until
> There, in the glacial silence of sunrise,
>
> We saw the ranks of serried archers stand,
> Their arrows sharp and pointed, hand by hand.

The poem, for worse but mostly for better, is a microcosm of *A Map of Verona*, showcasing many of the distinctive themes and devices which seduced the collection's early reviewers. These are evocative in individual passages but frankly become tedious when the volume is considered as a whole. In two of its quatrains and its couplet, the poem is certainly beautiful, like most all the poems in the collection; it is pleasant to the eye and ear with its graceful Shakespearean rhymes and prominently iambic rhythm. Reed preferred a cold to a warm milieu: this poem outlines the setting of 'Winter's white labyrinth' in its first three words. He preferred tableaux: quiet scenes of limited or no action. In a later poem, 'Three Words', Reed personified 'the small word "silent"' as following two other words he had most favoured in his poems, taking his hand gently, and pleading, 'Do not forget me:/ I have also been yours'. As Reed drafted 'The Forest', perhaps no pleading was necessary. Silence infuses the scene. The night sounds 'found their place, lay quiet, and were still', respectful, it seems, of the 'mute' lovers. The 'disturbances of night' are 'soft', and the sunrise which closes the scene makes no sound at all.

After the two arrive at their love-spot, the only movement in the poem is insubstantial, nearly imperceptible. The motions of forest life seem as mere 'shadows rustling to their place'; the only progress is of the 'hours'; and the movement of the sunrise when it comes is 'glacial'. However, as in 'Hiding Beneath the Furze', the sense of security is false. The narrative of the quatrains has set up the reader for the revelation of a sinister presence in the archers 'serried', that is, pressed together in rows. Characteristically, the poet leaves us with a scene of static tension. The archers 'stand', with their arrows sharp and apparently trained on the lovers. And, Reed's many protestations of the inferiority of allegory notwithstanding, this poem, among many others in *A Map*, leaves itself open to a second level of interpretation: neither character is named in this forest pageant, nor is a specific kind of tree or animal identified. The poem's publication date, just a year after V-J Day, suggests that the poem may be a reflection on the pre-war tension of the late thirties. The lovers—of each other, but also of quiet, stillness, and beauty—are loving on borrowed time, for the menacing purveyors of war have been insidiously massing on the borders of their idyllic world.

These three poems erect the most solid narrative frameworks of any early Reed poem. The longer poems from 'The Desert' wend obscure, almost impossible-to-trace pseudo-stories which serve merely to prop up Reed's symbolic, lyrical, and meditative designs. Similarly, a thin narrative underlies the 'Tintagel' sequence, poems viewing from four different angles the familiar Tristram and Iseult story. As always, Reed demands much from his readers. As it is, there are three Iseults in the saga; in a further complication, the poems are choked with antecedentless pronouns, including second-persons which seem to modulate freely from singular to plural to informal substitutes for *one*. The poet also assumes the reader knows all of the particulars of character and incident in the tale. Thus only a few clearly identifiable places and events crop up, at widely spaced intervals: Brittany and Cornwall; a lovers' tryst; the episode of the white and black sails (covered in a mere four lines). And one of the incidents in 'King Mark', the poet tells us in his notes to the New York edition, evidently appears in only one of the many Tristram and Iseult retellings, Godfrey of Strasbourg's. As in most Reed narratives, the story itself holds little fascination for the poet; he wrote in his notes that the 'Tintagel' poems 'represent four aspects of a problem known in one or more of these aspects to most men and women' (in Stallworthy 158).[13] The emotional range of Reed's version of what many consider the greatest love story in Western literature is tightly circumscribed. The story as told by Malory and retold by the likes of Wagner, Arnold, and Swinburne conveys the agonized, hopeless love of the two principals; a profound sense of duty, as Tristram is bound by oath to obtain for King Mark the hand of Tristram's beloved Iseult in marriage; and the gross treachery observable in the various endings of the tale. In one, Tristram is murdered by Mark, his uncle, while playing the harp; in another, he is lied to when he asks if the ship's sails are white, signifying Iseult's return to his side. The power of their love is so great that Tristram dies when told the sails are black, and Iseult dies when she sees her dead lover.

Only Henry Reed, it seems, could have so refined and intellectualized such a story into a series of quasi-lyrical meditations—melancholy, wistful, and almost completely removed from Iseult and Tristram, never mind the potent human passions inherent in their story. Often the meditations are on a favourite Reed theme, the Romantic truth of the power of the memory, imagination, or perspective to 'half-create' reality, and sometimes these passages succeed. The poems were inspired in the Wordsworthian way by an actual visit, in Reed's case to the ruins of Tintagel castle on the north shore of Cornwall and, also true to Wordsworth, 'recollected in tranquillity' years after the visit. In the first poem, 'Tristram's tower' itself prompts the meditation. We enter it through Reed's heavy-footed words—'The ruin leads your thoughts'—but the meditation is successful in lyrically expressing two truths about the workings of memory. 'Sometimes', says the speaker, Tristram's tower

> . . . comes unsummoned as if by magic.
> And sometimes when we could best prevent, we let it
> Form and rebuild itself before our eyes.
> For some, at each return it comes more faintly,
> Less echoing . . .[14]

On the other hand, we

> . . . cannot learn to forget as sometimes we learn to
> remember,
> To compose an oblivion like a memory,
> To capture carefully an empty future,
> As we recapture, fragment by fragment, the past.[15]

Part of the beauty in these lines is their gentle reminder that memory is a re-collection, often imperfect but more potent for that, of artifacts and shards from our past.

Henry Rago described 'Iseult la Belle', the fourth of the 'Tintagel' poems, as 'a lovely, liquid thing', and indeed all the poems of this group do have isolated passages which appeal to one's ear and sensibilities; but Rago was also right in asserting that 'only a few short lyrics in this volume'—assuming he is taking 'Lessons of the War' as lyrics—'are what could be called mature poetry' and that the longer poems do not have 'a sufficiently fresh intelligence' to sustain their full length (353). 'Iseult Blaunchesmains' does make a nice doff of the cap to the worldview of Leopardi, Hardy, even Stephen Crane as Iseult surveys the foreign coast of Cornwall with its 'valleys not hostile, but their hillsides/ Turning themselves indifferently away'. But too often the indictment A. T. Tolley made against 'Iseult Blaunchesmains' sticks: the poems are literary and precious. Part of the problem is Reed's tendency to ask his abstracts to do too much and his readers to strain too hard to envision them. In 'Iseult Blaunchesmains' the title character says, 'they [antecedent unknown] come with their griefs,/ They come with their years around them in a leaden circle,/ Fatigued and baffled with the stress of understanding'. In the fourth poem Iseult la Belle speaks lines attempting to elicit a world which for G. D. Klingopulos was 'plainly unreal' (143):

> . . . I come, in whatever season, like a new year,
> In such a vision as the open gates reveal
> As you saunter into a courtyard, or enter a city,
> And inside the city you carry another city,
> Inside delight, delight.

When the *vehicle* of a metaphor (in I. A. Richards' sense) is abstract as in 'like a new year', and readers are asked in the space of two lines to envision someone carrying a city into a city and delight inside of delight, they are clearly overtaxed. The last eleven-plus lines of 'King Mark' are whispered to the King by 'the heat of summer'. Here, as elsewhere, Reed has taken pathetic fallacy and hyperrefined it: the nature which he artificially invests with human emotion is not even tangible nature like flowers or birds but abstract elements of nature like heat and time.[16]

In 'The Desert', too, fragile narrative structures serve as conduits for good and, more often, bad lyrical musings. 'The Place and the Person' is a bizarre, surreal tale (or more properly a collection of images) with echoes of 'The Rime of the Ancient Mariner':

> From the far horizon . . .
> A ship comes forth, with supernatural haste
> Parting the waters; and with grace the waves
> Draw from her painted sides.

The unpiloted ship, 'cargoed with a love/ That has broken through virgin seas',[17] docks with all the bustle one would expect: ropes being cast, gang-planks descending, and cargo being unloaded (here, flowers and oil delivered by fantastic 'women in green and purple'). It is the disintegration of this vision, one too deceptively bright, that Reed describes so beautifully:

> . . . the sails, their powerful and striding canvas,
> And the riding fortress of timber which is the hull,
> Are changing there in the sunlight, undone and mastered
> As all is undone and mastered that comes this way;
> Dislimning, falling, dissolving, canvas to satin,
> Satin to sunlight turning, wood to paper,
> The masts to cobwebs, women to wraith and phantom,
> Failing mirage of the noontime . . .

But this poem too suffers from manipulative pathos similar to that found in 'Tintagel': it speaks of rock 'Which cannot weep, . . ./ And cannot turn or yield, but suffers and endures'.

'South', though, the third poem in 'The Desert', is most representative of the excesses to which Reed was prone. Perhaps it does vaguely address the question 'by what values should the truly civilised man live?' as one reviewer suggested (The *Listener*, 23 March 1946, 690), but the poem is as 'recondite' as the stars which brood over its main backdrops of ice, a rock, and the sea.

The token narrative premise of this poem, which the incisive Roger Savage safely speaks of only as 'Reed's Antarctic exploration poem' (172), concerns a sailor who separates himself from his crewmates and takes an isolated position on a rock, where he has some manner of epiphany and, clambering down off the rock 'after the others,/ Face[s] the full day'.

As in other unsuccessful Reed poems, highly abstract concepts, impossibly, do things. 'He opened his eyes,// And there was a world'; later, suspense is built, but '[t]he world remained'. This little sub-plot is completed when the man speaks and '[t]he world broke at his words'. The manipulative emotion is here as well: the man weeps 'hot tears' and cries, 'Where is my love?' So are the incongruous images: 'His coasts henceforth would calve in change unceasing'. The two mesh in several of his images involving the heart. It is usually safe to say a movie or somesuch 'tugged at my heartstrings', because the metaphor is long dead and summons up no absurd image in the listener's mind. But some of Reed's metaphors in this conspicuously serious poem are little removed from that which Coleridge attributed to 'a young tradesman': 'No more will I endure love's pleasing pain,/ Or round my heart's leg tie his galling chain'. In 'South', through the man's 'waiting veins' the 'silent bay/ And the great black rock passed . . ./ The shock of peace'. By the second and third such effusions only bathos is elicited by the jarring of abstract and concrete. The ice, rock, and bay '[s]howed him through glaciers the heart's still unforgotten/ Knocking of blood'. Later, '[n]ot peace but like it' is available to this heart which 'like a ship . . . would shake and tack/ To a varying port'.

Reed attempted also to conduct his lyrical and philosophical musings, again with varied success, through the medium of dramatic poetry. Five poems from the 'Preludes' section lightly sketch a dramatic situation by promptly addressing a 'you'. Though the second person is intentionally nebulous in 'Outside and In', both 'A Map of Verona' and 'The Return' are apostrophes. In the title poem, the listeners are the cities of Naples and

Verona; in 'The Return' the speaker mentally addresses his friends before his arrival at their home on Christmas Eve, speculating how he and his party will be received upon their return from a long voyage. In both cases, of course, the dramatic sense is softened, since those addressed cannot respond, in fact are not even present. 'Morning' and 'The Door and the Window' have more conventional listeners, announced in the poems' first lines: 'Look, my love, on the wall, and here, at this Eastern picture'; 'My love, you are timely come, let me lie by your heart'. All five are subdued poems which intend not to limn sharp dramatic portraits, but to showcase the poet's affection for the lyric, that is (returning to the *American Heritage*), for subjectively, sensually, and musically expressing deep feeling. They ask the reader to share emotion with their speakers, emotions meant to be felt deeply, though they are quiet emotions: a sense of strangeness, mild dislocation, peace, calm, friendship, longing. Because of various failings—wordiness, affectation, clumsy word choice, obscurity—three of the poems fall short.

X. J. Kennedy has defined sentimentality as 'a failure of writers who seem to feel a great emotion but who fail to give us sufficient grounds for sharing it' (*Literature* 747). Reed is not asking us to gush unwarranted tears for a child who 'choked on a piece of beef' as Julia A. Moore did in 'Little Libby'; still, the weakest of these poems do suffer from something of the high-brow sentimentality seen in by 'The Desert' and 'Tintagel'. In some ways the title poem, Reed's stylized account of how he has absorbed the charms of Naples and is now sitting 'under the still lamp-light' with a map of Verona pondering how he will court his new love, is a fine piece. Embedded in it is a beautifully expressed, well-earned aphorism about the limitations of maps, perhaps of all expectations: 'Maps are of place, not time, nor can they say/ The surprising height and colour of a building,/ Nor where the groups of people bar the way'. But again the poet asks too much of his reader. Before we even begin the poem we must process a French epigraph (from Rimbaud, translated and adapted by Reed as part of his last stanza) for a poem by an Englishman about the charms of Italy. Moreover, few readers can be expected to be as moved as Reed purports to be by the sentiments of stanzas three and four:

> My youthful Naples, how I remember you!
> You were an early chapter, a practice in sorrow,
> Your shadows fell, but were only a token of pain,
> A sketch in tenderness, lust, and sudden parting,
> And I shall not need to trouble with you again.

The scant concrete details are not enough to justify the first effusive direct address in the poem ('how I remember you!'), nor the self-pity in stanza four. We are rather told, not shown, through abstract language, the five emotions Reed associates with Naples. And we can only expect similar effusions when he courts (stalks?) his new mistress, that is, Verona:

> The train will bring me perhaps in utter darkness
> And drop me where you are blooming, unaware
> That a stranger has entered your gates, and a new devotion
> Is about to attend and haunt you everywhere.

We do not quite care.[18]

Nor does the poet allow us to care much about 'Morning'. One of several aubades that Reed wrote, this poem tries to set the lovers in the ideal Reedian world, a calm still quietness so profound that not even shadows, reflections or echoes can disturb it. There is some beauty in both the scene depicted and in Reed's words, but the beauty is undercut by the clumsy image of the lovers' mouths 'assembled' and by the haziness of stanza two, in which the speaker asks his lover to

> . . . look away, and move. Or speak, or sing:
> And voices of the past murmur among your words,
> Under your glance my dead selves quicken and stir,
> And a thousand shadows attend you where you go.

Moreover, as readers we feel at least twice removed from 'real' love by the straitening conventions of the aubade and by the poet's entreaty to have us meditate on second-hand reality, in this case a work of art that we cannot see and that is described in far less detail than, say, Keats's urn (which Reed may have had in mind).

'The Door and the Window' presents a humble little truth in its first stanza, that 'at some dark time or another', we have all felt a nighttime disorientation, have awakened 'to find the room not as [we] thought it was,/ But the window further away, and the door in another direction'. This unpretentious aphorism is welcome in a love poem that fails in many ways. Though Henry Rago's scorn fell on these lines as slavishly Eliotesque, and he singled out a passage from 'Outside and In' as particularly wordy, how could he have missed the prolixity of lines two through four, in which forms of the verb 'to wake' appear four times? Rago does properly isolate the 'grotesque fault' in lines seven and eight, in which we are told that the speaker, before being united with his lover, 'woke' (that word again) in 'the icy grip of a dead, tormenting flame'. The motley mix of images seems even more unfortunate when held up against the parodic line in 'Chard Whitlow' warning of 'the frigid burnings of purgatory'.[19] Even the title of this poem seems pretentious. In the 1930s and 1940s, writers were fond of titles linking disparate elements with *and*: Roger Savage cites *The Root and the Flower* and *The Light and the Dark* among his examples. Reed himself was later to satirize the vogue through the novels of his own radio creation, Richard Shewin: *The Bang and the Whimper*, *The Quick and the Slow*, *The Up and the Down*, *The Arse and the Elbow*.

Perhaps this line of argument is unfair; moreover, the poem which precedes 'The Door and the Window' in the collection has a similarly designed title, and it succeeds. As with 'The Door and the Window' and 'The Forest', in 'Outside and In' a hint of menace surrounds an outpost of sorts. But here the speaker is alone and not at peace, in a house 'vulnerable and divided, with/ A mutiny already inside its walls . . '. We never learn who or what is threatening the house from without; rather, we see and hear signs of its imminence: 'The twig gave warning, snapped in the evening air,/ And all the birds in the garden finished singing'. In the poem's only misstep, another manifestation of the threat's nearness is packaged in maladroit syntax: 'The trees went silent you were prowling among . . '.. Why, one wonders, was the subordinate clause not placed right after the noun it modifies? Still, the poem more than adequately conveys 'the intense apprehension at the prospect of a fate we would rather endure than continue to endure the apprehension' (Kermode 17). The precise nature of that fate is left ambiguous and perhaps more frightening for that. And while in *The Novel since 1939* and elsewhere Reed protested his disdain for allegory (which in fact plays an integral role in *A Map*), this poem should be viewed as he probably would have preferred it to be: as evocative, suggestive, but not allegorical of anything in particular.

The best of these semi-dramatic lyrics is 'The Return', a melancholy poem of twenty couplets that was read on the BBC Home Service, Christmas Eve 1944. The 'we' in the poem are in a snowy harbour, having travelled far, but unlike the Magi, bring no prizes, 'no pearls or gold'; all they can offer friends back home is their 'glad return'. The speaker has no wish to extort any pledges of undying love and devotion from his friends, whom he imagines to be blithely dancing the evening away, nor does he expect such a pledge:

> And though you have turned [from] us, and have taken
>   your release[20]
> From us and all thought of us, yet on this night of peace
>
> Pause for a moment, put by your dance and song:
> Take to us kindly, and we shall not stay long.

The poem escapes the sentimentality of others in this group. That was one of the features that most impressed E. M. Forster, who heard the broadcast and immediately wrote to Reed. The poem reaffirmed for Forster 'the idea that the only reality in human civilization is the unbroken sequence of people caring for one another'. Forster insisted that the idea 'cannot be prettified into reciprocity or faithfulness, nor is there any such prettification in your poem' (in Stallworthy 157).

The music of the poem is muted. In fact, it might have difficulty holding up to Reed's own charge, levelled a year earlier in a critical piece, that contemporary poets' inclination to relax an 'already liberal' rhythmic pulse was conspiring to blur the distinctions between prose and verse ('End of an Impulse' 121). In 'The Return' the consistent and exact rhyme is underplayed by frequent enjambment and by wide metrical variations in the lines, from ten to seventeen syllables. These variations, however, seem consonant with the poem's melancholy mood.

The early Reed's most direct grappling with the Aphoristic strand of his poetic persona took several forms. Part of him was rather embarrassed, as one might be by a public belch; it was simply bad manners to make pronouncements, least of all in one's poetry. If they were to be made, they must be tossed off casually, as if one had little interest in such things, though some cub reader might make use of them. The frequent result was what might be called anti-aphorism: far from asserting, the poet offers choices, leaving it to the reader, ultimately, to fashion the poem.[21] Reed believed strongly in the power of memory and imagination to shape and re-shape truths, a theme that shows itself prominently in the 'Tintagel' and 'Triptych' poems. The theme is introduced in the last two poems of 'The Desert'. In Reed's 'The Place and the Person'[22] the narrator speaks not to a distinct listener; rather, the *you* is the reader, who is directly addressed in lines two and three: 'So much like other empty places, you yourself/ Must paint its picture, who have your own such places'.[23]

The narrator of 'The Place and the Person' makes only one stipulation to us: though the main character's 'surroundings do not matter: they are yours or mine', we must '. . . paint alone the central figure faithfully'. 'Envoy' makes even less of a demand in depicting *its* main character: it is 'You, I, or we'. Reed positioned this poem at the end of 'The Desert', as Stallworthy, over forty years later, placed '[*L'Envoi*]' at the end of *Collected Poems*. An envoy, of course, is a messenger. But in a narrower sense it is the closing stanza, as of a ballade, serving to dedicate the work to a patron or summarize the poem. It is thus in this usage too a messenger. But what a message 'Envoy' delivers!

The poem, comprising just two sentences spread over thirty-seven lines, concerns a garden that the speaker and his listener ponder building, presumably in their imaginations. The entire second stanza is concerned with the features the garden should not have. Stanza one offers two options for each of five various features, for example, whether the garden will be 'shaped' (a neoclassical garden?) or 'disorderly' (a Romantic garden?), or whether it will be '[b]uilt over ruined shrines' or 'on virgin ground'. Considered mathematically, there are thus $2^5$, or 32, gardens that might be conceived.[24] The third stanza introduces three more options, expanding the possibilities to $2^8$, or 256 gardens. After all the features have been offered for consideration, the minimum criterion for the garden is outlined. One wonders, though, if Reed has victimized us with a shaggy-dog story: with all of the qualifiers and parentheticals removed, and slightly paraphrased, stanza three delineates the essential feature of the garden: 'certain ways/ Wherein . . ./. . . we/. . . may/. . ./ Wander and praise'. In this final poem of a long sequence, wherein the reader is directed to seek some meaning in the previous five difficult poems, he or she is left mystified: is this an encomium to the myriad possibilities engendered by imagination, or merely a joke?[25]

In other poems it is clear that Reed *was* striving after truths, was trying to nurture the Aphoristic component of his poetic being. The efforts are often embarrassing, especially when he wedges laboured paradoxes or other cryptic statements into a poem and comes off, at best, sounding like himself doing Eliot in 'Chard Whitlow', and silly at his worst: 'They are here and not here'; 'remembered weathers/ Which they will always forget'; 'the familiar place, familiar,/ And desperately unknown . . '.; 'it is so bright you cannot call it darkness'. In 'Philoctetes' the title character speaks of a wound which no longer pains him: 'its death/ Is dead within me'. Granted, nearly any Eliot paradox would look as pretentious and pseudo-profound out of its context, but we cannot forgive the statement that opens the poem, for setting it in that position, with a period at the end of the line, the poet intends for it to stand alone, without contextual support. Says Philoctetes, 'I have changed my mind; or my mind is changed in me'. A. T. Tolley writes that such mannered phrasings 'become a staple of Reed's style without the firm resonance of inner meaning that redeems them in Eliot's poems'. As to the first line of 'Philoctetes', Tolley continues, 'the play on words through the correction of the customary phrase does not alert the reader in any important way' (49).[26] Similarly, for his character to say the 'death' of his wound 'Is dead within me' is an affected and convoluted rendering of 'it doesn't hurt now'.

Another instance of Reed's awkward use of aphorism is found in 'The Builders'. This long, obscure poem takes a circuitous route in presenting its truth about man's insignificance in the scheme of things. The three-line stanzas take us through a cloudy tale of natives and explorers, reminiscent of *Heart of Darkness*; perhaps the poet's intent is to make our goal uncertain and the 63-line trip arduous. The last stanza offers our dubious reward:

> What marks in time have we made? 'None, none, . . .
> All we could find was the space in the forest and only
> The cross on the temple, islanded above the waters'.

Not all aphorisms need express wildly original ideas—in fact, most do not—but in 'The Builders', the exhilaration at finding the clearing after hacking through the jungle is not commensurate with the difficulty of the journey.[27]

Reed was sometimes able to bring his aphoristic tendencies under control, as we see in his lovely poem 'Lives'. The first two stanzas begin with peremptory assertions: 'You cannot cage a field'; 'But you can cage the woods'.[28] These aphorisms serve as topic sentences for the verse paragraphs, and they are amply and gracefully supported. The woods, on the surface more imposing than a field, you can fence, 'Hold', 'Confine', 'alter', 'Press to your own desires'. The woods' response to your aggression is to 'succumb', 'retreat', 'withdraw'; they 'Betake themselves where you tell them and acquiesce./ . . . their protest of leaves whirls/ Pitifully to the cooling heavens, like dead or dying prayers'. The less imposing field may also be bullied for a time yet

> . . . never dies,
> Though you build on it, burn it black, or domicile
> A thousand prisoners on its empty features.
> You cannot kill a field. A field will reach
> Right under the streams to touch the limbs of its brothers.

The truths about nature are authentic and convincing, but Reed's title, of course, suggests more: how different human personalities respond to life's buffetings, to its conflagrations, oppressions and imprisonments. The *Listener's* reviewer called the poem a 'simple Robert-Frostian' allegory (690), but perhaps it is something a little different. Frost preferred to call himself a 'synecdochist' rather than an allegorist. 'Always a larger significance', he explained. 'A little thing touches a larger thing'. The larger thing in 'Lives' is the resilience of human beings. Those who are even more resilient than the fields are 'touched' by another little thing: a stream, the subject of the poem's third stanza. Somehow Reed manages to charm us with the personality of coursing water, which responds to interference not so much by resisting the pressures or seeking sympathy with kindred spirits as does the field. The stream personality wins our respect by asserting its streamness not in a showy but rather an almost cavalier manner, simply not deigning to acknowledge the powers which attempt to coerce it:

> The stream announces its places where the water will bubble
> Daily and unconcerned, contentedly ruffling and scuffling
> With the drifting sky or the leaf. Whatever you do,
> A stream has rights, for a stream is always water;
> To cross it you have to bridge it; and it will not flow uphill.

The stream is pliable, tolerant, adaptable—almost Thoreauvian in its resistance: 'You can widen it here, or deepen it there, but even/ If you alter its course entirely it gives the impression/ That this is what it always wanted'.

Unlike the stream, which is spontaneous, almost philosophical in its careering downhill, Henry Reed's poetic course did not meander. In the early years the poet was so preoccupied with being lyrical, in fact with labouring under a highly constrained conception of what was lyrical, that he failed to nurture his obvious gifts for the comic and dramatic. William Matchett, a poet and teacher who knew Reed at Washington, speaks for many in calling him 'the funniest person I think I've known in my lifetime' (in Fountain and Brazeau 217). But in his poetry Reed gave free play to that humour and wit in only four of his *Map* pieces and in no poems published after 1950. Granted, there are faint evidences of his comic side elsewhere in *A Map of Verona*. Some feeble wordplay, for example, glimmers in the title poem's last stanza:

> And in what hour of beauty, in what good arms,
> Shall I those regions and that city attain
> From whence my dreams and slightest movements rise?
> And what good Arms shall take them away again?

The capitalized *A* gives the reader a poke in the shoulder that is absent in the wry word order in 'Sailors' Harbour' as seamen 'Wander through the suburbs, with quiet thoughts of the brothels,/ And sometimes thoughts of the churches'.[29]

But Reed's published poems, for the most part, are unrelenting in their earnestness and their complete suppression of an essential part of the poet's being. Thus, it is comforting to read some short prose-poems that Reed had completed before 1940—as part of a sequence called 'Green, Spleen, & c.'—but chose not to include in either edition of *A Map*. All three are drily comic. All three are studiedly unlyrical, in metrics, and in diction—sometimes stilted or jargony but always at least prosaic ('apparently', 'informed', 'fact', 'anaparanoiac') or jauntily casual ('One afternoon in Naples', 'frightfully annoyed'). There are no conventions followed in rhyme, metre, or even capitalization at the beginnings of lines; indeed, the major consideration in line divisions (which may, it is true, be those of Reed's editors) seems to be approximating right-justification. And although the poems facilely allude to figures of classical myth and literature, the allusions are not to the obscure personages honoured in his more self-conscious or academic poems, figures like Chrysothemis, Simaetha, Perimede, Philoctetes, and King Mark of Cornwall; they are, instead, the Furies, Ulysses, and the women of *Lysistrata*. What is so refreshing is that these poems reveal a Henry Reed who can write little pieces from a narrative or dramatic perspective, pieces written with wit and apparently with real joy, pieces with no pretensions of allegory, sensitivity, or lyricism.

'The Eumenides' has something of a dramatic sense; at any rate, its first-person, present-tense narration gives it that effect. The title, which could entangle a critic in a web of allusive suggestions—of the drama by Aeschylus, of Orestes, guilt, murder, women coiled in snakes—is merely suggestive of someone being pursued, as Orestes was by the frightful Erinyes. The speaker says that 'those/ things which true paranoiacs/ think pursue them really do/ pursue me . . '. But he simply ignores the pursuers. The speaker's last words are vernacular, unflappable, British: 'They/ get frightfully annoyed about it,/ too'.[30]

'Lysistrata' and the untitled piece which falls third in the sequence are both past-tense narratives. The women's ultimatum in 'Lysistrata' is updated for World War II: 'Either/ throw down those guns, or abjure/ the pleasures of our beds!' But the men turn the tables on the women, much as they might in a James Thurber story. Accustomed to the pleasures of brothels, the modern warriors take the ultimatum as sanction to continue enjoying them. The last lines of the piece are spoken with mock-patriotism, and one almost hears stirring, martial music in the background:

> ... accordingly
> we shall not sheathe the sword until
> we have freed the smaller nations of
> Europe from the perpetual and recurring
> threat of German aggression.

The poem's amusing irony and possible sexual double entendre ('sheathe the sword') that we see in Reed's other war poems might have been welcome amidst all the gravity and all the ethereal love in most of *A Map of Verona*.

The 'lively sense of comedy and of the absurd' which Douglas Cleverdon's obituary remarked in Reed (in Stallworthy xv) comes through too in the untitled piece. The assurance of the 'large bright lady' is as absolute as that of the speakers in the other prose-poems as she seems to lean over conspiratorially to the narrator and inform him 'of the fact' that she is the virgin nymph Parthenope (on the authority of Ulysses, who has appeared to her in a vision). Unlike so many of Reed's poems in at least the first two parts of *A Map*, whose unnamed narrators and characters cry out Universal Condition, this piece unabashedly names her three sons: 'Peppino, Vittorio/ and Fernando'. The unarguable concreteness of her sons helps reinforce the comic incongruity of this one large, very un-nymphlike woman—mother of three very unvisionlike, tangible sons—claiming to be a virgin nymph.[31]

Reed's comic strand had a generous number of satiric fibres in it, as readers of 'Chard Whitlow' will vouch. Reed's second most recognized poem was the winning entry in The *New Statesman and Nation*'s contest #585, April 1941, responding to the following prompt: What would contemporary poets have written for *The Postscript* (the BBC's regular Sunday evening uplift show)? The choices included Dylan Thomas, John Masefield, Cole Porter, and of course T. S. Eliot. The poem was published in May and hailed by G. W. Stonier, the formulator of the contest, as 'a brilliantly funny Eliot' (422). The unanimous praise for Reed's piece has come from many quarters since, including Eliot himself. 'Most parodies of one's own work strike one as very poor', Eliot said, citing 'Chard' as the only one that 'deserves the success it has had' (in MacDonald 218). Dwight MacDonald listed 'broadness' as 'the sin of most Eliot parodies' (218); Elizabeth Jennings agrees with MacDonald that Reed's poem escapes it, satisfying its readers by being 'uproariously funny' while also 'shrewdly ironic' (1253).

From even before the first line, the poem does its comic work, some of it independent of Eliot, but most of it rewarding those readers with a sensitivity to Eliot's manner in *Four Quartets*. The title suggests a character of lesser intelligence, 'low wit', and/or a place that has been 'charred', presumably in the Blitz. The subtitle (*Mr Eliot's Sunday Evening Postscript*) cleverly alludes to the radio programme on which the piece will have its mythical reading and to Eliot's own short poem, 'The *Boston Evening Transcript*'. The poem itself is brimming with Eliot trademarks: the glib use of dead languages, the acknowledgement of religious authority, both Eastern and Western, and the abstruse musings on the nature of time. 'And this time last year I was fifty-four', Reed's speaker declares, 'And this time next year I shall be sixty-two'. Eliot also had a fondness for homely English place names. As parallels perhaps for Eliot's 'Clerkenwell', 'Putney', and 'Ludgate', three of the seven hills of London listed in 'Burnt Norton', Reed gives us 'Stoke or Basingstoke' (with further play on fire imagery). Eliot was never loath to juxtapose such mundanities against his deepest meditations on the loftiest issues of God, time and the afterlife. For Eliot, the juxtaposition rarely occurs in neighbouring lines, though it might, as in 'Burnt Norton', where 'Garlic and sapphires in the mud/ Clot the bedded axle-tree' and where we also find 'Eructation [violent eruption, as in a belch] of unhealthy souls/ Into the faded air'. In Reed's condensed Eliot, the yoking of high and low necessarily comes in the same poetic clause. His speaker chides us: 'the frigid burnings of purgatory will not be touched/ By any emollient'. Likewise, we are reminded that hell cannot be extinguished by 'the simple stirrup-pump', the modest device, resembling a bicycle pump, used to put out small fires from incendiary missiles.

Stylistically, Reed has matched Eliot's long, unmetronomic line, his propensity for paradox and a rhetorical method also favoured by Faulkner: a sort of progressive reconsideration of words—not merely worked out in drafts, but appearing in the final versions of their works—much as one might roll a gemstone around in one's palm to inspect all its facets. In 'Chard' the device is seen in the speaker's concession that even fewer precautions than one can take against the 'blast from bombs' can protect one 'against the blast from Heaven, *vento dei venti*,/ The wind within a wind, unable to speak for wind'. The pun in that second line is exquisite: in one sense, the wind has no tangible mouthpiece to speak *for* it, but Reed also hints that perhaps God, or more likely Eliot, is something of a windbag whose message is obscured by his 'wind', or bombastic language. In 'Chard' too we see Eliot mirrored in Reed's 'cautious and admonitory phrases' (Stonier 422), his hesitations, parentheticals, and qualifiers which tend to soften hard aphorism and harden soft lyricism. One might set, for example, a characteristic passage from 'East Coker'—'There is, it seems to us,/ At best, only a limited value/ In the knowledge derived from experience'—against the halting manner of Reed's lines: 'And I cannot say I should care (to speak for myself)/ To see my time over again—if you can call it time . . '. Add to all these features the morsel of literary history that Reed's response to the Blitz actually pre-dates Eliot's—'Little Gidding' was not drafted until June 1941—and it is easy to recognize 'Chard Whitlow' as a work of sheer genius.

Even the more formal framework of the sonnet proves an apt vehicle for the satiric wit which Reed rarely allowed in the poetry collected in *A Map of Verona*. Written apparently in 1939, 'Dull Sonnet' is listed by Stallworthy as part of the 'Green Spleen' sequence, though its manuscript was found in a separate folder of poems Reed evidently had rejected from a proposed second collection. It fits some singularly mundane language into the almost perfectly iambic lines of a hybrid sonnet: the first eight lines promising an Italian sonnet, the last six lines a Shakespearean quatrain of alternating rhyme followed by a couplet. The word choice in the first four and a half lines is comically lifeless:

> I have always been remarkably impressed
> By the various sights and sounds of trees and birds
> Respectively; have always thought that words
> Could not express the beauties of the West
> With much exactitude.

The four syllables of filler in line one (remarkably) and the monumental vagueness of line two are outdone by the pompously superfluous adverb *Respectively* so perfectly placed at the beginning of line three and followed by a caesura. This pause and the ploddingly exact iambic rhythm reinforce Reed's satire of imprecise diction in bad poetry. The satire is furthered with a parenthetical 'not seldom' in line seven and the labelled choices in line fourteen, the *(a)* and *(b)* meant to be spoken and serving to fill out the metre. More specifically, the poem may represent an act of counterrevolution against the revolt of Auden and others calling for the admittance of flat, 'unpoetic' diction into serious poetry.

'Dull Sonnet' is an excellent piece of satiric poetry. Why then was it not considered for any collection, least of all a poet's first collection, one that needed all the excellent poetry that could be mustered? An answer can be found in one critic's opinion that the inclusion of even 'Chard Whitlow' in *A Map of Verona* was an unwise decision. Henry Rago's implication—that in 'Chard' Reed is unconsciously parodying *himself* parroting Eliot—has validity when short lyrics like 'The Door and the Window' and nearly all Reed's long poems are held up next to his great parody. Similarly, the abstract diction of line two in 'Dull Sonnet' might have exposed that of even one of Reed's better lyrics, 'The Forest'. In that poem's generic group of trees various sights and sounds are made (and then stop being made) by 'each beast and bird'. Setting aside the insistent Shakespearean rhymes of 'Dull Sonnet', we also recognize the same lacklustre diction and syntax, along with pointless line divisions, that mar serious poems like 'Sailors' Harbour': 'In the eating-houses we always contrive to get near to/ The window, where we can keep an eye on the life-/ Bearing sea'.[32]

The dilemma Reed might have faced over the inclusion of 'Chard Whitlow' in *A Map of Verona* is prefigured by a review he wrote in early 1946 of a collection of V. S. Pritchett short stories. He had the highest praise for all the stories, but detected a 'false note' in Pritchett's inclusion of a satirical fantasy among their number. Certain adjectives of subtle connotation in Reed's other reviews regarding the 'slickness' of certain 'little' satires hint at the relatively low position of satire in Reed's literary hierarchy. Reed was also perhaps overly fastidious about consistency of tone. 'Chard' and the three 'Lessons of the War', his four poems of satiric character in *A Map*, appear together in a sort of ghetto at the end of the miscellaneous section called 'Preludes'. And the fact that 'Lessons of the War' does not merit an all-caps label in *A Map*'s table of contents—while 'The Desert', with its six wretched poems, and 'Philoctetes' do—is further evidence of Reed's inability to assess his early work lucidly and disinterestedly.

Such misjudgment may be part of the reason three other fine sonnets did not appear in *A Map*, or it may have been simply good judgment that kept these ribald poems off the printed page. The references to certain visceral matters are quite bold in these pieces, as opposed to the 'exceedingly improper' (Ackerley *Letters* 84) but extremely subtle bawdiness of

'Movement of Bodies', which Reed did publish in 1950. All are nevertheless artful pieces, rich in high and low comedy.

Each poem is addressed to a woman by her lover, a term we must use most loosely for the speaker of 'Spleen', whose revulsion at the figure of the woman rivals Gulliver's upon encountering the huge 'dug' of a Brobdingnagian woman. This is the low comedy, as the speaker 'with kindly forethought' removes his boots and joins her in a field, all the while bemoaning the features of his 'Surrealist Love', distorted far from the 'splendours of the classic norm' like a Picasso painting. 'I do not love the lobster in your loins', he confesses in the first line, presumably alluding to the reddish pinch of her vagina, nor the hiss from her navel (flatulence?), nor 'the great suction-pump that always joins/ Its mouth to mine to intercept my kiss'.

Though all three poems abound in sexual imagery, more or less graphic, devices of high comedy dominate. All three are written in the tradition of the Metaphysical Poets, seeking to match their brand of sharp wit and striking conceits that allow God to 'ravish' recalcitrant believers and introduce fleas and worms into love poetry. 'Green' is the most conventional of the three, a carpe diem appeal in the manner of Herrick and Marvell,[33] in which the speaker reminds his love that

> . . . Time will not roll back.
> When thirty winters shall besiege your brow
> And the little nymph be nymphomaniac,
> Don't be surprised to see Love's ancient trick.

The couplet holds his final entreaty: 'Ere Autumn whirl you to a worse newcomer/ Hold while you can, my Love, the shaking summer!' 'Spleen' seems especially to glance at Donne, specifically at 'Song' (the reference to mandrake-roots) and, in the speaker's imperative 'For God's sake change your form', to the opening line of 'The Canonization'. The poem also contains one of only two slant rhymes in these perfectly English sonnets, and it is a rich one: the word *drawers* in line eight directs us to *laws* two lines back and invites us, in keeping with the tone of the poem, to give it the working-class west English pronunciation. The pun in lines eleven and twelve juxtaposes the relative loftiness of 'Love's right true end'—intercourse as the necessary consummation of true love—with his lover's 'right true end'—her vagina, swathed in mandrake-roots, notoriously foul-smelling.

The wittiest of the sonnets is 'Falange', which maintains an ingenious (and historically and geographically accurate) conceit of the woman as Loyalist Spain and the man, especially his fingers, as the rapacious insurgents reasserting their dominance. Perhaps it is unfair to expect an upstart poet to include such a daring piece in a first collection the way, for example, an established poet like Ben Jonson could get away with including a 196-line scatological romp called 'The Voyage' among his *Epigrams*. Ironically, more than its ribaldry, the partisan politics of 'Falange' may have been a greater factor in its exclusion. In 1937, when each of the sonnets was written, Reed was in the early stages of his own rebellion, already cultivating his aesthetic, apolitical stance against Auden and other poets of the thirties.

In 'Falange''s rebellion the first victory is secured 'in the North'; this is mere foreplay, as the speaker commands the woman to part her 'smiling regiments' to greet his 'insurgent tongue'. The next victory is gained a little further south, in Seville and Burgos, her 'shining breasts', by the speaker's 'five advancing armies'. 'Falange', the name of the fascist organization which eventually took power when the Loyalists were defeated in 1939, is Spanish for *phalanx*, a closely knit deployment of advancing infantry, and is etymologically related to 'phalanges', which are bones of the toes or fingers. Reed brilliantly makes use of all these denotations and connotations. The fingers 'manoeuvre' to stimulate her nipples, raising on 'both fair crests' a 'new cathedral', alluding to the return to power of the Roman Catholic Church, whose collective property valued at $500 million had been confiscated by the Republic. The woman resists, and although the 'garden suburbs' (pubic hair?) fall easily, her 'Red centre is a very Hell'; indeed, the leftist troops held on grimly to Madrid (almost exactly in the geographical centre of the country) for the rest of the war. From the imperative in line one ('clean your teeth') to that in line fourteen ('open: let your conquering Hero come!'), Reed has succeeded in depicting the fascists as vile and arrogant aggressors interested not in the woman/country for herself but in power. Their violent domination of Spain, though not consummated until two years after the poem's composition, is portrayed as the most repugnant of rapes.

Reed undervalued certain sub-genres inherently. Allegory and fantasy were two he seemed to sneer at, and satire ranked nearly as low. As he undervalued satire as a whole and his own aptitude for comedy, so he misjudged his dramatic gift, failing in his early poetry to give that side of himself free play. There really is a much keener dramatic sense demonstrated in the fourteen-line, unpublished 'Spleen'—a clearly identifiable listener, one whom we can see (all too well!); a definite scene; strong emotion—than in 'Antigone' and 'Philoctetes', the long second and third poems of Reed's 'Triptych'. Both purport to be dramatic poems, the first a dialogue and the second a monologue, but the language of both is too often quasi-lyrical and empty. When in 'Antigone' one of the two onlookers asks what kind of world Antigone has left behind after her suicide, the other unnamed citizen's overly wrought response heaps intangible upon wordy intangible:

> —I am that world, oh listen.
> A drooping wind has been set to sigh on the silence
> And disappear into darkness; there is a pause
> Of waiting till it sighs again and goes.

In 'Philoctetes' the title character utters a similarly nebulous lament which makes its vague, self-pitying way

Through a catechism of ghosts and a toiling litany,
To the ultimate sanctum of delerium, unremembered,
The recapitulation of the bitterly forgotten,
And then forgotten again in the break of day.

These poems, like some in 'Preludes' and 'Tintagel', are marginally dramatic, but the drama is inert, entirely intellectual and abstract. *Drooping* promises some real emotion, but it modifies *wind*; something is 'toiling', maybe even sweating, but no, it is a 'toiling litany'. The only *break* is of dawn. As with most of the 'Tintagel' series, these poems focus on characters whose stories are inherently powerful, but manage to wring most of the emotional intensity out of them; what is left is limp lyricism.

Somehow, though, the first poem of the sequence works. Where 'Chard Whitlow' and Reed's early sonnets and prose-poems trumpet Reed's aptitude for the comic and satiric which manifested itself in his highly amusing radio comedies of the 1950s, 'Chrysothemis' shows that Reed was also capable of creating serious dramatic situations, involving named characters that are more than just amanuenses for Reed's own delicate thoughts. Chrysothemis was just a bit player in *The Oresteia,* 'the passive, evasive sister of Electra' as Reed describes her in his notes, yet his poetic treatment of this woman lends her a dignity of near-tragic proportions.

Reed asks us to consider what happens to those characters who are left to bear 'the sins of the fathers' in the same way that Sophocles in *Antigone*, for example, ponders the fate of the children of incestuous union. 'Chrysothemis', Reed's drama of another ill-starred woman, is set in a distinct place, the 'falling, decaying mansion' where Agamemnon, Clytemnestra, and Aegisthus have been murdered; at a distinct time, sunset; and in a distinctly powerful dramatic situation, outlined by Chrysothemis herself in the first verse paragraph of her soliloquy: 'I have set myself to protect/ Against the demons that linger inside our walls,/ [The] saddened, quiet children of darkness and shame'. This determination, to care for children brought into the world by the woman who had cuckolded then murdered one's father, in the house where both crimes occurred, would not be in anyone's nature. But it is even more out of character for Chrysothemis, who we learn in the fifth and sixth lines of the poem is the kind of person who '[s]uffered the winds [she] would not strive against,/ Entered whirlpools and was flung outside them'.

In the third and fourth verse paragraphs, Chrysothemis recalls a time of truce in the family (comfort enough to a non-confrontational daughter), a time when in

> . . . the long broad days of summer,
> . . .
> The gardens glittered under the sweeping sun,
> The inmates kept to their rooms, and hope
> Rose in the silence.

After the murder of Agamemnon, Clytemnestra had annealed herself to the new order, Electra seemed to be resigned to it, and she and Clytemnestra had '[c]alled off their troops to bury their dead'. Faithful to her nature (and Henry Reed's), Chrysothemis had moved from room to room to peer through 'slotted shutters' at her mother and sister in the garden, hearing no words but alert to the nuances of gesture as the delicate armistice was maintained. (Reed preferred a tableau, but a dumb show was next best.) But true to the higher forces infusing the lives of the Greek aristocracy, Fate holds sway: 'The fragile dams would burst, indeed constructed/ Only for breaking down'.

Like all Reed's serious poems, 'Chrysothemis' '[seems] to sigh, and then again' emit a 'sigh and another silence'. Nobody does much. Still, a great deal distances 'Chrysothemis' from the other two poems of 'Triptych' and indeed, all the quasi-dramatic poems in *A Map*. Though given in soliloquy, Chrysothemis's words remind us twice that there are others present, the sleeping children of Clytemnestra and Aegisthus, not to mention the 'demons' of the adulterers and others haunting the household. Chrysothemis is not just a Woman Thinking or a Woman Feeling: there is some stage business, as she moves to and from a window, and wipes dust from a mirror to examine her reflection. Yes, she meditates and considers and remembers and regrets, but these lyrical passages work because they are not too far removed from common human speech and experience. The cruel paradoxes of the house 'decaying but not dying' (like Tithonus?) and both 'preserving and embalming' the 'shuttered rooms, the amulets, the pictures ...' are affecting also because they are within, not refined from, the dramatic situation, of which Reed keeps us aware through images: 'the hanging gardens carved on our mountain', 'terraces, groves, and arbours', the 'great bronze doors of the bridal chamber'. The poet's carefully placed images invite us to see a contrast between the glittering gardens of the relative idyll before Orestes' return and the empty gardens of the present time. The idle 'furniture covered with sheets' contrasts too with the furniture that was so integral to an earlier scene. This is the scene of Agamemnon's death, and though Chrysothemis reports it to us only as she has pieced it together in her imagination, it is nevertheless a crackling scene, unusually violent:

> My father rises thus from a bath of blood,
> Groping from table to chair in a dusky room
> Through doorways into darkening corridors,
> Falling at last in the howling vestibule.

Here is the poet showing us (and himself) that he is prepared to paint big scenes, as he does in his radio play nearly ten years later in describing the death agonies of terrified Pompeiians, fleeing the 'hot wet ash' as it

> pressed them down, surrounded them, engulfed them, found out every curve of their bodies ... The last fraction of breathed-in air passed out again in a bubble from their mouths into the filthy blackness ... (166)

'Chrysothemis' is a good poem, not a great one. But as poems like 'Dull Sonnet', 'Lysistrata', and 'Chard Whitlow' show what Reed could accomplish when he allowed the comic and satiric strands into his poetic fabric, so does 'Chrysothemis' represent the early acme of Reed's understanding of his Dramatic strand. We see this poem better than most of Reed's, and we also hear it better. John Lehmann recognized the dramatic element in Reed's early poems, citing 'Chrysothemis' as one that 'read aloud remarkably well' (168). The poem may touch our soul, but to do so it more immediately reaches our senses first, as nearly all good poetry must. Though it is less self-consciously lyrical than Reed's other efforts, 'Chrysothemis' succeeds, perhaps ironically, in its lyrical passages because it allows them to grow out of the dramatic situation. Lehmann saw too a hint of the Aphoristic in the poem: to him it could be viewed as a '[parable] of the artist's predicament in a world given over to violence' (168). Chrysothemis is something of an artist, at least in the sense that Reed and apparently Lehmann viewed artists: she is a sensitive person, cast out of the 'whirlpools' of life, left to observe her world through slots and frames or the gauze of imagination. In all these respects, 'Chrysothemis' symbolizes the next directions of Reed's career: his fascination with the lives of artists; his interest in drama; and his abiding faith in verse, from both the radio studio or the stage, to carry that drama to people of taste.

1 According to Roger Savage, even at the peak of his success, Reed kept 'a low profile in the London literary circus' (158).

2 Melville's poetic gift is not to be gainsaid, though one wonders how Reed might have chosen these relatively unimpressive samples from all the choices in Melville's novel.

3 Shewin's embarrassingly purple prose, however, is not to be taken as corresponding one-to-one to Joyce's. From *A Hedge, Backwards*, for instance, comes this sample:

> There, by the familiar shining stream, in that glade as verdant and fresh as the groves of Avalon, Peter looked at Paul. It was as though he were seeing him for the first time. Or no, not seeing him for the first time, but for the first time realising, realising like some slowly delicious, slowly flickering delicious flame, that Paul . . . was his brother. The words flamed in his thought like some utterance from Holy Writ: THOU ART MY BROTHER. Peter had never known it so innerly . . . (109).

4 Significantly absent in Reed are epic and tragic strands. Certainly many worthy writers do not have or do not nurture these impulses in their poetry. Reed borrowed his epic and his tragedy from others, as seen in his radio adaptations of *Moby Dick* and Hardy's *The Dynasts*.

5 By 1949, at least, Reed had forgiven and forgotten, expressing his appreciation of 'the admirable *Scrutiny*' (in Savage 181).

6 Reed the romantic, who never drove an automobile, is partial to ships and the occasional horse as means of transportation, but one is hard-pressed to find cars, planes, or trains playing any major role in his works.

7 Perhaps ironically, it is often Reed's shortest poems which maintain the strongest narrative pulse.

8 Unless otherwise indicated, all quotations of Reed's poetry are from *Collected Poems*. Page numbers for poems in *Collected* will be cited only for Reed's two longest poems, 'The Auction Sale' and 'Psychological Warfare'. Page numbers will of course be provided for all other quotations from secondary and primary sources.

9 As 'a faint, barely detectable story-line' (Dedicatory Letter) runs

through the four comedies Reed collected in *Hilda Tablet and Others*, so might a similarly silken band of plot bind the poems of 'The Desert'.

10 The Captain' is the kind of poem whose composition may have followed the model of T. S. Eliot, who once told a critic: 'The conscious problems with which one is concerned in the actual writing are more those of a quasi musical nature . . . than of a conscious exposition of ideas' (in *Literature* 702).

11 So pronounced is the allegorical sense of the poem that the one phrase including the specificity of a proper noun ('The evil captain had fled defeated to Norway') seems incongruous and silly.

12 Reed seems not especially interested in specific nature description, either in itself or for symbolic suggestiveness. Thus, in his poems one will not find a linnet, raven, skylark, nightingale, or hermit thrush. The generality of 'beast and bird', moreover, invites allegorical reading.

13 I defy Harold Bloom himself to pinpoint these four aspects.

14 That Tristram's tower 'Rises and falls and rises' suggests not only the speaker's vantage point — a rocking ship off the coast — but also the literal decay of the walls and the imaginative rebuilding of the walls in one's memory.

*15* Though Henry Rago and Alan Jenk cite the first of these lines as evidence of Reed's attempting paradox in the manner of Eliot, they are taking as to mean 'while'; rather, the line is more simply paraphrased 'We cannot learn to forget (unfortunately) in the same way, or as easily, as we can learn to remember'.

*16* 'The Wall', in 'Preludes', is likewise full of abstracts *doing* all kinds of things, having things done to them, and trying to have personalities. It is ironic that in a rare Reed poem with actions, those actions are not made or received by people; instead, 'flower and weed caress/ And fill our double wilderness'; 'The tangled thickets play and sprawl'; the *riot* of the flowers and weeds is 'undismayed/ And unreproached' and '[t]he months' are 'unaccompanied by fears'.

17 Here again, note the overburdened abstracts.

18 Elizabeth Jennings disagrees, finding in 'A Map of Verona' 'nostalgia without a trace of sentimentality' (1252).

19 Rago says the 'grotesque fault' of mixed metaphor is rare in *A Map*, but instances are all too easy to locate, as in 'The Wall', where the speaker again is trying to convey a sense of menace threatening him and someone else (a lover?): 'some dark, unseen hand of stone/ Hovered across our days of ease/ And strummed its tunes upon the breeze'.

20 *Collected Poems* shows *for* in this line, which must be an error. The text in *A Map of Verona* reads *from*.

21 This may or may not be what Klingopulos meant by his cryptic remark (on 'Lessons of the War', oddly): 'The appropriate reader composes the poetry' (142).

22 Again, the abstraction of Reed's language can be maddening. Why 'the place' and 'the person'? Why not North Grubshire and Bewick Finzer, or Tilbury Town and Eben Flood, or even Smithville and Bob?

23 Some readers may see an analogue in Ursula K. Le Guin's short story 'The Ones Who Walk Away from Omelas', in which the narrator gives the reader license to paint the joys of the utopic city as 'your own fancy bids, . . . for certainly I cannot suit you all'. The citizens may have 'floating light-sources, fuelless power, a cure for the common cold. . . . As you like it'. And if you want the Omelasians to have *drooz*, the drug which among other things heightens orgasm, that may also be part of your own vision of the city.

24 48, more properly, if one takes the first feature — that is, whether 'You, I, or we' build the garden — as a choice of three options.

25 Quite inexplicably, the *Listener* reviewer contends that 'The Desert' contains the best work in *A Map of Verona*.

26 'Eliot's Heir' is the snide title of G. D. Klingopulos's scathing review of *A Map*. Klingopulos, like most critics, found Reed, at least when he adopted his gnomic and paradoxical manner, not 'Eliot's Heir' but an Eliotaster.

27 There are 'tangled thickets' too in 'The Wall'. The poem is an allegory; it is really almost impossible to have a wall (or a garden) without one. But amidst all the clashing metaphors and vague, pretentious expression it is impossible to figure out what the referent of the allegory is, even when the poet closes with a couplet (' . . . such a wall/ Is based in death, and does not fall'.) offering a clue. 'The Wall' is pompous, and

we feel like reproved children: we know we've been given a lesson, but we don't get it.

28 Significantly, the 'you' in the poem (uncharacteristic for Reed) is not second but third person. True to the aphoristic spirit of the poem, it speaks not to a specific listener or a particular case but presents general, universal cases: 'One cannot . . .' or 'It is impossible to . . .'.

29 J. R. Ackerley, though obliged to return 'Sailors' Harbour', defended Reed's choice of *brothels* against another editor who wanted the word changed to *movies*.

30 The tone and style of these three pieces might remind some readers of Stephen Crane's poems along the lines of 'A man said to the universe', or 'I saw a man pursuing the horizon' (setting aside Crane's loftier subject matter).

31 This scene is later given a fuller treatment in *Return to Naples* (185).

32 One of the line breaks creates a pun on the Bering Sea, but why?

33 Klingopulos saw Reed's published poem, 'The Wall', as indebted to Marvell. He was right in suggesting that this weak poem's only tenuous resemblance to Marvell is in its attempt to be witty and its tetrameter couplets, reminiscent of Marvell's in poems like 'To His Coy Mistress' and 'The Garden'.

Given the five strands of Henry Reed's poetic fabric, with the sinewy toughness of some and the tendency of others to fray, the most fortunate, perhaps even the inevitable course for his career to take was toward radio drama. Granted, nearly everyone's career choices are affected by more than just the recognition of where one's talents lie: the pull of family and friends, the vicissitudes of the job market, how much one will be paid, of course. But it is possible that in the late forties and early fifties Reed had begun to recognize and sort through his literary gifts and deficiencies. He was good at comedy, and he was good at the 'dramatic', that is, setting up powerful scenes at emotionally charged moments, crafting ironic situations, and juxtaposing high and low or, even more delicately, the high and the not quite as high. His plays show how adept he was, along with the casts and production teams whose excellence he always credited, at conveying fine distinctions of class, education, and mood with only the barest use of narrative: instead, through the dramatist's primary tool of dialogue, along with music and sound effects. The Lyrical strand of his poetic personality, along which he had achieved sporadic success in *A Map of Verona*, works well in drama only in small doses, Reed acknowledged, when it grows out of, rather than being impressed into, the dramatic situation. Moreover, the Aphoristic, that part of his poetic character which Reed as heir to Auden and Eliot felt much obliged to cultivate, yet which remained in his work underdeveloped, is uniquely ill-suited to non-visual drama. A radio play is generally heard once; it flits through the air and disappears. Aficionados of theatre need help with aphorism, especially when it is tightly knotted in paradox or other complex wordplay. Aphoristic language is less suited to the airwaves than to the stage, where gesture, body language, and mise-en-scène provide additional clues to tone and multiple meaning, and where a good play has a run and can be viewed more than once. In fact, a few of Reed's plays were produced more than once, and he was fortunate in that, while so many worthy works by his contemporaries in the heyday of British radio drama in the forties and fifties did not reach print, over half of his plays now rest within hard covers, where a writer's more compressed expression may be reflected upon any number of times at the reader's leisure.

The Narrative, another mode in which Reed was unsuccessful or scorned altogether, also is poorly suited to drama, on stage or over the airwaves. Narration from a figure outside the drama strikes one as especially artificial, and even a voice-over from a character in the story often seems pretentious.[1] Through the medium of dialogue, narration takes a new name: exposition. But unless the playwright wholly justifies it by, say, having old friends bring each other up to date after a long separation (and sometimes not even then), the relation of events seems clumsy and not well integrated into the dramatic whole.

Reed came to know that the highly charged passages of lyric poetry (as with aphorism) can be taxing on the ear of even the most intent radio play listener. In two radio talks of 1951, Reed warned that listeners (even more so than readers) of verse drama have limits, much as Poe and Coleridge had reasoned that a long poem cannot be *all* poetry; even Eliot's *The Family Reunion*, in Reed's view an intensely poetic play, 'contained about as much fine poetry as one could reasonably expect or put up with in one evening' ('Towards "The Cocktail Party"' II, 804). He insisted 'that the verse drama must not be regarded as exclusively the prerogative of the lyric poet; and indeed that the initial practice and habits of lyric poetry may prove strongly deterrent or misleading to the verse dramatist' ('Towards "The Cocktail Party"' I, 763). Reed felt it was 'necessary to remind ourselves that what we want in the theatre is good drama' and that the 'dramatic transactions' behind the playwright's words must have meaning in themselves, no matter how beautiful and fraught with emotion those words are ('Towards' I, 763). Presumably Reed's cautions have to do with the strain this most condensed sub-genre of poetry places on the mind of the listener (one possible reason, too, for his disdain of poetry readings). In his Radio Notes column, Reed commends C. Day Lewis for reading a new poem 'twice straight off', recognizing that 'lyric poetry is notoriously difficult to grasp when read aloud for the first time' (*New Statesman* 10 January 1948, 28). But Reed knew too that the challenges of listening to lyric poetry are perhaps balanced by the joys: the sheer beauty and musicality of the words. Even so, as in 'Chrysothemis', those passages of highest lyricism in Reed's radio plays emerge from the situations which the playwright has manipulated to be most 'dramatic', those in which the characters' emotions (and the listeners') are pulled the tautest.

Of course, Reed's best works for radio are dramatic in the plainest sense of the word: they are plays, despite his protestations that 'the things are neither plays nor poems' and despite the BBC's label, 'features', which he also disdained (Foreword to *Streets*). They are not essays or short stories. Nor are his biographically faithful studies of the Italian poet Giacomo Leopardi or his dramatic tour through *The Streets of Pompeii* mere documentaries.[2] In all six plays collected in *The Streets of Pompeii* volume, too, there is well-orchestrated conflict, good 'drama' in the more abstract sense, as for example when we listen painfully as Leopardi falls in love with Fanny Targioni, a silly, insubstantial young woman, or when Reed artfully withholds 'from his sightless audience until the last and most poignant moment' (Savage 185) the revelation that young Leopardi, in his self-imposed, health-breaking labours in his father's library, has made himself into a hunchback. There is too a wonderful episode in *The Great Desire I Had* in which 'Guglielmo' Shakespeare stands in the Duke Vincenzo's palace in Mantua, envying Giulio Romano's sprawling depiction of 'lascivious Helen' and all the principals and scenes of the Greek-Trojan saga, lamenting the paralyzing writer's block which has limited his own production to theatre 'hackwork' and stymied the work he envisions for his epic poem on the siege of Troy. Reed draws out his dramatic irony for six and a half pages as Vincenzo himself enters the room and faces numerous impertinent questions and remarks from Shakespeare, who believes the Duke is a low-ranking palace functionary. Finally, the listener hears the '*clink of coins*' as Shakespeare tips the great nobleman for his wise advice to abandon the epic.[3]

Reed's keen dramatic sense is also showcased by his deft management of the playwright's eternal problem of exposition. In the *Leopardi* plays he contrives to incorporate nearly all pertinent details of place, time, and previous events into the words of the characters themselves, augmented by the music of pianos and drums, the sounds of doors and windows and of distinctively tolled bells. The difficulty is circumvented (in what some may see as compromise, others as creative or pragmatic theatrical problem-solving) through the use of choric figures in nearly every other play, certainly all his works with serious aims. Only one play succumbs to giving such a pedestrian label as 'Narrator' to the figure; in all the others, at the least, the narrator also doubles as a character in the play, as is the case with Herbert Reeve in the comedies. But the choric commentary is usually more intricate, possibly owing a debt to Hardy, whose epic-drama *The Dynasts* Reed so lovingly adapted for radio in 1951. That play includes a complex cast of 'Phantom Intelligences' who comment on the drama and, as one might expect of the Spirit Sinister and the Spirit of the Pities for example, often tug in divergent directions. In Reed, the action is frequently stopped for commentary, usually in verse, from two counterpointed perspectives: those of Ishmael and Father Mapple in *Moby Dick*; two commentators identified simply as 'HE' and 'SHE' in *Pytheas*; and in *Streets* the Sibyl of Cumae, a priestess of Apollo who speaks in verse, set against the prose of a Henry Reed figure called the Traveller.

Reed's other great poetic gift, for the Comic, shows mightily in the plays, too. Even in the plays which Roy Walker too tidily labelled those of the 'thinking' Reed (presumably those collected in *The Streets of Pompeii* plus *Moby Dick*) versus the 'winking' Reed (380) can be found passages of wit and humour. And in *The Great Desire I Had* plus *Pytheas* and the four more conspicuously winking plays in the *Hilda Tablet* collection, comic and satiric songs and poems periodically burst through the predominant prose. Some of these can only be called wacky, as for example a song from the unpublished *Pytheas* called 'Jolly Snowballs', which is all the more wacky in contrast to the grave introduction a pre-Christian Briton gives to Pytheas and his crew:

> (SADLY) There be times of the winter, the time of snow and frostcold in the hall, when our mood is bounden with sorrow, and the ice lieth heavy around the heart. Ye shall hear our songs of that season, oh strangers from over the swan's way. (61)

The '*VERY CHEERFUL*' song follows, sung as a madrigal by a choir of female voices. Eight of its twenty-one lines go a long way:

> Hey, jolly, jolly winter,
> And jolly, jolly winter,
> And jolly, jolly winter,
> And you have come too:
> And we will throw our jolly, jolly snowballs,
> And our jolly, jolly snowballs
> And our jolly snowballs
> At YOU. (61)

Other verses in the comedies are amusing doggerel of a bawdier nature as, for instance, the ballad-stanza piece which Stephen Shewin, a highly maladjusted psychologist, attributes to his brother Richard, the 'poet's novelist'. Written in the persona of Stephen's wife Connie, these 'unsavoury ditties' (*A Very Great Man Indeed* 16) purport to chronicle the sordid passion of Connie for Richard. In the last stanza 'Connie' (we suspect Stephen is the actual author) justifies her infidelity:

So that's why I leave poor old Stephen
  And hop over to Richard instead:
Psychology's all right in the proper place,
  But I know what I like in bed.
(*Great Man* 17)

Stephen, whose marriage is childless (unless you consider his wife's brood of cats), attributes other 'unseemly verses' to Richard, revealing Stephen's own bitterness at what he views as his other brother's scheme to gain the lucrative inheritance:

While Stephen does no more than read
Little books on How to Breed,
On the other hand my brother Ned
Mistakes his home for an oyster-bed.
(*Great Man* 42-43)[4]

In other verse from the plays, the comedy is subtler, as in a parody of A. E. Housman in *Pytheas* and the exquisitely trite pop lyrics of Brian Shewin, one of the twelve children of Edward 'Ned' Shewin:

You are my chance of happiness,
  Please don't turn it into distress.
Oh, moon, just stay . . .
Five minutes longer,
Four minutes,
Three minutes longer,
Two minutes,
One minute.
Oh! Oh! (*Private Life* 91-92)

As with 'Jolly Snowballs', Brian Shewin's lyrics (set to his brother's music) are all the funnier for the deadpan framing Reed provides. Brian modestly labels one cliche-ridden piece as 'experimental' and '*avant-garde*' (*The Primal Scene, As It Were ...*

171-72). Another piece, Brian and Owen Shewin's foray into black dialect ('Yeah, boss, / Dem weeds/ Grow ride up'n ole home-door') is followed by young Owen's sage caution: 'Of course, you have to be very careful with that type of lyric. It can be done, of course, but you have to be very careful with it' (*A Hedge, Backwards* 124). The banality of 'Don't Hurt My Heart' is set in relief by the reverent tone of Herbert Reeve's narration:

> How very easily, how very lightly the young write of sorrow's touch! It seems that youthful genius has *instinctively* a knowledge of those depths which experience has not yet, thank God, led it to. One thinks at once, of course, of the youthful Leopardi, of Rimbaud, of Keats . . . (*Great Man* 47)[5]

The song itself appears less than a page later. Its refrain alone should illustrate the witty absurdity of Reed's juxtaposition:

> Baby, don't hurt my heart, baby,
> Baby, don't make me sigh.
> Baby, don't make me smart, baby.
> Baby, don't make me cry. (48)[6]

These passages of rhymed verse are noteworthy exceptions for Reed the playwright; verse as a dramatic medium steadily gave over to prose as his career burgeoned and then began to wane in the 1950s. Indeed, Henry Reed wrote only two plays entirely in verse[7]—fittingly, perhaps, his studies of the Italian poet Giacomo Leopardi—but incorporated significant verse portions into three other early dramatic works: his adaptation of *Moby Dick* in 1947; *Pytheas*, his 'dramatic speculation' from the same year; and his award-winning *The Streets of Pompeii*, first produced in 1952. But the simple equation of verse to poetry is overly simplistic, we would all agree, and even though he was not entirely consistent on the subject in his critical writings, Reed generally was quite vigilantly protective of the distinction between verse and poetry. Though the present study insists on admitting the Comic as an important element of Reed's poetic character, it is hard to see much 'poetic' in a bawdy little song he ascribes to a street urchin in *The Great Desire I Had*:

> And now it's two in the morning,
> And I hope nobody will pass,
> For she's taken my Sunday breeches off,
> And she's kissing me on the . . .
> Oh Teresa, Oh Teresa,
> She's a girl to know . . . (239)

The steady meter and rhyme (or at least the suggestion of rhyme) no more qualify this as poetry than they do the '*i* before *e*' jingle. In contrast, no one would gainsay the poetic character of the play's opening lines, which happen to be written in prose:

> This is the air . . . That is the glorious sun . . .Westward from Venice the blind bronze eyes of Verrocchio's horseman, high-mounted in the square of St John and St Paul, glare toward the domes of Padua. In Padua, city of learning, the eyes of the horseman of Donatello, in the square of St Anthony, glare eastward back. The servitors of violence. Between them plies the peaceful river, the Brenta, charged with boats . . . (229)

With the opening puns, the alliteration, and the rich connotations of words like *glare*, *plies*, and *charged*, this is highly lyrical language.

Such passages, in fact, belie arbitrary distinctions between verse and prose. In choosing material for Part IV of *Collected Poems* (selections from the radio plays), Jon Stallworthy seemed to labour under a very narrow definition of poetry. He neglected any passage which appeared in a script as prose: he was apparently beguiled by any passages with jagged right-hand margins and upper-case letters along the left margin. Further, when he did excerpt passages written in Reed's distinctive and often praised long, unrhymed verse line, he admitted no rapid exchanges among characters and muted the dramatic character of his selections by editing out the names of the speakers, as in the verse from *Pytheas* and *Moby Dick*. From *Leopardi*, he scoured 112 pages of blankish verse, some very good, and selected only a little song performed by Fanny Targioni's children:

> Little bird, my little dove,
> Little dove, as white as snow:
> See, I have you in my hands,
> And I shall not let you go.
> And I shall not let you go.
> And I shall not let you go. (*Monument* 92)

Granted, William Shakespeare's songs seem thinner when taken out of their natural environment, but even in its context (which Stallworthy does not acknowledge in giving these six lines a page to themselves in *Collected Poems*), 'Little dove' is inferior to dozens of other passages of less formal versification in *Leopardi*. From *The Streets of Pompeii*, Stallworthy's selections seem equally mysterious. He passes over the sophisticated prose meditations of the Traveller, the highly lyrical prose soliloquy of an old man facing death from the creeping lava, and even the tetrameter verse of the Sibyl of Cumae in favour of the paired sonnets of the young lovers, Francesca and Attilio. These pieces, though quite moving in their context, are also somewhat prosy, in their trite love-talk, for example. Francesca admires Attilio's 'dark hair, .../ The curve of his silent cheek', and 'the golden splendour/ Of his throat ...'. Moreover, Reed pads seventeen syllables into Francesca's last line, which takes its time trying to get to a rhyme for 'above him': she will avoid looking at her lover, 'Lest he should see, when he wakes, dear Attilio, how dearly I love him'.

Unquestionably, many prose passages elsewhere in the Reed dramatic oeuvre possess more 'poetic' qualities than these pieces. Most occur in Reed's choric interludes, and their excellence grows in part out of Reed's artful circumvention of 'the blandness and buttonholing of conventional narration'

(Savage 185). In addition to keeping his Dramatic strand free from the taint of pure narration, to preventing his radio plays from sounding like dramatized novels, which he felt were nearly always failures ('Towards' I, 764), Reed managed to make these speeches highly lyrical.

'The most virtuosic choric narration', Roger Savage believes (185), is found in *Vincenzo*; it is given by four of the Mantuan nobleman's women: his wife and three mistresses. The first of these in *Vincenzo*, termed a 'meditation' in Reed's stage directions, directly precedes the hero's initial entrance, shirtless, into the rose-garden of Barbara, the Countess of Sala. Barbara has admiringly likened Ippolita, another of the prince's lovers, to a rose, before Reed leaves Ippolita alone with her thoughts, tinged with self-irony:

> So I stayed and looked at the roses and was like a rose myself. Oh, roses; roses of Colorno. In the windless summer air, millions of them, calm and unshaken. . . . with the soft full blooms of yellow and red about me, as I cupped my hands gently over this one or that, . . . I knew how many kinds of jealousy can be felt at one and the same time . . . How often? Where? And what had he called her? He never believed in real names; we were unreal to him until he had found his own names for us. Me, he called Andromeda. (If I could only mislay jealousy, if I could lose mistrust ...) (278)

Ippolita's speech provides exposition, to be sure, but in its acknowledgement of her setting, and in its pained series of jealous questions, it is dramatic; it is lyrical in the parallelism of her parenthetical remark and in the lushness and suggestiveness of its descriptions: the roses 'calm and unshaken', 'million-petalled' (and, later, as Vincenzo makes love to her: 'Roses above me. Yellow un-nodding heads, and golden beneath them his, bending to mine. Reprieve. Or red, open roses, circling his head. Reprieve. The soft flesh of roses, kissing me, caressed by the warmth of roses ...'. [281]).

These small samples of *Vincenzo* cannot do justice to the cumulative dramatic artistry of the play's multi-voiced chorus. Taken by themselves, any one of the women's speeches runs dangerously close to the kind of insubstantial lyricism Reed was vulnerable to in *A Map of Verona*: 'precious', in the words of one critic, mere 'fluency at low pressure' to another. We find a tougher, surprisingly political lyricism in *Return to Naples*, whose central consciousness is again more than just a 'narrator'. '*H.*' is not just a generically aureate host for some BBC documentary; specifically, he is an older, wiser Henry Reed looking back at, and directing his words to, his youthful self through each of the five visits. In one passage, he concedes that the 'high clean rooms' of his beloved Neapolitan family insulate him from the 'noise, the squalor, the crowdedness' of the lower floors' denizens. 'The cities of Hell must be built thus', he muses,

> on hillsides, where none can escape the upward or downward glance of his neighbour. High up, you seemed aloof from where, below, Naples stank and festered, but in two minutes you could plunge into a *vicolo* of descending noise and horror between high tenements, the bottom floors of which were, cave-like, open to the view. And always the same scene in the dark interior: the huge matrimonial bed, a single chair, a picture of a holy face. (184)

In a later meditation *H.* remarks on the 'oddly unfamiliar' Italy which greets him in 1939:

> Here and there had sprung up smooth huge featureless modern buildings, which seemed to say: whatever we make let us make it big, and let it be all surface, let it have no features, for features betray human idiosyncrasy and weakness. We will build in perfect cubes and spheres and ellipsoids, buildings so big that all who enter shall know their own smallness and despise their own separateness. All shall be big. The letter-box at the new post-office shall be so wide that

> in your sleep you shall dream you are posting yourself in it. (197)

The passage is so accomplished that Reed is able to incorporate into it a hint of aphorism without the usual fuss or pretentiousness.

Though the language of these passages is fluent and artful, Reed would have blushed at any excessive adulation for the prose of his plays. As evidenced by most of his poems in *A Map of Verona* and in his critical observations of the forties, he tended to set up sharply delineated parameters and unwavering hierarchies for literature. In two radio talks on verse drama, he worked hard to distinguish the effects of prose and verse and further to erect a sharp partition between 'poetry' and 'verse',[8] for example in chronicling Shakespeare's development as a dramatist, his mastery of the power of verse which necessarily came after his education in the power of *poetry*. 'Bravely attired language', Reed believed (and so much of the language in *The Streets of Pompeii* collection qualifies) was not even essential to good verse drama. Such beautiful and affecting language Reed concedes to playwrights of the previous generations like Shaw and Ibsen and, in his more generous moments, might have acknowledged in O'Neill and even in Tennessee Williams, toward whom he was quite sneering. Though ironically he was to travel the same route, Reed laments Ibsen's abandonment of 'the sharp and delicate instrument of verse' that made *Peer Gynt* such an 'expansive and penetrating work' ('Towards' I, 764) for the blunter instrument of prose in all his later plays. To Reed it must have seemed like giving Seurat a four-inch housepainter's brush to fashion his masterpieces of pointillism.

Rhythm gave Henry Reed something that even the best of his prose in *The Streets of Pompeii* collection could not provide. The rhythm of verse, Reed would argue, always pumping away, comes to the foreground, like a heartbeat itself, during moments of greatest emotion (in somewhat the same way that strict rhythm asserts itself in prominent positions in 'Naming of Parts', in the last line of the stanzas). To Reed, 'the poet's rhythm' was necessary for the audience of a play 'to put part of its mind at ease with the poet' ('Towards' II, 804). He went further, suggesting that until a 'common norm' of rhythm is established, not necessarily the blank verse of the Elizabethan playwrights but a conventional verse form of some kind, 'the dramatist cannot hope to be heard. He may be enthusiastically listened to, but he will not be heard' ('Towards' II, 804).

Audiences have not agreed. We know, forty-plus years later, that verse drama has never reasserted itself as Reed had hoped. The comeback has never materialized, in great measure because people's listening skills, never as hale as Reed's anyway, have atrophied, in part from the bombardment of noise from popular music, advertising and television. Perhaps he was preaching to the unconvertible.

Nevertheless, Reed tilted at the windmill of the masses until 1952, when his last play with significant verse portions, *The Streets of Pompeii*, was given its first production.[9] The only plays in which Reed attempted to use the sharp instrument of verse throughout are his pair of studies on Giacomo Leopardi, generally regarded as the next great Italian lyric poet after Dante and Petrarch. The dramatic diptych is extremely faithful to what we know of Leopardi's life (even in its finer details, such as a chess match Leopardi describes in his *Diario d'amore*) from the writings of his sister, father, and good friend Antonio Ranieri, as well as from Leopardi's notebooks and an unpublished autobiography which he intended to title *The Story of a Soul*. The first play, *The Unblest*, was originally produced in May 1949 under the direction of Rayner Heppenstall. It dramatizes the poet's early life, from his tenth birthday in 1808 to his departure from an oppressive family situation in provincial Recanati as a young man of twenty-four. The warden of *casa Leopardi* is the poet's mother Adelaide, a grotesquely autocratic woman who for years will not allow Giacomo even to leave the house.[10] Leopardi's sheltered existence leaves him vulnerable to heartbreak: when he finally does get out into the world among guileless street-girls and the infinitely more dangerous sycophantic women (dramatized in the second *Leopardi* play) who seek his attentions once he has achieved literary renown, he is overmatched.

In part to escape his mother's tyranny, Leopardi throws himself into a severe apprenticeship for poetry. Though 'across [his] pages/ Flickered' the laughter of his younger brothers and sisters at play, after a youthful vow he 'was never tempted' to waver from his rigorous hours of study in Monaldo's library. So obsessed is Reed's Leopardi to know all the books and languages of the world that he is oblivious of his progressively stooping spine. One day, he remarks in brief soliloquy,

> I looked up from the page and saw myself,
> ...
> The bent bone in the breast.
> *(shortly and sharply: the word can no longer be suppressed)*
> Hunchback...(28)

Leopardi waits with paralyzed excitement to meet finally his ambassador from the outside world (ironically a priest, Pietro Giordani). That meeting provides a miniature climax to *The Unblest*; that the visit and Leopardi's subsequent day-trip to nearby Macerata are even countenanced is testament to the belated but refreshing assertion of will by Monaldo. Three months after the visit, Monaldo has waited for Leopardi's late return from one of his now customary walks through Recanati. At the end of the play's only extended father-son talk, Monaldo closes the scene by tenderly offering to guide the suddenly tearful Leopardi to his bed. Deftly, Reed leaves a potentially maudlin scene off 'stage' and closes the drama with Monaldo's report to the incredulous Adelaide that he is sending his son to Rome.

Obviously, Reed found much that was 'poetic' in the early life of Giacomo Leopardi. His companion plays are the first fruits of his fascination with the lives of creative artists, a wide range of whom he celebrated in words, from *The Great Desire I Had*, his speculative play about Shakespeare in Italy, to the hundreds of pages he wrote on Hardy for his never-published critical biography, to the *Hilda Tablet* comic pieces showcasing the off-centre life and work of a serialist composer. Particularly in *The Unblest*, Reed shows his great admiration for the way such beautiful poetry could have sprung from the prosaisms which surrounded the young poet-to-be. One is the lack of intellectual and aesthetic stimulation in little Recanati, a village of 'thirty thousand windows' (*Unblest* 11) on the Adriatic Sea. Among many even harsher descriptions, the historical Leopardi once called Recanati 'the deadest and most ignorant city of the Marches, which is the most ignorant and uncivilized province of Italy' (*Poesie e Prose* in *Selected Prose and Poetry*, 18). Leopardi's chief obstacle, though, is the repression of Adelaide, who squelches all childish gaiety in the house and views all of life's materials for artists as 'snares', both the seemingly positive materials—'cleverness, wit, and beauty'—and the tragic ones: in Leopardi's words, emotions such 'as ordinary beings are touched by:/ As shame or pity, remorse, penitence or guilt'. All these are choked out of the Leopardi household by Adelaide's 'extreme displeasure and grave offence' (56). In one instance she exhibits shock when an attractive visitor, Countess Geltrude Lazzari, suggests that Giacomo is handsome and Paolina will be pretty. Later, when Geltrude's husband remarks upon the priestly black cloaks in which the Leopardi boys are attired, Adelaide reacts with indignation:

> How else should they be dressed?
> Like children who flaunt their limbs about the streets?
> And shout indelicacies to one another? (38)

These words accentuate the total austerity which Adelaide has imposed upon her children, a completely prosaic life where beauty is sin.[11]

Such a 'poetic' subject as the portrait of a young artist demanded a proper medium, one with the flexibility to contrast the 'prosaic' with the 'poetic' in Leopardi's life. The ideal to which Reed aspired was reached, in his view, only by Eliot's *The Cocktail Party*, first staged in the same year as the second production of *Leopardi*. In Eliot's play, Reed saw 'a verse equidistant between prose and poetry [which] can with equal consistency move toward the state of either' ('Towards' II, 804). One manifestation of the flexibility of the *Leopardi* verse is in its metrics. The lines (with the exception of one song sung by children in each play) are unrhymed and set into a pentameter so pliable that any kind of pulse is almost impossible to detect. Naturally, in one hundred pages of verse drama, even in the dramatized life of a great poet, not all moments can be transcendent. There are scenes, for example, in which conventional greetings must be negotiated, as when out-of-town guests arrive in Recanati. The exchanges are functional and little more:

*Adelaide* (*abruptly*) You must allow me to introduce my children.
*Geltrude* We feel we know them very well already.
This is Paolina. Paolina, my dear, kiss me.
*Paolina* (*shyly*) Welcome to Recanati.
*Geltrude* Thank you, my dear. This is my little Vittoria.
You must look after her for me while we are here. (36)

Robert Frost once defended his insistence on metrical regularity by likening the free verse of most of his contemporaries to 'playing tennis with the net down'. In passages such as these Reed kept the net low, leaving his hand at the ready, though, to crank it tauter at moments of greater emotional intensity.

Both Savage (170) and A. T. Tolley (200) refer to *Leopardi*'s pentameter as 'sprung', borrowing Gerard Manley Hopkins' concept which recognizes that much verse takes its shape from the number of accents per line rather than the number of syllables. But a study of the play's opening reveals neither a traditional nor accentual meter: its first ten lines, for example, range from nine to fifteen syllables and from four to (depending on how one counts) nine stressed syllables. Yet behind this, the longest soliloquy of either *Leopardi* play, the metronome slowly and subtly begins to tick, and from about halfway through, in nearly every line can be heard five stresses:

> Oh morning, morning, across the twittering rooftops,
> Oh slumbering, umbered city, oh Recanati,
> Wake! You may celebrate. I have set you free.
> You may do today as you please, I shall not rebuke you.
> Only do not brawl and quarrel in the morning light,
> And treat your children kindly. Peace, gentle city. (11)

The soliloquy puts on display much of Reed's poetic genius and a few of his failings, along both his Dramatic and Lyrical strands. His dramatic instincts are immediately in evidence with the reinforcement of young Leopardi's joyous welcoming of the morning through the six chimes of the town watchtower. Reed would use the device later in his curtainless radio drama to mark changes in locale: '*the Recanati bell cross-fades to the louder one of Macerata*', where Leopardi is trying to pack as much life as possible into his day with Giordani. Later, when the Macerata bell strikes the quarter-hour, Leopardi's sense of desperation that his Cinderella-like experience will end becomes apparent, and the almost immediate striking of the quarter by the Recanati bell whisks us to a concurrent scene at home, where Carlo, Paolina, and Luigi look longingly out the window, wondering of their brother's fate and their own.

Reed the careful dramatist sets up our sympathies with the lead character (initially referred to in the text as '*Giacomo*', later as '*Leopardi*') by making his first speech bright and full of an innocent optimism; if we know the intense pessimism of the mature poet, we will be inclined to believe that it was forced on him by harsh outside forces. Reed also makes his soliloquy beautiful and affecting, even sophisticated, while keeping in focus, for the most part, that its speaker is ten years old. The boy savours his new age, testing its novel sound over and over: 'I am ten, at last:/ Ten, ten, ten'. He is completely frank and without guile in his brief capsules of family members, including his parents, who have not yet 'begun the day's first quarrel' and himself, 'the cleverest leopard,/ With the softest footfall, and the sharpest ears . . '.. But perhaps Reed's own sharp ears fail in some lines, as when Giacomo says, '. . . my morning lies/ In honeyed ladders across the marble floor' (11). Reed had the luxury of a precocious boy for his protagonist, a young man of letters who in six short years would have mastered Latin, Greek, French, and Hebrew and in four more had completed a *History of Astronomy*, numerous translations, and had published his first volume of poetry; still, these lines seem obscurely Reedian rather than genuinely pre-adolescent.[12]

Reed's musical and dramatic sense are on display through the remainder of *The Unblest*. And, in fact, in concluding the second of his radio talks on verse drama in 1951, he insisted that they must work in concert, with the dramatic driving the lyric and not vice versa, though he observed that 'many poets approaching the stage at the moment are still inspired with the prime wish to precipitate lovely verse on to the stage' (804). He conceded that even in responding to *The Cocktail Party*, 'no one, without the book in hand, could for the first fifteen pages of the play identify the fact that it is constructed as verse' (804). Yet listeners are 'intermittently getting caught up into more concentrated moods of expression', are 'relaxed from them, and again caught up'. The goal of verse drama is not to 'precipitate' beautiful verse in a theatrical medium: 'What we far more desperately need', Reed maintained, 'is a means of direct and powerful dramatic communication' (804).

Thus, in *Leopardi* there is much of what Reed called in Eliot 'passages of uninsistent verse' ('Towards' II, 804). But it seems to be important to him that the passages be printed as verse, because 'even if the delivery is barely affected' by such packaging, 'the thread of rhythm' must be always present, no matter how thin, so that the expression may easily 'move up once more into moments of passion' ('Towards' II, 804). Reed's adherence to the conventions of printed verse seems quaint at times, as for example, in an exchange between the eleven-year-old Giacomo and his brother:

*Carlo* Giacomo.
*Giacomo* Yes?
*Carlo* Have you finished your lesson?
*Giacomo* Yes.
*Carlo* Giacomo.
*Giacomo* Yes?
*Carlo* Are you lost in thought?
*Giacomo* Yes.
*Carlo* Oh . . .
(20)

This is a cute passage, not a 'poetic' one it seems, but at least to *readers* of the play, the positioning on the page underscores the parallelism in Carlo's endearing interrogation.

Often in *The Unblest*, prosy language and moods resolve themselves quickly into something more powerful; 'the high moments of the poetry . . . are likely to emerge in an unpredictable and discontinuous way, much as lyric poetry does' ('Towards' II, 804). The shifts are often reinforced by the metrics of the lines. In one early scene, for example, Paolina is literally counting to one thousand, after which she promises to say her prayers 'twice over'.[13] We hear nineteen of her numbers along the way before she is cut off by an impatient Giacomo, who is trying to tell her it is his birthday, between 684 and 685. Of course, it is impossible to maintain a consistent rhythm in a series of three-digit numbers, but when Paolina responds '*in rapid anger*' to Giacomo's charge that she is 'impossible', her words resolve into nearly perfect iambs:

And so are you.
Don't be so rude. What have you come here for,
If only to be rude. . . . (12)

The iambic pulse also rises to the surface in a soliloquy spoken just after Geltrude Lazzari and her family have departed, leaving the teenaged Leopardi more keenly aware of the sterility of his Recanati life. He looks out the window and laments that his only experience is vicarious. 'You hide your bending breasts with that brown hand', he apostrophizes in perfect iambic pentameter to a girl bending to drink at a fountain. 'And other, special pleasures I have known', he continues self-mockingly and iambically. In much of the impassioned conclusion of this soliloquy, the iambic rhythm predominates, punctuated effectively by trochaic imperatives:

Help me, incredible God! unmake my fever,
Give me my unhorizoned innocence,
Or send me him who shall restore me to it,
And it to me. Send me Giordani. Send him . . . (42-43)

Lyrical language admits attention-demanding nonce words like *unmake* and *unhorizoned*, though in any writing of vitality, readers and listeners will be more or less conscious of literary 'devices', both sound effects and figurative language. Some may be subtle, some even accidental; in fact, it is possible that more of such devices appear proportionally in Reed's prose, even a critical piece, than in *Leopardi*. In any case, Reed would not have been bothered if they do appear in a lower proportion in *Leopardi* than elsewhere; his discussions of verse drama in *The Cocktail Party* radio talks and in a 1946 review of two verse plays hammer at the point that 'verbal sensitiveness' must always take second place to two 'principal requirements of drama': telling stories which embody 'impressive truths' and creating 'credible and important characters, whose actions and changes of mood compel attention' (*Listener*, 11 April 1946, 486).

*The Unblest* sometimes compels the wrong kind of attention when Reed's control slips and drama oozes toward melodrama, though Reed did his best to mitigate the tendency. Certainly, we can forgive as boyish excess Giacomo's expressions of self-pity—'my birthdays are all snatched from me', for example—and his abdication from the war games that have so entertained him and his siblings:

> I want
> Neither to be a king nor to act as one. . . .
> I am old enough to make a decision and keep it.
> In future you and Carlo will have to find
> Another king to lead you against the French.
> I have other things to do. I shall work underground,
> And rich in knowledge I shall emerge again:
> Omnipotent and great. (23-4)

Reed assuredly had great sympathy for what can only be called the romantic pessimism of Leopardi, yet at some points in the play, where Reed apparently finds beauty and nobility in Leopardi's emotions and in his expressions of them, readers might be more inclined to slap or spank the young protagonist. Leopardi frequently bemoans the provinciality of Recanati; to Paolina he wonders how many people live, as he does, 'far from their kind' (29), though both concede that many people are forced to live in this condition. The self-pity in Leopardi's remark, 'We don't have opportunities in Recanati', is tempered by the bantering tone of his conversation with the Countess Geltrude Lazzari over a game of chess, a tone which brings a laugh from Geltrude to close the scene just seven lines later. Readers and listeners might find unfairly manipulative the newly deformed Leopardi's repeated command to his parents—'Behold your son!'—and his claim that Adelaide, 'with perverted joy, with hideous mounting triumph', has allowed him to blind and cripple himself through excessive study. But in fairness to Reed, this melodrama is defensible in that Leopardi has been tyrannized by his mother all along, most immediately by her aggressive and provoking interrogation, from which Leopardi has genuinely tried to escape:

*Leopardi* I shall not come down from the library.
*Adelaide* And why not, may I ask? . . . Giacomo, answer me!
*Monaldo* What do you mean by this nonsense, Giacomo?
Answer your mother.
*Leopardi* No, father, or I may be tempted
To speak in words she may not care to hear. . . .
*Adelaide* I have asked you a question, and you will answer
it:
Why should you not come down to meet the
Lazzaris? (33-4)

Yet in this, perhaps Reed's bleakest play, a surprising proportion of comedy wriggles free. To be sure, most has a tone of bitterness. Some is outright mordant, as Carlo's response to the rare news of visitors: 'What an eviscerating round of gaiety we move in, don't we?' And while Paolina is helping Luigi dress, his remarks sound like a parody of the Home Shopping Network: 'It is the latest *fashion* in cassocks, didn't you know?/ "Seductive model for the well-groomed novice./ And in size eighteen for cardinals and archbishops"' (30). Adelaide's despotic management of her children and domestic affairs is laid bare in a lighter spirit by at least two visitors to the household. Monaldo's mother dryly comments that her children 'were so contented, I'm sure I can't think why,/ For I'm afraid I never looked after them in the way that you do' (32). Adelaide 'sells all Monaldo's wine,/ And gets this stuff made up at the chemist's', jokes her brother Antici, who recognizes 'her hand in anything. She treats the cellars/ Just as she treats Monaldo and the children,/ She won't let 'em mature' (39).

There are other manifestations of Reed's Comic strand, even more characteristic in their subtlety and mildness. We see the familiar witty redundancies, as with the frequent recurrence of young Carlo's pet phrase in one early scene, twice in one speech: 'As a matter of fact,/ I am a very light sleeper, as a matter of fact' (14). In using a sharp segue spanning two days, one that a stage dramatist could never implement, Reed sets Monaldo's idealistic portrait of his guests against the reality:

*Monaldo* They are gentle people and exceedingly well-bred.
You will see that they do not out-do you in politeness.
The Countess herself is an extremely well-bred woman.
They are *all* well-bred . . .
(*pause*)

*Geltrude* Ah, what bliss to get free from that beastly carriage:
It has given me the worst indigestion I have ever had.
And my husband is convinced it has given him bedsores. (35)

Here is that characteristic Reedian brand of humour which gently deflates the grandiose by juxtaposing it against the base.

*The Monument*, hardly a less serious play than *The Unblest*, begins comically, with a two-page exposé on four bandwagon-riders, two men and two women, of the kind against which Pietro Giordani had warned Leopardi in the earlier play. When Leopardi, now 28, finishes reading a fragment of poetry,[14] after '*much respectful, genteel clapping*', the men respond:

*Old Gentleman 1* (*deep voice*) What ... was the poem ... *about?*

*Old Gentleman 2* (*deeper still*) Truth. Truth, and that sort of thing.

*Old Gentleman 1* (*profoundly*) Yes, I see. (*cautiously*) It was very good, don't you think?

*Old Gentleman 2* Oh, very.

*Old Gentleman 1* What's the fellow's name?

*Old Gentleman 2* Ah ... *Count* Something or

other.

*Old Gentleman 1* Brilliant! (65)

The women soon engage in a catfight straight out of Moliere or Oscar Wilde. Countess Malvezzi, the older of the two, professes a great interest in Leopardi's intellectual gifts and in his poetry (over which he and she have 'spent many hours together', she makes sure of remarking). In tangled syntax, rich in subordination and dubious metaphors, she gushes that the 'rhetorical force' of the poem '[w]hich carries the verse through the most complex reasoning,/ And deposits it, like an athlete depositing a torch,/ Into the mind of the reader is of a kind to equal which, *(pause)* ..'. (67). Though here Countess Malvezzi never quite gets her rhetorical torch deposited, she has scored some points in an earlier exchange with her rival Rosa Padovani, in which both women claim superior intimacy with Leopardi:

*Malvezzi* Is he an acquaintance of yours?
*Rosa* Yes, quite a friend.
*Malvezzi* How strange that he should never have mentioned you.
*Rosa* Ah, you know him too? (65)

Rosa's greater interest is in Leopardi the man, as further witty dialogue reveals:

*Malvezzi* I was wholly absorbed in the poet's thought and expression.
*Rosa* I prefer his private thoughts and expressions myself.
I could write a book about some of the things he says;
I mean if I *could* write.
*Malvezzi* Exactly, yes.
*Rosa* But it wouldn't, I'm afraid, be a book for publication;
Or at any rate not in Bologna.

*Malvezzi* I am very glad
He goes in sometimes for lighter diversions. (66)

The repartee shows two formidable women tearing at a man's fame, each staking a claim to a different part of Giacomo Leopardi.

Another brief scene in the play also reminds one of Moliere's particular brand of comedy. Leopardi sees through the actors who have gathered at the home of his friend Ranieri, where 'they sat in their unreal, well-learnt postures./ They had forgotten how to live, so much each gesture/ Came from some other life they had enacted' (93).[15] Leopardi has them 'all anatomised', in the way Célimène of *The Misanthrope* presents her devastating satiric portraits of the French men and ladies at court. At the gathering, Leopardi observes, Fabrizi was always caressing his 'lustrous hair', while 'Pavesi sat/ Sideways to the dark wall, presenting his best profile/ With practised nonchalancy'. The poet recognizes that one of the players cares less about his appearance than the others: 'Sound is enough for Biffi'. Indeed, 'He lets down into a well/ A voice deeper than any human feeling ever called for' (93-94).[16] Although these miniatures are sharply drawn, Reed as usual comes off second-best when his work is compared to that of his influences. The couplet rhyme and more distinct metre give Molière's word portraits a keener, more epigrammatic quality than Reed's.

Perhaps *The Monument*'s greatest manifestation of the Comic strand in Reed's poetic character is one of 'a remarkable number of performances-within-the-performance' (Savage 183) in Reed's plays.[17] In a scene which also allows Reed to show off his gift for translation, at Ranieri's party the troupe performs the suffocation scene from *Othello*, translated and 'improved upon' because, according to Biffi, Shakespeare's original 'words don't give [actors] very much help of course' (89).[18] Reed's own stage directions help the Florentine players transmute the tragedy into melodrama by summoning a musical backdrop, loud kisses, and a sob. He also directs Maddalena's lines to be spoken, in rapid oscillation, *'loudly'*, *'vox angelica'*, and *'passionately'*, and Biffi's actually to make a *'crescendo'* from *'loudly'*. In Biffi's interpretation, Othello's 'Hum!' becomes 'Berrrumph!', delivered *'like a drum-roll'*. The bad translation of Botti, one of the players, somehow converts Othello's opening lines of the scene—'It is the cause, it is the cause, my soul./ Let me not name it to you, you chaste stars!/ It is the cause. . . '.—to something like the twentieth-century bureaucratese Reed was so fond of satirizing: 'Oh my profoundest soul, the reason is as follows:/ I need not mention it, you bright fugitive stars;/ But the reason is as follows...'. (91). The most virtuosic comic translation, though surely some of the joke must have been lost when the words whisked as quickly out of as in to English living rooms at mid-century, is of Othello's play on the word *light*. As Shakespeare's Moor compares the light of Desdemona's life to that of a lamp burning in her bedroom, he refers to it as the 'cunning'st pattern of excelling nature'. Botti apparently takes the more modern, less flattering definition of *cunning* to portray Desdemona, or perhaps her death, as the 'unscrupulous plan of Nature'. If Othello kills her, nowhere, says Shakespeare, can be found 'that Promethean heat/ That can her light relume'. In Botti's unfortunate rendering, again reminiscent of some of the malapropisms in Reed's war poetry, 'Not even Prometheus's omnipotent pants' could revive Desdemona (91).

The ludicrous image of 'Prometheus's omnipotent pants' would be hard for even a radio audience to miss. But, as in *The Unblest* and Reed's other radio plays, the author who let his Comic personality run free in short bursts was aware of the need to rein back Aphoristic or Narrative inclinations in his writing aimed at listening audiences. In *The Monument*, as in the first part of the *Leopardi* diptych, there are none of the more or less baldly narrative transitional passages found in each of the other four plays in the collection. Still, an affecting story, only occasionally risking melodrama, gets told.

*The Monument* begins in 1826—some eight or nine years after Leopardi's first foray outside Recanati and four years after the final scene of *The Unblest*—and highlights the last eleven years of the poet's life. The first play left Leopardi on his way to Rome; in the second, Reed takes Leopardi to five other cities, beginning in Bologna, and proceeding back to Recanati, briefly to Pisa, to Florence for the bulk of the play's action, and finally to Naples, the hometown of his friend Antonio Ranieri and the site of Leopardi's death. The conflicts arising in these settings are numerous enough to maintain listener and reader interest. To practice his literary art, the protagonist must face great physical hardships, most of which he battles with grim equanimity. When Monaldo asks after his health, his son replies,

> My blindness is not as bad as I have sometimes known it.
> A good deal of the time I can even see, which is rather
> refreshing.
> But what is most interesting is that I have given up
> coughing blood.
> I rarely have indigestion; and I rarely lose my voice. (71)

To these discomforts can be added asthma, the hunchback which has deformed him from an early age, and a malady he mysteriously refers to as 'father's complaint'. Emotionally, Leopardi agonizes over the fate of the siblings he has left behind: 'Paolina: unwanted by men, haunting the cold white walls./ Carlo: still trembling on the edge of his escape./ Luigi: watched, imprisoned, persecuted . . . Pietruccio . . '. (70).[19] An even more wrenching emotional trial for Leopardi is his unrequited love for Fanny Targioni, whom one of Leopardi's translators described as 'a lively, amorous, pretentious, commonplace coquette' (*Selected* 59).

Indeed, one of the play's themes is the ironic caprices of love. In this play, the notorious love triangle of the literary tradition seems to bud into a polygon of even more sides and angles. As Leopardi pines hopelessly after Fanny, a young woman who is more interested in poets' autographs than their poems and whose husband seems only vaguely aware of her existence, Fanny directs her romantic interest toward Leopardi's friend Ranieri. Ranieri, for his part, is as indifferent to Fanny as is Targioni; his unfortunate love is for Maddalena Pelzet, like Fanny a wife and mother, an actress who claims to be in love with her 'Art' but seems to draw her greatest satisfaction from manipulating men, chiefly Ranieri. A second theme of the play contrasts the selfish passions in these relationships, as well as the parasitism of those in love with Leopardi's fame, with the genuine, abiding love between friends like Ranieri and Leopardi and between these men and their families. A third theme concerns the ineluctable and ineffable tug of 'home'. Despite all the emotional repression of his youth at *casa Leopardi*, Recanati and the trials of his sisters and brothers reside in Leopardi's heart wherever he is in Italy. Like *The Unblest*, besides its surprising proportion of comedy and its deftness with the dramatist's tools, *The Monument* displays both Reed's mastery along his Lyric strand and his occasional excesses. He could not, for example, resist his rather insubstantial puns, often marked in the printed text with upper- and lower-case letters, like Giordani's remark about what Life (in general) has made of a *life* (Leopardi's) or Fanny's mediocre paeans to *Home* with a capital *H*. Reed, who should have known better, tries to buttress his themes of home and family with dense, hard-to-hear wordplay, as when the not-yet-jaded Leopardi asks God: 'Help me to help them', that is, his siblings; 'deliver their deliverance/ Into my hands' (79). The title metaphor of one's family likened to a sculpted monument, which is introduced by Ranieri and then expanded upon by Leopardi, is a rich one: 'They have that permanence; and when they die,/ They are only stilled'. Some personalities, 'winged and free' like Ranieri's, can 'hover/ Over the immutable carven group'. But Leopardi recognizes how he is burdened by his family: 'I am grounded./ I carry their stone with me'. So far, so good; but in the last line Reed puns, with questionable success, on one of his favourite words: 'And there they are *still* . . . And here they still *are*' (98). Roy Walker's 'winking Reed' was, broadly, the funny Henry Reed, but these passages do a more particular kind of winking; the capitalization and italics flatter readers and ask them to find the puns more clever than they are.

*The Monument* presented to Henry Reed a greater challenge perhaps than any other play because its protagonist is a gifted, mature lyric poet. In some of the love-words he scripted for Leopardi, Reed seems not up to the task. 'Her face could twist my heart', Leopardi agonizes after his first meeting with Fanny, 'and turn my days to fever' (91). Later, he gushes, 'I could build up whole cathedrals of thought about her' (92). He comes back to stone imagery to develop a sort of cosmically ironic contrast between his passion and nature's indifference: 'And now she goes/ Between the insensible stone and the heedless fountain' (99). In Reed's defence, Leopardi's documented words of love were excessive; in 'Aspasia' he wrote that in Fanny he had found 'a new heaven and a new earth, almost a divine light' (*Selected* 59). The historical Antonio Ranieri wrote that Leopardi would return to his room in the evenings and glut himself with 'vain and unrestrained soliloquies of love, unworthy of the dignity of so great a man' (*Selected* 59). We must remember, too, that when John Keats wrote to *his* Fanny, there was much more sentiment than art to the words. Keats and Leopardi are not poets in these moments: they are merely lovesick young men.

On subjects from which Leopardi could achieve a somewhat greater emotional distance, his words, in the verse of Reed, have a truer lyricism. Readers may not be prepared to share in the hero's lyrical plaints earlier in the play, but by the end of Leopardi's Florentine period, we can more readily accept them, especially when uttered '*with great simplicity*' as is the soliloquy given immediately after Fanny's rebuff ('I did not hear it') of Leopardi's declaration of love. In Florence, says Leopardi, 'I am lost among iron, clanging streets,/ Which proffer to me only a choice between/ This prison or that' (110). An earlier prayer had been directed to God, but this time the poet pleads to a heaven 'emptied of God' to buoy him enough to go with

Ranieri to Naples: 'Give me the strength of the damned/ To shift my place in hell' (111). From Naples he issues his last soliloquy, a fine one in which Leopardi, like Reed himself, imagines his haven, his 'house of peace', with the 'servants docile and good, a beloved view from the window./ A cypress-walk, the sun on the balustrade,/ The distant sea, and a daily boat-sail plying' (116). Though Tasso, Ariosto, Petrarch, Cavalcanti, and Dante were denied their house of peace by the whims of patrons—both nobles and churchmen—driving the poets to exile and 'the torturer's rack', Leopardi admires and hopes to emulate their courage: 'In the breathing-spaces of such worlds, they forced/ Their words from out of their hearts' (116).

Thematically and technically, much comes together at the end of *The Monument*. Shortly after Dr Mannella has sent for a priest a virtuosic sequence begins (to be performed with increasing speed) in which Ranieri and his sister Lina subtly give way to Carlo and Leopardi's sister Paolina as respondents to Leopardi's repeated imperative: 'Open the shutters!' Only in radio drama could the '*near*' voices of Lina intertwine so rapidly with the '*echo*' of Paolina's voice and, within seconds, the voices of Carlo as a boy and Carlo as a man. The Naples characters are soon silent and an apparently delirious Leopardi is left with the 'monument' of his own family. 'They cannot move, they try, they cannot move', he says. His father, he observes, is 'hard as stone' (121). The poet, it seems, is coming to 'take up [his] position on the plinth,/ There in the vacant space' that waits for him (110). Listeners of the 1950 Douglas Cleverdon production of *The Monument*, broadcast only a week after *The Unblest*, must have appreciated the verse in the play's last minutes more than first director Rayner Heppenstall's audience (who heard the second play nearly ten months after the first), for it comes full circle, repeating many lines from *The Unblest*, including much of Giacomo's first soliloquy. Each family member 'exits' with one of his or her signature lines (the precocious Pierfrancesco's is 'Don't you find us all rather provincial?'), and we are left with just 'Giacomo' and 'Leopardi' vying, as they had also in a brief coming-of-age sequence in *The Unblest*. In the play's last words, both cry together triumphantly, 'Oh morning, morning . . . and it is morning again!' (121) All the Reed strands except the Comic have converged to raise the 'characteristic Reedian lump in the throat' (Savage 172).

The *Leopardi* plays are fine pieces of work, certainly deserving of more than the faint praise given by *Listener* reviewer Philip Hope-Wallace: 'Henry Reed's *Leopardi* pieces were well done, for that sort of thing' ('Laying a Ghost' 492). On the other hand, *Leopardi* probably deserves less than the description of its script by Heppenstall as 'huge and marvellous' (in Coulton 91). It is, however, easier to dismiss Heppenstall's assessment of a play he directed than the diverse, independent laurels bestowed on Reed's radio version of *Moby Dick*. Hope-Wallace calls Reed himself the hero of the 1947 production of *Moby Dick*, though along the way he credits, as Reed himself had in his preface to the printed text, the musical score of Antony Hopkins and the 'precision, clarity, and evocative power' of Stephen Potter's direction ('Live Whale' 169). Hope-Wallace also gives plaudits to the acting, especially that of Cyril Cusack, Harry Quashie, and Sir Ralph Richardson, and both he and Reed of course recognize the massive presence of Melville behind the production and the near-blasphemy of compressing his huge novel into a radio play of eighty undersized pages. However, as David Wade, a scholar of mid- to late-century British radio drama, would also contend thirty-five years later, Hope-Wallace argues that the joint effort of Reed, Potter, Hopkins, and the cast 'rises to the status of creative art'; more than mere reshaping, 'it was as independently and sensually "alive" as a new film or opera or play' (169).

With so many collaborators, how much of the production's independence, creativity, and originality are owed to Henry Reed? Even setting aside the music, acting and direction, since Herman Melville had already done so much of the artistic legwork, there would seem to have been little left for Reed. The narrative, of course, is Melville's; his prose, as Reed remarked in his preface, is highly lyrical and, as he commended Melville in his review of 'Billy Budd' (*New Statesman* 31 May 1947, 397), not afraid to make wise pronouncements, to be aphoristic; he also had a sense of theatre, creating his own gods-defying Byronic hero on a quest that can only breed grumbling and conflict from his men, and even setting one of the chapters in the form of a play; and as anyone knows who has read his portraits of the biorhythmically challenged law copyists Turkey and Nippers in 'Bartleby, the Scrivener' or appreciates the image of Queequeg bringing his harpoons to church, Melville can do the comic, too.

Even Reed's original verse passages owe a debt to Melville, and much of the predominating prose he takes from the novel verbatim; still, Reed's contributions as playwright and adaptor are many. It is the dramatist's task to select from Melville's voluminous material and arrange it for the most powerful effect. Reed is at his best, for example, in saving the famous opening of the novel for a later scene between Ishmael and Elijah which occurs in Melville's nineteenth chapter. In the novel, the prophet's name is long withheld. The kind of satisfaction in the revelation of a character's name is even stronger in Reed's version: Elijah discloses his name, then asks the young seaman his, eliciting (after a pause), 'Call me Ishmael' (22).

Reed discusses further instances of dramatic resourcefulness in his preface to *Moby Dick*. While arguing the validity of Melville's technical chapters and seeming digressions from the plot of the novel (and indeed giving Melville his highest praise by likening his devices to those of James Joyce), Reed concedes the necessity of deleting them from his radio adaptation. He omits these sections and many other elements of the novel—including all but 'a hint of the touching friendship between Queequeg and Ishmael' (9) and all of the business of Queequeg's illness and his coffin—'at the risk of appearing to try and tidy up Stonehenge' (10). Dramatic necessity also prompted Reed to expand the roles of the 'Manxman' and Pip; the 'felicitous ear' of Reed's that V. S. Pritchett praised in his review (102) deemed a 'treble voice' to be a 'great help in a wholly male cast' (9). Perhaps the most vexing problem Reed needed to solve was how to retain as many as possible of 'the most exciting and dramatic scenes' (and Reed insisted on including all three days of the chase) without producing 'merely a series of roaring climaxes', a 'tumult of nonsense' (9). Melville had the luxury of separating these climaxes by fifty or more pages. Reed had to attack the problem differently. He fairly evenly spaced six verse passages, including a song by Cabaco, throughout the drama's two or so hours. The last of these, which Reed terms an 'intermezzo', is Ishmael's highly lyrical narration of the second day of the chase. Reed, albeit somewhat equivocally, saw this change in medium as necessary, amid all the frenzied dialogue and sound effects of the play, 'to give the ear a rest (if it can be called a rest)' (10). Pritchett, admitting that he had rarely heard a radio play that he completely understood, saw the same function being served: the lyrical interludes 'are periods of spacious calm which are required in a narrative as stormy as this is' (102). Indeed, Pritchett saw *Moby Dick* as 'full of suggestions for those who are experimenting in this art', and one of Reed's most successful experiments to be the use of 'the long, explanatory chorus or prologue . . . to calm and to focus the reader's agitated inner eye' (102).

Dramatically, then, these interludes work very well. Regrettably, they are wanting in other poetic qualities. At least two contemporary critics saw great merits in the verse portions of *Moby Dick*. To the *Times Literary Supplement* reviewer they 'stood up like buoys, constant and illuminating' (632). Pritchett unreservedly called them 'the most instructive and enjoyable things in the text' and applied to them four glowing adjectives: 'exalted, refreshing, vivid and excellent' (102). But there is not much that is either vivid or illuminating, in the first verse section, which immediately follows Bildad's whispered warning, 'If you touch at the islands, . . . beware of fornication' (26). 'And my to-morrow came', begins Ishmael's section of verse, the slight concretization of the abstract by use of a possessive pronoun serving no apparent purpose. Worse than his pain, Ishmael continues, is 'the thought of the light round the harbour, the warmth feeling out in the darkness,/ The voice of the hidden singer' (27). There are some concrete words in these lines, but their force is rendered impotent by their obscurity in combination and by the seemingly chaotic mix of literal and metaphorical which we saw in *A Map of Verona* and which prevents the reader from shaping in his mind any coherent images. The line ending in *darkness* is downright irascible in its metrics, a baggy monster of nineteen syllables. Reed's rhythm and metre, at least in his lines that most strive for lyricism, are like near-rhyme in the hands of a clumsy poet: they are too far from Whitman on the one hand and too far from iambic pentameter on the other to sound like anything but bad poetry. The weak phrasing of Father Mapple's last sentence of this section, embarrassingly, states the essence of this first verse interlude: 'The spring has begun to enter'. There is some arresting imagery in these sixteen lines: 'The slow dead bite of the cold, the jaws of the blind ice closing,/ The claws distending and binding their fiend's grip tighter and tighter' (27). But on the whole they fit Reed's own unflattering definition of 'heightened speech': 'no more than normal speech carefully rendered abnormal in the pursuit of beauty or remoteness' ('Towards' II, 803). In their emphasis on coldness and in their opaqueness, they are reminiscent of the worst poems of 'The Desert'.

Certainly there is some powerful poetry in *Moby Dick* that nearly justifies Pritchett's adjectives. Reed's dramatic sense heightens the lyricism of the second interlude. Whereas Melville placed a chapter between Pip's plea for 'the big white God aloft' to 'have mercy on this small black boy down here' at the end of Chapter 40 and 'The Whiteness of the Whale' (Chapter 42), Reed turned his medium's limitation of time into a strength, artfully modulating Pip's desperate words 'White squall, white squall, white whale!' into Father Mapple's measured 'Whiteness is lovely' (40-41). The aphorism and its counter-truth 'Whiteness is terror' are Melville's. So are most of the supporting examples, though some are original with Reed. The loveliness of white is illustrated by a pearl earring, the white stones representing joyful days in Rome, and the 'transfixed delight' of snow on a winter morning. But in counterpointing Father Mapple's two speeches in this section, Reed has used his dramatic and lyrical gifts to tighten and sharpen Melville's voluble chapter. The contrasts between Mapple's two speeches are accentuated by their length—each is nine lines long—and by the one-to-one juxtaposition of a terrible whiteness and a beautiful one. The whiteness which looks so lovely when it 'lies on the city roof-tops' is terrible when it shapelessly drapes a barren landscape. When 'Alabaster/ Gleams white on breast and thigh in the marble temple' it is beautiful, but the same colour is terrible on '[t]he leper's breast and thigh' (41).

Reed seems to have chosen the leper as his alternate for Melville's Albino, to whose repulsive whiteness the novelist devotes a short paragraph in Chapter 40. A leper is obviously and not subtly shocking to the eye. The Albino, on the other hand, 'is as well made as other men—has no substantial deformity', just as Moby Dick is perfectly whale-like in every respect but one. And yet the 'mere aspect of all-pervading whiteness' makes the albino 'more hideous than the ugliest abortion' (997). It is unfair to compare Reed's five words to Melville's seventy-eight, but the novelist's seem so much the better to aid the reader's appreciation of the subtle, visceral, and unaccountable terror of whiteness. Reed similarly falls short in much of the third interlude, in which his verse is often less lyrical than Melville's prose. Its refrain is thin: 'Can you think what that [the whaling] life is like?' Granted, refrains do not have to hold to the same standard as verses, but the best seem richer than this or 'We are hunting a white whale', a refrain of Ishmael's that appears before and after it; at least they offer some variation or gain a cumulative force as does, for example,

Mark Antony's 'They are all honourable men'. But no momentum seems to be gained in the three repetitions of this chorus or in the three additional repetitions of its first three words. The sixth instance of the 'Can you think . . .?' query introduces the weakest passage of this segment, one that rivals *A Map of Verona*'s 'Philoctetes' in its stacking up of empty abstractions:

> Can you think of what that life is like? Even across the sea
> The winds blow tales of death, of other deaths
> Than the deaths that surround us. Rumour and mystery
> Weave a way like a fog about us. Every strangeness
> Carries a warning inflection. (57)

These verse paragraphs do go some small way toward serving the function of Melville's expository chapters, and they are sometimes interesting verbally as well. Father Mapple speaks of 'The reek of blood through the mist, and blood baked in sunlight,/ The slither of blood on the deck' and Ishmael of how the whale's carcass 'will be picked and peeled by midget men' (50). The more idealistic mission of the *Pequod* Reed captures less successfully, as in Father Mapple's talk of 'the mad grey lust of a captain' and in the strained syntax of a parallel speech by Ishmael: 'Can you think of the weeks/ Drifting through sunlight or storm, no vessel spoken,/ Or spoken, quickly gone on a jealous quest?' (50)

This and the next interlude reprise some familiar Reedian themes; while some are derivative and some tedious, some are affecting. Along with Hardy and Leopardi, Reed was taken by the idea of a powerful but apathetic Nature; and Melville's last words before the Epilogue of *Moby Dick* show his sympathy with this worldview: after the destruction of the *Pequod* and all but one of its crew, 'the great shroud of the sea rolled on as it rolled five thousand years ago' (1407). Reed does Melville justice, though he incorporates the sea's apathy into a verse speech given earlier by Ishmael after the crew has taken a black whale. In

Reed's rendering, the 'enormous creature' in its 'final flurry' is not the *Pequod* but this black whale, insignificant against 'the vast seas rolling/ Indifferently over defeat, of creature or man' (50). As Jon Stallworthy observes, Reed expressed in much of his poetry a sense of longing for the 'Great Good Place' (xxii) which in life he had found only fleetingly in Seattle, in Dorset with Michael Ramsbotham, and in the 'high clean rooms' (*Return* 184) of his adoptive Neapolitan family. Despite the increasing madness of the quest for the white whale, Ishmael admits he feels 'sensations of highest bliss' as he looks to the sky beyond the hunk of 'whale-flesh hanging from the maintop' (60-61). He and the Manxman, to whom he speaks of Pip's madness, and Ahab's of a different kind, are part of a narrow strip of existence, 'a lonely surface world,/ The world of shadowed life' (60). In the world above them soars the majestic albatross, but the more wondrous haven is 'another world, becalmed and charmed/ *Under* the water'. The most powerful verse in the play describes this Eden, where 'the Leviathan/ Innumerably and ponderously keeps/ His breeding-ground; here his vast roving courts/ Pause in a giant circle'. We can 'with our darts bring fright and consternation' only to the 'borders' of this world (62). In the 'still blue waters at the centre', says Mapple, 'The young whales suckle calmly—'. Ishmael continues,

> —and their great mothers
> Float in the heavenly depth; our boat is only
> A drifting shape across their upward glance. Our bloody wars
> Stir not a ripple around them...Central delight;
> Eternal mildness of joy. (62-63)

The 'heavenly depth' of these passages, their lyrical and aphoristic quality, is rivalled in only a few passages from the last verse interlude and Ishmael's epilogue, added for the 1979 production of *Moby Dick*. Given the novelist's advantage over the dramatist in sheer number of words, Reed does creditably in his adaptation of Melville's two brilliant paragraphs on the *Pequod* crew's singleness of purpose by the second day of the last chase. As their ship, wrote Melville, though wrought of disparate materials—'oak, and maple, and pine wood; iron, and pitch, and hemp'—is nevertheless unified by its keel in a single direction, so its seamen 'were welded into oneness, and were all directed to that fatal goal which Ahab their one lord and keel did point to' (1389). The men in Reed's version, Ishmael now realizes,

> . . . dream as one, as one they stir in their dream.
> We are a ship no longer: we are Ahab.
> . . . a single doom
> Presses upon us. (86)

And much as 'the twain' are drawn together by the Spinner of Years in Thomas Hardy's poem, the *Titanic* and iceberg 'being anon twin halves of one august event', so, says Reed's Ishmael, does Fate direct the players in his drama: 'And here in the night they onward move, the three,/ Ahab, the whale, the sea, our trinity' (86).

Much in the climactic sections of verse, unfortunately, is disappointing. Ishmael's last passage of verse in the 1947 text begins with the third instance of that rather lame chorus, 'We are hunting a white whale', followed by a prosy set of words whose line break gives undue emphasis to one of its weaker words: 'He is not such a beast who may be caught/ Easily . . '. (86). Other words are artificially dressed up by the mere omission of articles. Ishmael says 'The men breathe fitfully in bunk and hammock', as in an earlier passage Father Mapple had marvelled at the white gleam of alabaster 'on breast and thigh in the marble temple/ Under shine of planet and star' (41). The 1947 *Moby Dick* had ended powerfully with '*a strangling cry*' from Ahab and, soon after, his words: '*Hemp! . . . Hemp!* . . . Moby Dick . . . Moby Dick . . . *Moby Dick!*' (96) Reed's judgment in adding a verse epilogue for his 1979 production is questionable. He passes up some of Melville's finest phrasing: the 'sheathed beaks' of the sea-hawks, for instance, and the passage on the

*Rachel*, who, 'in her retracing search after her missing children, only found another orphan' (1408). Instead, he adapts some of Melville's more dubious language: 'the unharming sharks/ Go by, as though with padlocks on their mouths' (in Stallworthy 94). What he adds is some heavy parallelism and entreaties to deity:

> (Let me live, oh God!)
> Even with every hand
> Against me, mine against all, even alone . . .
> Even alone, if only to tell a story . . .
> Even alone (oh, thou, fair Christ in Heaven!)
> even alone . . .
> Even alone, *let me live!* (94)

Reed has distorted Melville's intentions and transformed drama into melodrama. This is not Ishmael in the middle of the ocean; this is Scarlett at Tara.

After the (not always successful) high seriousness of *Moby Dick*, that Reed set his sights much lower for most of *Pytheas*, his next dramatic venture, is refreshing. Reed's 'dramatic speculation' follows the adventures of Pytheas, a 'brown-limbed Greek', on a quest that, like Ahab's, metamorphoses into something more than just mercantile. Circa 300 B.C., a profit-minded Massilian named Melanthius commissions Pytheas to find tin on 'certain unnamed and unspecified islands, situate [*sic*] at an unknown distance beyond and probably to the north, or to the north-west, of the Pillars of Hercules' (13). But Pytheas is a poetic soul more interested, for example, in a little conflict on the quay between a crab and a starfish than in his employers' grosser preoccupations with war and commercial competition with the Carthaginians. He is more concerned with tracking down the source and meaning of the play's theme song, '[I go my way]', than profits for Massilian coffers. Pytheas takes his crew to the Azores, to Britain, and finally to the far north, 'the edge of the world' (68). 'I do not want to bring back loot and pale slaves from those lands', he tells his friend Ctesiphon,

> Or to tie between that sunless world and us
> The gaudy ribbons of commerce, every year
> Growing a little more grubby with grime and sweat
> From the anxious hands of the dealers.

His motive is more ethereal, not unlike that attributed to Sir Edmund Hillary: '*I want to see what is there*' (10).

It is only in his shorter poems that Reed can resist juxtaposing ironically, sometimes at his own expense, the very low against such lofty and lyrical themes and language. But in no Henry Reed work is the low *lower* than it is in *Pytheas*. One of the running jokes is the contrast between the grandeur of the mates' names and the baseness of their breeding and manner. Ctesiphon is 'deeply honoured' to meet Ajax, the first mate, whom he assumes to be 'one of the Ajaxes, without a doubt' (23);[20] Ctesiphon declaims a bit of *The Iliad* to refresh the sailor on his lineage. But Ajax must allow that the only Homer he knows is 'a ship's carpenter by the name of Omer' (24). Ajax refers to the second mate as 'that little Egyptian bastard' (22); his name is Osiris. Ctesiphon's reverence has given both men a disproportionate self-esteem, which emerges especially in their verbal duel conducted in heavy Cockney accents just after the crew shoves off from the Azores. Ajax, feeling very superior to 'slinging about in an old tub like this', by rights should be 'Governor of two provinces of Southern Greece and four islands in the Arkypy Large; or so I'm give to believe' (45-46). Osiris, of course, can do Ajax one better. With 'BEDRAGGLED SUPERCILIOUSNESS', he counters that he would be 'sitting on the Frone of Eaven, with the goddess Ices olding my ead in er lap' (46). At the end of this scene we first learn the name of the cabin boy, whose head, according to Ajax, Ctesiphon has been 'stuffing . . . with nonsense' (47): it is Orestes.

Orestes figures prominently in two other bits of farce in the play. Convention calls for a cabin boy to yell things, and he is the first to finally sight Britain through the fog. Ctesiphon, who seems to have been born jaded, chastises, 'I've begged you a *hundred* times not to scream like that' (51). Later, when Orestes twice raises a cheer after the sighting is confirmed, Ctesiphon scolds him into a polite and subdued pair of hurrahs. In an earlier episode we find that Orestes and all the mates have become seasick, with the cabin boy blubbering like Pip from *Moby Dick*, for reasons that do not arouse quite the same pathos: he has vomited down the inside of his flute. Low comedy also insinuates itself through the speech impediments of Cleomenes, one of Melanthius' advisers, and a pedantic lecturer who provides background information on the Pillars of Hercules as the ship passes through the Strait of Gibraltar. The scholarly debate she outlines is an interesting encapsulation of one of the play's themes: the poetic versus the profitable. But her difficulty with the *r* sound serves no apparent purpose—other than perhaps to undercut ironically the grandeur of the theme—as when she describes the pillars' 'inscwiption in an unknown orfogwaphy, vawiously interpweted as weferwing to mystical doctwines or to wecords of expenditure' (30). Likewise the poor speaking and hearing of Cleomenes seem gratuitous. Cleomenes' chronic mispronunciation of the *s* sound as *h* (he is apparently a harelip) and his misunderstanding of 'taradiddle' as 'parrot fiddle' receive much more play than they are worth.

Thankfully, *Pytheas* is rich in high comedy as well. Satire and subtle wordplay abound. In addition to the chill, sunless British climate and the bland starchiness of its diet, objects of Reed's gentle satire include the profit motive, bureaucracy, and bluestockings. Melanthius's insistence that the men of his company are all idealists (and the claquish concurrence of all his yes-men on the point) becomes funnier when set against his earlier qualified defence of the virtue of idealism, 'especially if it is kept in its right place, and is of the right kind: and is not continued too late in life' (10). When Pytheas and his crew seek to open negotiations for surplus tin in which no other merchants have shown interest for over three months, the island bureaucrats insist on going 'through the usual channels' (54). Pytheas (in a double pun, tellingly misnamed 'Captain Purchas' by one of the bureaucrats) is asked to fill in 'the relevant scrolls', including 'B 1429, AP 273 (the pink one) and J 86 . . '. (55). Reed also presents a brief comic portrait of a bakewife, who offers her terrifying recipe for pudding, the island delicacy. Her prose description, ironically perhaps, contains more rhyme proportionally than all the verse of Captain Pytheas himself: her pudding calls for flour, 'two pound of suet, and four of lard, or a little extra if it runs to it' (60). In contrast is an even more satiric portrait of a 'LADY' who wants to set up 'something in the nature of cultural interchange between our two countries . . . We might just at first, say, send over little drama groups: even a solo performer, perhaps . . . (*FADE*) (59).

Reed seems to find great sport, too, in puns, parodies, and literary in-jokes. In attempting to paint his venture as altruistic, Melanthius has stressed how vitally important is tin to her 'that Bears the Brunt' of managing and cleaning kitchen utensils, that is, the Housewife. Ctesiphon and Ernest the bureaucratic Briton complete the pun in a later exchange:

| | |
|---|---|
| CTESIPHON: | (*BORED*) Have you any housewives? |
| ERNEST: | A large number, yes. |
| CTESIPHON: | Do they bear Brunts? |
| ERNEST: | It's not always realised by the layman just<br>how *many* brunts they bear. . . . (55) |

When Ajax gets hold of the famous passage from *The Iliad* quoted by Ctesiphon earlier, we find it severely mangled: 'Boldest of men, 'e stood there, the old Babylonian Ajax, Rumtity, rumtity, rumtum' (32). And one of Ctesiphon's speeches seems to play on some of the late lines from Tennyson's 'Ulysses': 'The seas may be different, there may be sunless lands; we may find men whose heads grow from their armpits, or from quarters of their persons even less savoury. Again, there may not' (26).

Aside from the allusion to the English adventurer and travel writer Samuel Purchas is a sly pun on Proust embedded in the Beowulfese spoken by the diplomatic Briton; he gives a prologue of sorts for the rendition of 'Jolly Snowballs' to the strangers from across the 'swan's way' (61). Characteristic of 'the lively sense of comedy and of the absurd' that Douglas Cleverdon praised in his obituary for Reed is the outrageous anachronism of one exchange between the mission's leadership and a Briton, who commands his sons Throthwulf and Thrithwulf to

> Bring the flagon of mead and let it pass gaily from mouth to mouth. Don't spill it . . . An it be Fate's will, thou shalt not suffer harm nor harrowing under my roof-tree, though the winds blow chill from Thule.
>
> PYTHEAS: Didst thou name Thule?
>
> BRITON: Though the wind thunder from Thule, bane shall not betide thee. An it be Fate's will.
>
> CTESIPHON: And what if it isn't? (53-54)

One thousand years before *Beowulf* and nearly two thousand before Shakespeare, Renaissance phrasing (not to mention twentieth-century cynicism) mixes freely with Old English theology and poetic devices.

Another comic tour de force, spoken by the 'chorus', comes right after Orestes has first sighted the island:

> SHE: It is said they landed in Cornwall.
> HE: It is said they landed in Kent.
> SHE: There are many conflicting reports of the places
> to which they went.
> HE: It is said they wintered in England.

SHE: It is said they summered there.
HE: It is said the weather was filthy.
SHE: It is said the weather was fair.
HE: One can imagine the wild rough hills, the roadless plains, the bogs.
SHE: One can imagine no end of bogus dialogues. (53)

Just as the rhyme enhances the comedy of this exchange, so it does in the play's most wicked parody, a song in the manner of A. E. Housman which unfortunately had to be cut from the broadcast version. When the chief Briton calls for a song of 'sooth, but not sorrow, bliss, but not bale', a ballad of characteristically bitter irony is performed by a baritone soloist. 'OH, lad', he sings, 'the sights of summer/ Along the land are strown . . . '; why, then, 'are you idle,/ Why do you pine and moan?' The youth has reason for feeling glum: his beloved has

...doffed her Sunday gown
　　And laid her sadly down.
Not [by] her sunny window
　　That looked on Knighton Crest,
But in a lightless chamber
　　She lies and takes her rest,
　　Her hands across her breast.

Reed was no doubt aware that the twentieth-century ear had become uncomfortable with such grim themes carried by the music of common metre. Housman set so many of his most pessimistic poems—'With Rue My Heart Is Laden' and 'When I Was One-and-Twenty' are two familiar ones—in this precisely iambic form, alternating seven and six syllables, with an ABCB rhyme scheme. And Reed added a fifth line doubling the rhyme and meter of the fourth, as Housman had in his most famous poem about a lost love, 'Bredon Hill'. By the time we reach the final stanza, the discrepancy between the sad message and the 'pretty' medium renders comic the song's ending:

Then lad, why should you carry
        Your woes about the land?
Here is a simple razor;
        Come, take it in your hand.
        And we will understand . . . (57)

Rhyme, in fact, is used more prominently in *Pytheas* than in any other Henry Reed play, including quite a bit of its serious verse. Pytheas himself speaks in rhyme only in the play's last four lines, but all of the inter-scene narratives and ruminations by 'HE' and 'SHE' are written in hexameter couplets. Rhyme is imposed even more strongly on the ear of the listener by the short-lined triplets of the play's fine theme song, '[I go my way]'. As we discover much later, the song's persona is the wind, which goes its own way 'Through sun and shower/ Through brake and bower/ Through day and hour': not the fierceness of the wolf, the guile of the snake, nor the strength of the bear can *stay*, *delay*, or *waylay* the independent wind (3). Perhaps overinsistently, Reed makes numerous rhymes of two and even three syllables:

And swelling and lifting,
And pausing and shifting,
Caressing and drifting,
        I go my way.
You cannot belie me,
You cannot defy me,
You cannot deny me,
        I go my way. (5)

It is possible as well that the song hints at one of the play's motifs: the mind's wonderful wont to conjure up its own images of the past, to amend or at least expand upon 'the dead and pompous words' of the history books (2). Like the wind and like the stream in Reed's early poem 'Lives' which make their own course, the imagination fashions its own way. SHE says, as part of a prologue to the play's action, 'Images came and went, like the darting wings of birds,/ Places and buildings rose, flashed through the mind and were gone,/ Every ancient place-name was something to build upon' (2). The rhymed musings of HE and SHE, along with the theme song, consume the first three and and half pages of the script, setting the tone for *Pytheas* which, aside from *Leopardi*, contains more verse than any other Reed play. Much of it is relatively straightforward narrative from HE and SHE, commenting on the stages of the journey, through the Carthaginian blockade at Gibraltar, to the Azores, the island of Amnis, Britain, and north to Thule.

The more earnest verse is less consistently successful than the comic verse of Pytheas, but it does have its moments. One is Pytheas's first extended blank verse speech, condemning the rapacious power of Alexander and his cronies. Disdainfully spoken of as 'our earth's great man', Alexander brings his 'prowling armies' to

> . . . a land of mountains
> With gilded cities in their steaming valleys.
> They call it India. He will call it Greece. . . .
> Under his ministrations, unprotesting,
> Civilisations die. (9)

He beats his soldiers before him, and 'the tangled knots' which unsettle their consciences he 'weaves as simple skeins in a giant whip/ Which cracks from Scythia to the Indian mountains' (9).[21] Behind him, 'a respectful distance after', come the promise-givers, 'The merchants, speculators, and accountants,/ The moneylenders with the gleaming teeth,/ Ready "to put the East on its feet again"'(9). This verse, unusually sharp in its political satire, is contrasted by the lovely lyricism several scenes later as Pytheas describes the pre-dawn of his departure day, musing on the cherished Reedian theme of finding and seeking to hold a place and time of stillness and peace. 'The flowers and stones/ Have been there all night, tree, grass and flinted wall', he says. It is a scene worth holding:

> The houses are still, and wrapt in their white stone
> sleep.
> The hills are mute, colour and light of day
> Drained into silence. Only the slow wide sky
> Moves its great fan of stars over the town. (17)

When the music behind this scene falls away, Pytheas implores the dawn to hold off, though he has 'prayed/ For this one day' to arrive:

> Dawn, come not
> To stretch your fingers through the heavy streets;
> Oh waking shepherd-boy, it is not time
> For your cold flute and bell to climb the hill.
> Droop still, oh flower; oh dews melt not in morning. (17-18)

But as the affecting passage closes, Pytheas realizes he 'cannot stanch the day. The day must come,/ And the highest tower glow: the flood of morning/ Creep down the waking trees' (18).

As always, however, Reed's hand at the lyrical and aphoristic is less deft than his comic and dramatic sense. *Pytheas* begins with pseudo-profound, but ultimately rather thin meditations on the nature of time. As with the most winking passages in *A Map* and *Leopardi*, Reed marks his wordplay with capital and lower-case letters, in this instance to distinguish between 'the Past' and 'the past'. In between this and Pytheas's last two blank verse speeches, which also disappoint, reside in the verse more than a few incidences of the kind of prosy or wordy language Reed might himself have satirized in his more puckish moods. 'It is interesting to find that one feels . . . ' begins one of the long couplets, for example. Another line of serious verse is padded with the word *ostensibly*, which seems like a word to be uttered only by a character Reed sought to ridicule. Other lines show these faults and the characteristic Reedian obscurity, partly engendered by his habit of overburdening abstract nouns and adjectives: 'And now: how far a distance,/

How far have I come from my troubled, ageing south,/ Where even happiness is a resentment . . '. (65) These lines are not punctuated as a question, but they could be taken as an interrogative, one of many issued by Pytheas in these last speeches. 'Does the sea reach out/ Its arms', he enquires, 'to clutch the land, or does the land/ Grasp at the roaring sea . . .?' Marveling on reports that men can live in Thule, he asks, 'How do they move?/ Shivering down to the waters. How do they breed?' (69) Sadly, none of these questions seems interesting enough for a listener to ponder overmuch.

Lines such as these aspire to 'the bravely attired language' which Reed found to be the wrong object of verse drama; Pytheas's last two speeches, in fact, fall well short of the true end of verse in a play, which in Reed's view is to heighten its dramatic quality. The little dramatic power in these last two speeches comes in contrast to the scene which falls between them, a lighthearted conversation between Pytheas and a slightly drunk Ctesiphon in which the latter, among other things, consummates a joke by announcing that the name of 'the third rower on the port-side' is Oedipus (67-68). Perhaps the high seriousness of the play's last few minutes is doomed to fail, coming so close on the heels of 'Jolly Snowballs'. Listeners expect the tone to be undercut at any time. Thus, the Eliotesque paradoxes do not (or cannot) succeed, as when HE says, 'an end from which one returns is, nevertheless, an end' (68) or when Pytheas muses, '*Thule*: a name for ever. *Thule*: a name for nowhere' (69). During the last speech of Pytheas, Reed calls for background music to come up and then back down nine times, presumably to lend even more weight to lines like 'Here may be there for them' (70). The referents for *here* and *there* and *them* are all rather obscure. I prefer the Henry Reed who wrote an earlier paradox that does identify the pronoun for its audience: 'It has many names, and it has no name; it is pudding' (58).

Reed made sure that pudding—along with speech impediments, snowballs, and seasickness—resides safely in the middle of *Pytheas*, which opens and closes with its very serious meditations on the nature of time. Reed's greatest play, *The Streets of Pompeii*, is similarly framed so that the funny Reed is subordinated to the serious Reed. *The Streets of Pompeii* concerns the roamings of five pairs of tourists through the excavated ruins of the ancient city, with flashbacks to the eruption itself and commentary by two choric figures, the Traveller and the Sibyl of Cumae. The range between the low and the lofty in the play is again wide, and though never quite descending to regurgitation into wind instruments, *Streets* does include a talking lizard and a foursome of tourists who speak in highly colloquial, clipped English—one doesn't like the *atmos* of the ruins, especially the tombs, which she finds very *morb*—and have their photographs taken in various embraces with the local statues.

But Reed, in pursuing his ambitious themes of 'fecundity and sterility, imagination and pedantry, love and death' (Savage 171), aims for a higher register as well. Along with the elevated prose of the Traveller he also gives us the short-lined verse of the Sibyl, which often resolves itself into iambic tetrameter and sometimes into rhyme, and the longer verse line of two teenaged lovers which, like the verse of *Leopardi*, settles into iambic pentameter at key moments and also into rhyme for their 'full-dress' sonnets (Savage 171). The generous mixing of forms in *Streets* might, in fact, remind some readers of *The Dynasts* or even Tennyson's *Maud*. Indeed, a *Radio Times* reviewer remarked, 'Though most of it is in prose, it has worked out as a sort of dramatic poem' (in Savage 169).

The dramatic quality of this 'poem' is evident in many ways, right from the start. A sober verse introduction is followed by a '*violent orchestral tutti*', which is '*almost at once reinforced by the voices of a great crowd in terrified flight*' (127). Out of the panic of the citizens fleeing the great eruption can be heard snatches: 'It is the earth and fire upon us. . . . My mother has fallen, fallen. . . . To the sea, to the sea. Is there time? . . . The mountain has burst!' (127-8) Against the unbearable agony of AD 79 Reed sets the tender, present-day scene of young Attilio ministering to Francesca's arm, scratched by a thistle. Later flashbacks to the terror of Vesuvius are effectively set off by the bourgeois concerns of the four English sightseers and by the charming soliloquies of the Lizard as he gives himself little reminders to handle his elemental needs: 'Stone, under belly. Good. Hot, all over back. Nice. Near leaf? Noise? No. Can wriggle? Yes. Safe. Good' (141). Another saurian soliloquy immediately follows the Traveller's description of the unspeakable pain exhibited on the faces of Pompeii's dead, alongside which 'the dead face of an ordinary person, even of a suicide, is triumphant in comparison' (154). 'Here is the naked form of a young girl', says the Traveller, acting as our tour guide.[22] 'Here is a dog, strangled at the chain, twisted on its back, its legs like those of an upturned stool, its long jaws open in agony . . '. (154). It is characteristic of Reed that the action eliciting such high emotion is not shown directly but implied from meditation upon still figures. But though big, loud sequences were not Reed's preferred mode, he could present them, judiciously. We have seen them, of course, in his adaptation of *Moby Dick*, but they burst through even his more static pieces like *Streets*. The last flashback to ancient Pompeii begins with a reprise of the orchestral tutti, eruption sounds, and panicked voices followed by an episode in which a greedy merchant commands his wife, daughter and six or seven increasingly insubordinate slaves to hold a torch and help him gather up his money, silver, and other treasures. In a '*sudden outburst*' one slave cries out, 'Take your statues yourself! And your money and your jewels. You'll be as naked as we are in an hour's time . . '. (165). Reed contrasts the callous, arrogant worldliness of the merchant with the innocence and loyalty of his daughter in the final two speeches of the scene. The merchant finally dismisses at least his wife but perhaps all his household: 'Go! Go! Go, if you want to; but, by God, if we ever get out of this, I can tell . . '. With the eruption crashing and drums pounding, the daughter interrupts: 'I can't see anything. Papa? I can't see anything!' (166).

Reed the dramatic artist stirs honest emotion in his readers and listeners through these characters and also through the last Pompeiian we meet, an Old Man, who, evidently suffocating in the rubble, becomes disoriented: 'I must have fallen. I cannot move my arms. Are my eyes open? I don't think so' (166). As might anyone's in times of duress, his final words take him progressively back through his life, from his time on a ship, to a nighttime kiss in a 'moonlit orchard' and finally to a place where 'all along the shore the waves bent back, ah, in a long white frill, and the water sparkled all the way to Sorrentum and you bounced me in the water, crying, "You are five years old today!"' (166-7) As a dramatist, Reed is no tragedian, but according to the strict definition his Guglielmo Shakespeare gives in *The Great Desire I Had*, few are, for they confuse tragedy 'with grief and loss and exile, with the breaking of the heart and the death or departure of the beloved . . . which are only minor ailments' (246). Pathos and hysteria, too, he saw as poor modern substitutes for the great tragic emotions of pity and terror (Foreword to Betti, *Three Plays* 8). But certainly grief, heartbreak and pathos, such as are aroused by the eruption episodes, are sufficiently noble emotions. As we saw too in some potentially mawkish situations in *Leopardi*, Reed was nearly always able to 'come within an ace of sentimentality without actually succumbing' (Savage 177). Reed's acute dramatic sense kept his drama from crossing over into melodrama.

Many of these touching scenes in *Streets*, as in all of Reed's serious plays, unabashedly lie adjacent to scenes of wit and humour. The talking lizard is almost an absurdist touch, and all the funnier because he is not anthropomorphized beyond his capacity for speech, limiting all his words to the parameters of his reptilian existence: breathing, temperature control, sleep, and camouflage. If we were to proceed up a hierarchy from lizard to the most obviously 'poetic' figures in the play, we would find the strongest comic elements at the bottom, with a proportional decrease as we ascend. The superficiality of the next lowest characters—Bill and Margery, and Walter and Judy—generates much humour. Judy announces her goal in touring the ancient ruins: 'I told Mum we'd get a snap of one or other of us, with every damned statue in Pompeii' (139). Margery bemoans the heat, contending that 'the real danger is', worse than sunstroke, that '*some* parts of you get browner than the others. . . . I mean, you don't want a sort of a *pattern*' (155).

The most consistently serious language is that of the humourless Sibyl of Cumae who, not incidentally, speaks entirely in verse. Attilio and Francesca are on the next rung below; there is some light banter between them, but since the purity of their love subsumes all, at least one possibly funny bit (Francesca's spoonerism, 'the Friangular Torum') is more endearing than comic. The Traveller is on the third rung down, adopting a hint of a satirical tone only when he slips into the language pattern of one of the pairs of tourists, as when he reports that the bourgeois couples have 'dismissed their guide. Rather glad he's gone, to tell you the honest. Nice chap, but enough is as good as'. (154-5). The two Scotsmen are given an almost wholly comic portrait by Reed. They have an ostensibly intellectual interest in all things visceral, and as they scrutinize some of the coarser paintings, sculptures, and appointments in the buildings, they quote scholarly authorities on, for example, chamber pots, 'the male organ of generation' (150), and 'what modern psychiatry would term Ho Mo Sexu *Ai*lity' (169).

Unlike the funny songs in *Pytheas* and the *Hilda Tablet* collection, as well as the verse in *Leopardi* and some of the HE/SHE passages in Pytheas, in *Streets* rhyme and metrics are rarely used to support the comedy. The one modest instance comes after MacFarlane has quoted a line from Catullus—'*nunc in quadriviis et angiportis*'—which he helpfully translates: 'Now in the quadrivia and the angiportae' (159). Soon after, Reed employs rhyme in the service of mild satire:

*Traveller* MacFarlane remembers another poem, which runs as follows:

*MacFarlane* *In great heat,*
*Never eat.*
*Traveller* This poem is not by Catullus. (160)[23]

The most consistently weak elements of Reed's poetic character, the narrative and aphoristic, also make appearances in *The Streets of Pompeii*. He 'is least convincing when he writes of the idea'; V. S. Pritchett wrote this of Honoré de Balzac, a man whose novels Reed translated, but he might have been speaking of Reed himself. The 'idea' that the play presses most insistently upon the reader is a kind of pessimism which is not original with Reed. It is an outlook that perhaps attracted Reed to Balzac, his 'belief that the world is a completely evil place' ('Balzac and the Human Appetite' 899), but one which in *Streets* Reed borrowed directly from Giacomo Leopardi. Whereas Balzac's pessimism grew out of his sense that the institutions of society were corrupt, Leopardi blamed Nature, 'the hidden ugly Power who orders our common ill'. At three separate points, the Sibyl speaks portions of 'La Ginestra' ('The Broom') in Reed's own translation. 'Let him come bravely now', she says in her opening speech, 'whose wont it is/ To praise man's power and chance; here let him see/ How the harsh Nurse covers her children's eyes' (127). And when such a man

. . . least fears her, she
With one light gesture shakes away half his life . . .
And with one other, and how little stronger,
Gives him annihilation. (132)

Later in the play, Reed plants a variation of the Leopardi philosophy, a worldview that attractively accounts for the second devastation of Pompeii when its inhabitants had struggled to rebuild it after an earthquake sixteen years earlier. But though such aphorisms *tell* us the Leopardi take on the universe, the other particulars Reed has assembled seem to *show* us a view more upbeat. His play is something like the student essay that announces one thesis in its first paragraph and offers evidence which supports another. By the end, Reed has contrived to peel away his least noble characters, leaving us with the four he wants us to admire most. Francesca and Attilio finally speak to the old couple whose silence, cleanness, stillness, and intelligence—those great Reedian virtues—the sensitive teenaged lovers have admired from afar throughout the day. There are no guarantees, for as in so many Reed works 'a vague sense of menace' has hung over the lovers (146), but that men and women two generations apart can possess these virtues leaves us with hope that, at least for a time, we can thwart that hidden ugly Power.

Of all his means of getting the narrative function accomplished, aside from the 'Narrator' in *The Great Desire I Had*, the Traveller is probably Reed's least imaginative and most obtrusive. For one, there was no way for a listener to know he is called the 'Traveller'; he sounds like just a narrator, and some of the information he provides is that which might be given in a documentary. In defence of Reed's use of the Traveller figure, that information is edifying and sometimes wittily presented. He gives speculative history lessons on the flourishing years of the public Forum under Nero, but also precise dates on the disasters. He provides analysis on the artworks and all kinds of architectural arcana. He even tells how the ruins were dug up and how plaster casts of the bodies were made. He is in fact our guide to Pompeii *and* its tourists, tracking their movements about the ruins like a security officer watching multiple television monitors:

> MacBride and MacFarlane have long ago returned from the Villa of the Mysteries, and for some time past have been carefully inspecting Region Six . . . Judy and Walter, followed at a distance of eighteen yards by Margery and Bill, have wandered along the Street of the Consul… (154)

Moreover, the Traveller's language is often highly lyrical, even when it is most educational. Just before the archaeological lesson on pouring plaster, the Traveller speaks in richly suggestive language:

> . . . the dead wait in their dead houses, their dead money scattered round them. The rain of filth that killed their bodies preserved their forms. Inside the black encasement that petrified quickly round them, the decay of flesh and blood proceeded, leaving only the skeleton therein, the dead butterflies inside the black cocoons. (154)

Elsewhere, the Traveller's word choice is as sharp and affecting as a poet's. He speaks, for example, of water once 'gurgling and clucking' in the streets (137), of how the Forum was 'admonished by temples', and of how its colonnades were tossed down by the earthquake 'like daffodil-stalks' (132). As in *Pytheas*, one of the themes is the imaginative conjuring of history, one that lends itself to lyricism. 'Fancies start up in the unreal heat', says the Traveller, 'are warmed for a moment in the glowing sun, and evaporate on the listless air' (142). One of these fancies is sparked by a well-preserved wine-bar:

> . . . jolly the smooth counter, jolly the big containers, jolly the brown earthenware amphorae, clean and stacked side-by-side in jollity, jolly the polished marble. Here the out-of-work sailor lounged, scratched his thigh, spat in the gutter, bored. And the owner . . . raised his eyebrows . . ., suggesting coolness, jolly coolness of room upstairs. Gay time with girl. Or agony with girl. Or boredom with girl. (141)

The options offered at the end, perhaps as the reverie begins to 'evaporate', remind one of those in the as-you-like-it fancies in Reed's early poems, 'The Place and the Person' and 'Envoy'.

There are many other attempts at lyricism in the Traveller's speeches and in the verse of the Sybil, however, that do not succeed. Some of the failings are familiar to students of Reed. Often he does make fine paradoxes, as in describing what the ruins both expose and conceal: each of 'the fractured grey boxes of strangers' houses' contains 'something we cannot see, even though all seems shamelessly and horribly broken open'; but often the wordplay is not worth the trouble: what the boxes are open to is 'the still, new air, the new, still air of the morning' (137). This is pretentious writing. Without a comma between *still* and *new*, readers might be better clued to a double meaning of *still* as 'yet' in the first instance and 'motionless' in the second, but so what? Some of the Traveller's light and dark imagery, too, seems superfluous, as if Reed wrote the passages in straight prose, then felt compelled to ornament them. After the eruption, 'the night of centuries fell over the place', the Traveller says (133); after excavation, says the Sibyl, Pompeii 'to the light of heaven returns' (131). When the Traveller reports that 'the sun is higher', he adds immediately, 'and the shadows in the street are shorter' (136). The excess metaphors become almost their own convention or part of a transparent code rather than legitimate lyricism.

Soon after Reed's chiaroscuro he pursues another contrast, again through the media of the Traveller and the Sibyl, this time of the 'clucking' water and babbling life of ancient Pompeii versus the aridity of the present summer day: 'Emptiness: water and fire gone; vacancy of earth and air' (137). Unfortunately, the description might double as a characterization of Reed's poetry at its weakest. One questions, for example, the purpose of the metaphor that follows all this meditation on lifelessness. As we hear for the first time the voices of Bill and Judy, the Traveller announces that 'again the light bright skeins of life are knitted together again' (138). The repetition of *again* in this passage seems merely careless. Similar redundancies lend to the lighter portions of *Leopardi* and the war poems, for example, much of their charm and satirical bite. But there is no doubt that repetition in the Sybil's opening speech is intentional. Granted, repetition is a hallmark of oral verse (as the chorus of a song is repeated for ease of listening), but Reed's opening pair of lines hammers out the phrase 'once more' four times and in the first stanza ten times total. The word *once* appears three more times in the second stanza even beyond its heavy-handed opening: 'And once, once, once:/ The garden and the palace and the noise/

Of the once prince, once powerful, broke this air' (127).[24] The use of poetic lines further reinforces the repetition: though the lines of the opening speech run as many as fourteen syllables, Reed twice places the word *once* on a line by itself, in one case following a line of only eight syllables: 'The sailor lolled in the wineshop/ Once' (127).

Hence, though his efforts at fashioning lyrical prose in *The Streets of Pompeii* are conscious and obvious, Reed was again very particular, almost obsessive about differentiating the play's verse from its prose. His most 'poetic' figures, the Sibyl of Cumae and Attilio and Francesca, speak verse, and when they have occasion to mix with the more prosaic characters, they elevate those figures to their level. Thus, even MacBride and MacFarlane speak in verse when they ask directions of Attilio, and the Traveller has two verse 'conversations' with the Sibyl. Reed had made some misguidedly high claims for verse, as opposed to poetry, one of them being that 'only the presence of rhythm will effect that state of communication' from writer to audience 'where the limited number of words can be disposed into speech that can bring the density and complexity of character and the progress of psychological action bearably and intelligibly before us' ('Towards' II, 804). He maintained that the well-exercised Elizabethan ear could pick up the distinction between the prose spoken by Antipholus and Dromio from Syracuse in *The Comedy of Errors* and the verse spoken by their Ephesian twins. But having Attilio's directions to the Villa of the Mysteries in verse seems more important to Reed than it is discernible to the ears of listeners in the era of the second Elizabeth.

Whereas Francesca and Attilio (whether he is speaking the tenderest love-words in an aside or pondering what shoes he will wear when he meets Francesca's father) always speak in the long irregular line Reed employed in his early verse drama, the Sybil speaks in shorter lines which frequently settle into iambic tetrameter. Although Savage calls her verse 'impressive' (176), much of it is not. Though perhaps the expectation is unfair, in short lines we anticipate greater density: more highly charged wordplay, more 'devices', more music. Reed tries to pack much in to these lines, but again, the paradoxes often fall flat: the 'seeding grass and arid bloom/ . . . shake in this unshaken air' (141); 'the grass and weeds/ Fight for and win their killing life' (137). Often a section of six or eight lines will contain only one end-rhyme: 'The ghost returning here has found/ . . . One shining corner that again/ Can stir once more an ancient pain' (142). The rhyming pair seems like a random stab or just a mistake, especially when one of the rhymes houses an unintentional redundancy.

However, the music in one of the two scenes in which the Traveller speaks in verse is powerful. For two pages in the printed text, the dialogue between him and the Sybil keeps to perfect iambic tetrameter almost throughout, including many instances in which one completes the poetic line for the other. The Keatsian theme of the scene is introduced by the Traveller, in prose, marvelling at the sense of movement and sentience among the figures painted on the wall of a room in the Villa of the Mysteries: 'Enter it quickly: see if you can catch a movement of drapery or limb among the figures that crowd its walls. You cannot. However softly you enter, all movement in the room ceases the second before' (147). Part of the depiction is of 'Silenus with the blank brute stare/ And the maiden's indrawn breath/ Of terror as she sees him there' (149).[25] Reed as always is fascinated by the tension of static scenes, of the immediate aftermath of action or impending action:

> Slowly round the painted wall,
> Spreads the cold voluptuous dream,
> Silence of arrested feast,
> Quiet of arrested dance,
> Anger of arrested lust. (147)

Although Reed's directive for a drum-roll behind seems a bit much, the trochaic rhythm of these, the oracle's first lines of the scene, helps them memorably encapsulate a theme: the power and permanence of art.

Reed's lyrical sense is also trustworthy in many of the verse speeches of Attilio and Francesca, and not just in the sonnets they speak at the transcendent moment of their love. It is the subtler gestures and words that Reed conveys more tellingly. Again, his line is usually of five stresses, falling into recognizable patterns only occasionally. The rhythms are most insistent in their initial meeting, as for example Attilio's first aside after he has cared for Francesca's scratch. His words resolve into almost perfect iambic pentameter: her arm 'was living and firm and white and smooth and simple,/ And cool and damp like mushrooms in my hands' (129). Reed's adherence to line integrity is not just conventional in this scene: the absolutely winning awkwardness and charm of the lovers' encounter is underscored by the positioning of the dialogue. Regarding the scratch, the two alternate rhythmically parallel speeches:

*Francesca* But it is nothing.
*Attilio* But it is bleeding.
*Francesca* Only a little.

Francesca tries to spare Attilio's handkerchief, but Attilio insists 'it is not a serious handkerchief' (128). In the following seven speeches (consuming only three lines), Reed manages to convey a wealth of fine psychology:

*Attilio* There.
*Francesca* Thank you.
*Attilio* *Niente.*
*Francesca* But it will . . .
*Attilio* You like Pompei?
*Francesca* Yes, very much. But I have not seen it yet.
*Attilio* I have been here five days in succession.
(128-29)

In these lines, we see Francesca's eagerness to please. We also see that, at seventeen, Attilio is a young man playing the role of protective hero who is shamed by thanks, but at the same time just an older boy (we find out earlier that his mother ironed his handkerchief) boasting to a younger girl. The anapestic rhythm of his last line is an apt medium to convey his basic innocence.

In reviewing *The Great Desire I Had*, J. C. Trewin contended that Reed's speculation on Shakespeare in Italy was too long by half an hour (701). With *Streets*, Trewin picks a similar bone: 'Henry Reed, summoning atmosphere eagerly, was excited about Pompeii, but he took a long time to fire us' ('Return Journeys' 487). And after the initial scene of panicked flight from Vesuvius's belchings, the play does saunter along at a rather leisurely pace. Trewin marks the second depiction of the eruption as the point at which Reed 'at length . . . startled genuinely in a reconstruction of the last hours of Pompeii under that engulfing flood of hot, wet ash. This was a real and terrifying return journey' (487). But Reed's gifts—comic, dramatic, and lyric—are on display several episodes before that, and then right on through the end of the play. This half hour, the indispensable half hour of *Streets*, is brilliant in its rapid segues, characteristic of the art of radio drama, and the impressive range of language and subject matter.

A scene or two after the Traveller's treatise on the plaster forms of Pompeiian beasts and citizens, Margery, in her inimitable clipped English, observes that Judy has 'found another statch, on a tombstone' (156). The Traveller describes the 'sad gaunt statue' who 'seems, from death, to be regarding life, and wondering if she has ever known it aright' (156-57). The question she asks through the Traveller, '*What were we?*', begins a direct lift of Leopardi's poem 'Chorus of the Dead', continued immediately by the Sybil: 'What was that bitter point in time/ That bore the name of life?' Reed modulates cleverly from the dark profundity of this poem into a scene of shallow banter among the two English couples:

*Sybil* . . . And as in life
Our souls drew back from death, so now they draw
Back from the flame of life.
(*no fade in*)
*Judy* (*in determined tones)* I want to be cremated. . . .
and have my ashes scattered.
*Walter* What, *now*, do you mean? (157)

In the episode, the four seem to be affronted that among ruins there would be 'all these *stones*' (157). When Bill is being photographed in an embrace with the statue, it is suggested that he 'pretend she's Marilyn Monroe'. 'Or Gina Lollobrij' (158), offers Margery, no doubt out of respect for Italy and period detail.

The short speech of the Traveller which follows begins with the word *Click*. Reed seems again to be freezing time as the Traveller captures with a 'click' the precise locations of all the tourists at that moment, including 'the clean old gentleman and lady [who] raise, click, to their silent lips a glass of white wine, served by an intelligent waiter'. He also implicitly contrasts the camera's baser freezing of time to that from a paintbrush or sculptor's chisel. At the end of this profound meditation the Traveller identifies MacFarlane's position as 'two yards nine inches to the west' (158) of his companion. That is because MacBride is urinating in a house on the Street of the Baker. The two rationalize the deed, then discuss sanitary matters throughout the ages before the Traveller returns us to Margery and company.

Here begins a little cadenza by Reed on sleep, first the 'low' sleep of the four English tourists, who have 'picnicked heartily' (160). Margery recalls having performed *A Midsummer Night's Dream* ('by Shakespeare', she adds)

> for Commem . . . in the open air, just outside the
> cricket pav . . . I did Helena—the tall one . . .

> I must have been awful . . . though I got a good crit.
> in the mag . . . (161)

Even the lizard is pondering sleep, ironically in the amphitheatre where the gladiators and the beasts contended and where now Attilio and Francesca utter their matching sonnets. In the second, Attilio tenderly asks the sleeping Francesca, '. . . can it do you harm,/ If I place a kiss, like a whisper, into your open palm?' (163) In parallel ballad stanzas both the Traveller and the Sibyl implore the lovers, 'Do not move. This minute hold' (163). This tableau is interrupted by the eruption scenes and Reed's portrait of the merchant's family and the Old Man. We then return to Francesca and Attilio, who indeed have not moved. 'Never, never, *never* have the buildings in the Oriental Quarter of the New Excavations shone more brightly than they do this evening' on the heterosexual love of a seventeen-year-old boy and a fifteen-year-old girl. Reed's transition is to the Scotsmen's debate on homosexual attraction and its causes in the ancient world, perhaps 'the comparative seclusion of the womenfolk from the men' or 'the custom of exercising in a nude state in the *palaestra*' (169).

While all of Reed's 'thinking' plays do their share of winking, in no other work except *Lessons of the War* does Reed so adeptly weave the lofty and the base, the profound and the superficial, the pathetic and the silly, the lyrical and the prosaic. But in all his radio plays outside of the Tablet-Reeve-Shewin comedies, the frame, especially the conclusion, must be serious: by the time the BBC announcer returns, listeners must have forgotten about childish Napoleonic wars, jolly snowballs, and bathroom breaks on nineteen-hundred-year-old buildings. And the ending must also be quiet, clean, still, and intelligent, like Reed's lyricism at its best and like the very characters in *The Streets of Pompeii* who are the last to depart his 'stage'. To leave us with his four most 'poetic' characters—the old gentleman and lady, Attilio and Francesca, and in the end, just the older couple—Reed contrives exits for all the loud and prosaic figures:

finally, the noisy Scotsmen and the even noisier Bill, Walter, Judy, and Margery, whom we last hear in the distance, singing 'Roll . . . out . . . the barrel,/ We'll have . . . a barrel . . . of fun . . '. (170). Though disaster may strike at any time, despite all of Reed's pessimistic posturing *The Streets of Pompeii*, like Reed's best early poems and his great *Lessons*, seems to say that men and women can prevail. The victory will not be won through the materialism of merchants; nor through sex, drink, or other Bacchanalian pleasures; nor through the 'red political slogans' (168) that sully clean walls, nor the violence that grows out of those slogans. It will be through love and the sensitive appreciation of beauty. The old gentleman and lady see much more in Pompeii than cute backdrops for snapshots to send to Mum; they see much in each other and much in the young love of Francesca and Attilio. After they exchange their good-byes with the young couple, the play's final lines are not a bang, nor a whimper, but as gentle concentric rings resonating from a stone dropped in a pond:

*Old gentleman* Good. Nice young couple.
*Old lady* As bright as lamps . . .
*Old gentleman* Yes . . . May they remain so.
*Old lady* May they remain so . . . Come, my sweet. (172)

The old couple themselves provide hope that love and the desire for quiet contemplation of beauty will last, that their benediction will bear itself out for such as Attilio and Francesca.

1 The film *Apocalypse Now* is a case in point.

2 Reed seemed always both endeared to and embarrassed by his radio productions. To him they were literary mulattoes, and his affectionate blushing over them reminds one of Anne Bradstreet's dual emotions toward her first collection of poetry, as expressed in 'The Author to Her Book'. It is noteworthy, too, that in the subtitle of his *Hilda Tablet* collection, Reed refers to the comedies therein as 'Pieces' for radio.

3 Readers necessarily are clued in to the ironic discrepancy right away by the name *Vincenzo* attached to each speech of the 'interloper'. The irony must have been more delicious on the wireless.

4 Although the much put-upon scholar Herbert Reeve is the most autobiographical character in the *Hilda Tablet* comedies, there is much Henry Reed in Stephen Shewin as well. It always seems to be *others* who are getting good sex: J. R. Ackerley in a Greek hotel while Reed makes himself scarce or one of the Neapolitan boys while *H.* is in a bookshop reading Freud.

5 Reed was certainly not superior to a little self-parody. Herbert Reeve is blinded by his devotion to the memory of Richard Shewin, and Reed seems in many of Reeve's passages to be twitting his own pedestal-building for certain artists, including the three cited by Reeve.

6 Again, Reed may be engaging in self-parody. Whether it is intentional is less apparent, but in his deathly serious poems in *A Map* he was capable of verse with similarly concrete images involving hearts: 'My love, you are timely come, let me lie by your heart' (from 'The Door and the Window').

7 The Reed entry in *The Oxford Companion to English Literature* (Ed. Margaret Drabble) incorrectly states that *The Streets of Pompeii* collection 'contains five verse plays'.

8 Though it is 'not an essential component of poetic or verse drama', maintained Reed, lovely phrasing was what, at mid-century, most theatre-goers and critics of the sub-genre were looking for ('Towards' I, 763). The use of the word *poetic* is unfortunate, seeming to unravel Reed's carefully knitted

distinction between verse and poetry.

9 *Streets* was also produced in 1955 and 1970; *Moby Dick*, first aired and published in 1947, was produced again in 1979 with an additional verse passage at the end.

10 Of Adelaide's absolute despotism, the historical Monaldo conceded in his autobiography, 'If I dared to conceal from my wife the reason for a single sigh, she would take my letters out of my pocket, sue me, raise an uproar through the whole town' (in *Selected Prose and Poetry*, 21).

11 It can be argued that Reed's Adelaide projects the view that life itself is sin. In her own mind a model Christian, she seems disappointed that her young son Luigi recovers from an illness, leaving her 'again frustrated', never having known 'that greatest blessing of mothers,/ The giving-back, the returning of the clean small soul,/ All uncontaminated into the hand of God' (17).

12 Reed recognized, too, that soliloquy is an authentic vehicle of expression for the melancholy, sensitive type, more so for a Leopardi or a Hamlet than for men of action like, say, Coriolanus or more social characters like Reed's own Carlo in *The Unblest*, as well as Antonio Ranieri in *The Monument* and Thomas Shewin in *The Great Desire I Had*.

13 The often irreligious Reed may have planted one of his in-jokes here: we pick up Paolina's counting at 666.

14 The poem is [' . . . and to this meditation I shall bear'], in Reed's translation.

15 The Reed comic figure who most dazzlingly illustrates Leopardi's remark is Giulio Pasquati in *The Great Desire I Had*.

16 In the next scene, Reed allows another actor, Ranieri's mistress Maddalena Pelzet, to expose her own phoniness. Milking her life story for maximum melodrama, she describes herself at sixteen, 'a poor girl,/ Orphaned, unfriended', pursued by unwanted men. She ends the speech with the question, 'Can you think what that means to a poor girl of fifteen?' Two speeches later, the fish has gotten even bigger: 'That was Maddalena, a poor girl of fourteen' (95-6).

17 Besides all the songs, of course, Savage cites among others Hilda Tablet's all-female opera and Richard Shewin's recently discovered play on 'a certain subject' (homosexuality).

18 Fabrizi remarks that *Othello*'s 'plot, of course, is anglicised beyond recognition' (89).

19 Another parallel Reed would just as soon have had hushed up is to the man he called 'Tennessee Whatisit'. Leopardi's backward glances toward home and his beloved but unmarriageable sister are very much like Tom's in *The Glass Menagerie*.

20 Before Ctesiphon learns Ajax's name he has remarked only that the mate 'seemed rather drunk' and spoke 'four coarse-sounding monosyllables in what I took to be a dialect of Northern Macedonia' (19).

21 This metaphor went the way of the Housman parody when the play was broadcast; perhaps one-tenth of the script had to be cut to keep the 11 June 1952 transmission at eighty minutes. Among several other variants between this script and the carbon typescript Stallworthy used for *Collected Poems* is 'Himalayas' for 'Indian mountains'.

22 Contrast the more venal tour guide that Bill and company encounter who wants to sell them a 'small bronce rrripproduction' of a phallus, with or without wings (140).

23 The Traveller continues, 'MacFarlane's grandfather composed it in the hot summer of 1870, the year of the Franco-Prussian War; and MacBride agrees that it would be folly in an unfamiliar country recklessly to overload the digestive organs and incur thereby the risk of enteric disturbance'. Here again the Traveller appropriates the language of the characters. Note too how Reed the fastidious grammarian keeps the infinitive intact: 'recklessly to overload'.

24 Repetition as a literary device has overstepped its efficacy when listeners begin to ponder how silly a word sounds and readers how its spelling is even sillier.

25 The first line is the Sibyl's; the last two, including the completion of an atypical rhyming pair, are the Traveller's.

Incidentally, this passage may exemplify Savage's contention that Reed's 'scholarship is not quite as dazzling as it appears' (183). Reed's Silenus is a satyr, but one mythology reference makes a strong distinction between the two, the Sileni being more equine than the goatlike satyrs and less prone to lechery.

# THE CONFLUENCE OF GIFTS: *LESSONS OF THE WAR*

True to Henry Reed's nature, in his poems of World War II no weapon is discharged, no man is wounded, no one goes insane from shellshock; there is no 'action' in the military sense, nor much even in the broader sense of the word. As always Reed was more interested in actions just completed or in the static tension of actions considered or impending. One of the five poems collected in the final version of *Lessons of the War* concerns, on one level, the return of issued military paraphernalia after the war, while the first four treat aspects of preparation for warfare. These poems are also a proving ground of sorts for Reed's unique poetic talents, a way of testing his poetic gear and recognizing what would serve him best in conveying his images, his characters, and his aesthetic. In too many poems in *A Map* and in some of the radio drama he is like a soldier trying to dig a trench with his canteen. In his overweening desire to be a serious lyric poet he too often ignored the dramatic and comic equipment in his knapsack.

The genius, then, in these poems is Reed's understanding and mastery of his 'issue'. For his purposes, he found the Aphoristic and Narrative wanting. He recognized that, at least for him, profound ideas were not to be blared over the loudspeaker, and there need be no overarching consciousness to present them, more or less directly, to the reader. In fact, in no *Lesson* is there narration, and in only one is there the faintest hint of a perspective outside that of the characters (the minimal 'stage directions' in 'Returning of Issue') to taint the sequence's brilliant Dramatic essence. Roger Savage speaks of 'the double vision of Reed the sensitive, observant intellectual, intensity and compassion balancing scepticism and irony' (184). In these poems Reed entirely trusts the words (and articulated thoughts) of the characters to project that vision. Through their dialogue and monologues alone are conveyed all the subtleties, ironies, and contrasts that arise when young people endowed with the virtues we saw in the exemplary characters of *The Streets of Pompeii*—silence, stillness, and intelligence—are thrust into the alien world of battle training. Though the purely Lyrical in these poems is sometimes affected, it is still more consistently affecting than in any other Reed work. And when we read the lyrical passages as they weave in and out of the clumsy military jargon of the sergeant and the witty and even erotically Comic improvisation upon that language by the recruit, we are appreciating a man in complete command of his craft. *Lessons of the War* is Henry Reed's most powerful and innovative work, a unique confluence of his poetic gifts.

The three *Lessons* collected in *A Map of Verona* had been published in *New Statesman and Nation* during the war years: 'Naming of Parts' in August 1942, 'Judging Distances' in March 1943, and 'Unarmed Combat' in April 1945. 'Movement of Bodies' and 'Returning of Issue' were published twenty years apart in the *Listener*, the latter in October 1970 just before all five came together in an edition overseen by Douglas Cleverdon, the man who produced nearly all of Reed's radio plays. For that Clover Hill edition, published by Chilmark Press in New York, Reed inserted 'Movement of Bodies' in the third slot between 'Judging Distances' and 'Unarmed Combat' and positioned 'Returning of Issue' as the fifth and final *Lesson*. The first 110 numbers of the limited issue of 530 were signed by the author (Reilly 273).

Both versions, that which appeared in *Map* and the sequence as completed in 1970, are dedicated to Alan Michell and take as their epigraph a minutely but significantly altered couplet from Horace's *Odes*. Title, dedication, and epigraph now appear on a separate page in *Collected Poems*. These three seemingly simple elements illustrate just how scant and careless Reed scholarship has been. No critic has attempted to identify Alan Michell, but six commentators manage to fumble the title, calling the sequence *Lessons of War* or worse, *The Lessons of War*.[1] That Reed was not one to disrespect the power of articles is clear from the lengthy justification Shakespeare gives Thomas Shewin in Reed's radio drama *The Great Desire I Had* for changing the title of a play from *The Taming of a Shrew* to *The Taming of the Shrew*. By playing loose with articles, explicators of the poems attribute to them a far broader and more didactic thrust than Reed's title *Lessons of the War* implies. The poet modestly offers *some* lessons of this one war, not the *only* lessons of *all* war.

Reed's epigraph tinkers with a single letter of Horace's couplet, which reads: '*Vixi puellis nuper idoneus/ Et militavi non sine gloria*'. Stallworthy translates the Latin to 'Lately I've lived among girls, creditably enough, and have soldiered not without glory' (xix).[2] Reed simply inverts the *p* so that *puellis* (girls) reads *duellis* (battles). His sleight of word is clever, though not as clever as most critics insist, notably Frank Kermode, who rewrites Horace and credits Reed with ingeniously changing *duellis* to *puellis*, to suggest, you see, the heterosexuality of one of the poems' speakers (rev. of *Collected Poems* 17).[3] In actuality, Reed's amendment has wrung some of the original wit out of the passage. Significantly, however, it sets a subversive tone for the *Lessons*, whose chief joy is in their playful piracy of the language of a mentor figure. To John Carey, *Lessons*—along with 'Chard Whitlow', Reed's good-spirited 'roast' of Eliot—'revealed a sensitive individual driven to retaliation by the lunatic bosses responsible for his education' (577). The retaliations are, to be sure, not frontal but flank attacks, using the weapons of parody and irony. In *Lessons*, these guerrilla tactics expose the 'tragic absurdity of training for war and death in the midst of the beauty and fecundity of an English pastoral scene', achieving 'an effect that is sometimes ruefully funny, sometimes sharply poignant, and sometimes both together' (*World Authors* 1198).

The first and best of the sequence, 'Naming of Parts', has also had the longest and fullest life outside the nest of *Lessons*. Somewhat ironically, Dylan Thomas helped give the fledgling poem its early wings with his theatrical and much-admired public recitations of the early fifties.[4] Apparently, Reed found

Thomas bombastic[5] and Thomas found most of Reed's poetry soporific. Nevertheless, 'Naming of Parts', along with 'Chard Whitlow' done in T. S. Eliot's reading voice, became part of Thomas's reading list, a repertoire of works from poets whose reputations have survived the buffeting forty years since. William Plomer is perhaps the one exception,[6] but Thomas also read from Auden, Belloc, Betjeman, Graves, Hardy, Alun Lewis (who vies only with Roy Fuller as the most highly regarded British poet of the Second World War), MacNeice, Pound, Ransom, and Yeats. And notable are his criteria of selection, bluntly stated in a preface to his reading at MIT in 1952: 'I like to read only the poets I like' ('I Am Going', 16). Privately, Thomas had chastised Henry Treece's 'ridiculous overpraise of Reed' and labelled most of Reed's poetry 'dull' (*Letters* 223). But it was the peremptory public words of an ascendant poet and poetic 'figure' that counted. As Wesley Wehr, a friend of artists and the arts for forty years, remarked, 'If Thomas read you, you were *it*'. 'Naming of Parts' has gone on to become, with the possible exception of Randall Jarrell's 'The Death of the Ball Turret Gunner', the most anthologized poem of the Second World War. The educators X. J. Kennedy and Dorothy Kennedy call it 'one of the most teachable poems ever written' (224).

Some teachers have viewed Reed's little drama as at least partly a reverie, in which the instructor—presumably a sergeant or other non-commissioned officer—takes both parts. As he ponders his instructions and labelling of rifle components, he is struck by the analogy of his own words to the more beautiful named parts (no instructions necessary) of nature. Surely, however, in the poem are represented the sensibilities of two distinct persons, the sergeant and a dreamy recruit. Such an insistence is more in line with the dual-voiced pattern of all the *Lessons* (with the exception of 'Movement of Bodies', which records only the spoken words of the instructor) and especially more consistent with 'Judging Distances', in which the sergeant undeniably directs a question to one of the recruits and receives a response.

The sergeant-voice which speaks all of 'Movement of Bodies' and which opens all the other poems is mechanical, prone to self-important use of military jargon packaged in tautologies and awkward syntax, inexpert in its attempts to use appropriate grammar, and blithely unaware of the rich sound effects of its diction. Responding in 1946 to *Four Quartets*, Reed wrote that 'One has to develop—and it is entirely worth while [*sic*]—an ear alert for subtle repetitions and transformations of single words' (rev. of Preston 435). The sergeant figure has clearly not cultivated that gift as had Reed and the character who seems to speak for him in *Lessons*. For example, an announcement like that which opens the first *Lesson*—'Today we have naming of parts'—must have brought a wry smile to the lips of 10557689 Pte. Reed, H. He must have savoured its suggestiveness and its rhythm: a perfect anapestic trimeter when 'And' and 'For' are added in the recruit's meditative reworking of the clause in lines 6 and 30. While the sergeant-voice drones about the previous day's lesson ('daily cleaning') and the next day's ('what to do after firing'), the meditation of the sensitive, daydreaming recruit emerges, observing that '[j]aponica/ Glistens like coral in all of the neighbouring gardens …'. His use of simile in likening one element of nature to another is one signal of a new, sharply contrasting worldview. Partway through the fourth line of each of the first four stanzas, this second voice intrudes upon the sergeant's pedagoguery and appropriates, at first subtly and then more openly, some element of the sergeant's phrasing to suit his own sensibilities, decidedly uncongenial toward violence and rote learning. But with a 'technical skill concealing itself under a perfect clarity and ease of statement' (Lehmann 168), Reed negotiates the shifts so deftly that though disorienting, the modulations are satisfying; though surprising, inevitable.

In his two-and-a-half-line role in stanza one, for example, the recruit is 'naming' a part of nature quite as precisely, in his own way, as the instructor is naming rifle components. Even the sounds of the parts so named, like the lilting four-syllable '[j]aponica', are more euphonious than 'cocking-piece' and 'breech' (with its alternate meaning of 'buttocks'), 'upper sling swivel' and 'piling swivel'. Like the language which describes it, the natural world in springtime is beautiful and bright: it '[g]listens', in contrast to the dull greens and browns of military garb and equipment. Nature is also more reliable. Whereas spring makes its yearly appearance without fail, the instructor is obliged to announce that, possibly because of bureaucratic errors, the men 'have not got' at least two of the rifle parts covered in the day's lecture. Ironically, the men are being trained to take life just as spring is resurrecting life from the deadness of winter. In the recruit's contribution to stanza two he admires the 'silent, eloquent gestures' of the branches in the garden as, later, he is wistful toward the 'fragile, motionless' quality of the blossoms. This appreciation exemplifies another contrast: what Michael O'Toole sees as 'the recruit's awareness of the STATE of nature' versus 'the sergeant's obsession with material action processes' (20).[7] Collectively, these oppositions are symbols—one might almost say an objective correlative—for what Reed undoubtedly suspected from his brief stint in the Royal Army Ordnance Corps and what the poem may imply, that in contrast to nature, the unnatural practice of war is full of inarticulate noise and action: sound and fury, signifying nothing.

The dueling perspectives of military and civilian life are counterpointed with greatest dexterity in stanza four. Here the sergeant is explaining 'easing the spring' of the rifle's magazine by sliding the bolt '[r]apidly backwards and forwards'. The second spring which is eased is that suggested by the capitalization of *Spring* when the phrase is repeated, that is, the season whose arrival is smoothed by the pollinating work of bees. Lost on the instructor, but likely not on his listener and certainly not on nearly all critics of the poem, are the unintentionally sexual connotations of the sergeant's language. A poet and World War II veteran, Vernon Scannell had sensed the 'pervasive and ubiquitous mist of sexual longing and deprivation that was part of the air one breathed in the atmosphere of barracks, camp, and ship during the war'(135); Scannell among many others recognizes that the recruit's mind, already transported from the sergeant's pointers about bolt oscillation to the backwards and forwards activities of the 'early bees', needs but a short step to envision a third kind of spring-easing. As O'Toole puts it,

> the shuttling movement of the bolt in the breech. . . appeals to the secret subversive streak in the minds of the pupils. It does not take much to make bored young men undergoing basic army training think of sex. . . . And erotic metaphors are everywhere to be found by those in the mood to seek them. Bolt and breeches, innocent enough as parts of a rifle, become perfect metaphors for sexual organs in action when the field shifts, when we get a 'naming of private parts'. (22)

Linda M. Shires carries the sexual suggestiveness of the language a precarious step further into Freudian analysis. The reader of 'Naming of Parts', she says, 'is consistently aware of the phallic weapon of war and the gardens it will penetrate' (81). Indeed, the gun becomes symbolic of the war itself, 'the diminished, endless, boring, hierarchical, stupid war' (81). But the anger in those five adjectives—or at least four, because I have no clue what she means by 'diminished'—is Shires' anger more than Reed's. His tone is closer to that Geoffrey Strickland ascribes to the poem: 'together with . . . acute nostalgia', a 'conscripted civilian's good-humoured acceptance of an inconvenient but unavoidable situation' (78). Undoubtedly Reed sought, or at least properly welcomed the serendipitous arrival of, the ambiguities which inhere in the language of the inductee's voice in stanza four which, O'Toole observes, connotes 'violence', even 'violation':

> the metaphors of pollination combine lexical items with strong connotations of both warfare and sex: *assault*, basically a military term, is most frequently encountered in the context of rape, and *fumbling*, the clumsy handling of

> equipment by untrained hands (say, army recruits), is often used in descriptions of awkward, inexperienced love-making. (22)

But do we then conclude, as Shires implies, that masculine, 'phallic' warfare is aggressively raping the world's gardens? And, further, that war is nevertheless 'impotent in comparison to man's private lusts'? (81)

Shires' reading is symptomatic of a number of excessive interpretations of 'Naming of Parts' that should be viewed with caution, for they privilege the Aphoristic over Reed's other poetic strands, particularly for the Dramatic, that somehow make this poem 'lyrical, satiric, meditative, and risqué all at the same time' (Savage 184). Shires, in fact, is one of the culprits guilty of giving Reed's sequence the too-big title *The Lessons of War*, an oversight that itself could be subjected to psychoanalytic scrutiny. Certainly there is a kind of truth in Shires' argument that individual lusts have more potency than collective lusts. But when he was at his best, Henry Reed could both accept those kinds of truths about the power of nature's beauty or man's sexuality, yet smile ruefully and resignedly at the equally compelling truth that a grenade in a split second could explode men and their private lusts. Readings besides that of Shires are similarly interesting and well meaning but misplace their emphasis and chafe against Reed's admonition at a 1966 poetry reading that his *Lessons of the War* 'were meant to be comic'. These interpretations exhibit the same 'yearning' X. J. and Dorothy Kennedy report in undergraduates to distort Reed's miniature masterpiece into 'a vast comment about Modern Civilization' (224). Stallworthy, for example, sees something about the gardens in Reed's poem as a modern 'extension of another symbolic landscape, the archetypal landscape of desire, that garden in which Adam *named* the animals' (xviii).[8] One reviewer, writing in the *Listener*, makes the meaningless, and therefore unassailable claim that 'Naming of Parts' is not just an allegory but a 'mixture' of 'explicit' and 'implicit' allegory (23 May 1946, 690).

Everything in Henry Reed's nature, if not always his practice, would have cried out against the view that his lyrical, comic, and dramatic gifts were serving as mere conduits for a message. By 1946 he was calling allegory 'the deadest of all literary forms' (*Novel* 33). His highly laudatory review of Billy Budd a year later takes a slightly discursive turn to a discussion of allegory and its literary cousin, symbolism. Reed clearly elevates the latter to a rung high above the artificial and ultimately inferior allegory: 'In symbolism, the real object is seen first', he wrote, whereas allegory 'takes a spiritual theme and *impresses* objects into the illumination of it' (397). The poet in Reed appreciated both meanings of *impresses*: 'presses, makes an impression', as a dentist might do in plaster; and 'puts into involuntary service'.

Although much of *A Map of Verona* seems open to the charge of allegory, 'Naming of Parts', at least, seems to escape it. Unlike Billy Budd and the recruit in Reed's poem, the words of his instructor were *not* put into involuntary service. They are the 'real object', if not seen first, at least heard first, rather than wrenched to fit some pre-conceived ideas of Reed's. As a critic of a fiction, Reed wrote,

> Some sort of philosophy or view of life, often with political implications, inevitably emerges from the work of a serious novelist; but it *emerges*; it does not insert itself, or stand there for the novel to drape itself round. (*Novel* 7)

Granted, it is dangerous to hold a poet to his own critical standard, least of all that for a different genre, but Reed's survey of the British novel was published in the same year as his poetry collection, and an intelligent young writer with a keen sense of his career as a literary man would surely have recognized that the two publications might be held up to the light together. To be sure, Reed was a leftist with strong anti-war sentiments (he admitted in a 1968 letter to being 'a Eugene McCarthy man') and a Freudian, specifically a follower of Melanie Klein. But he would have been, to say the least, distressed to have his poem viewed as draping for either of these points of view.

Reed was, in truth, 'an Ariel-dominated poet'. Scannell, borrowing from Auden, uses the term to describe an artist 'whose main interest in the writing of a poem is one of aesthetics and craft and whose concern with probing into the reality in which the poem originated is secondary' (135). Though neither Scannell nor I seek to argue that ideas did not matter to Reed, the poet in 1942 was riding the decade's literary wave, a wave that he himself described as breaking—in 'almost a dialectic process . . . against the politically-conscious, over-intellectualised writers of the early 'thirties' ('The End of an Impulse' 117)—away from the political toward the romantic and the aesthetic. As an artist who might easily be called a neo-Romantic, even an aesthete, Reed was more desirous of crafting an elegant work of art—with psychological, and perhaps philosophical and political truths gently emanating from subtle ambiguities—than in making overt pronouncements.

Thus, Reed's first *Lesson* ends with no statements of indignation and anger as found in poems of the earlier war. He does not rage as Owen did against 'the old Lie' that it is sweet and glorious to die for one's country, nor as Sassoon did in 'Glory of Women' against the mothers and lovers whose false view of their men often put them up to a such futile heroism. The last stanza, voiced entirely by the recruit, begins instead with a meditative repetition of that resonant phrase: 'They call it easing the Spring'. After Reed's favoured mark of punctuation, a colon, the recruit, without fanfare, gently corrects the sergeant's earlier misuse of an adjective—'you can do it quite easy'—to 'it is perfectly easy' (that is, if one has enough thumb strength). After a second colon, there is not even another independent clause in the remaining four-plus lines, much less a definitive one, besides the noncommittal repetition of 'Today we have naming of parts'. Characteristically, the poem ends with a dying fall, not the crash of a gong.

I cannot speak to the strength of Henry Reed's thumb. And I believe his poetic eye sometimes failed him even before he wrote in March 1985 that his literal eyesight was 'at rock-bottom': as beautiful as coral is, its color is flat and nonreflective of light; it does not 'glisten'.[9] His strength was in his ear. When 'Naming of Parts' made its first hardcover appearance in 1946, Reed was embarking on that part of his career that called for his keenest ear and laid the heaviest demands on the ear of those who sought to appreciate his art. That was the year his first radio piece, *Noises*, was sent through the airwaves, and the year *Moby Dick* was being scripted and rehearsed, to be broadcast in January 1947. Reed had come to see that radio drama required, as he wrote in a self-described fan letter to Louis MacNeice in November 1946, 'listening with an intentness [he] had never before been forced to give to anything except music on the wireless' (Coulton 82-3).

Reed's remarks on *Four Quartets* in a 1946 essay provide a gloss on his own best work, including, of course, 'Naming of Parts': it demands 'auditory attention' for its sheer 'verbal beauty' (435). To borrow Eliot's paradoxical manner, much of the sheer verbal 'beauty' of Reed's 'Naming of Parts', as of all the *Lessons*, is in the sheer verbal ugliness of much of its language. 'Naming of Parts', like the melange of sounds in Reed's first radio piece, reminds us that not all we hear will be beautiful, but everything we hear insists upon our attention.

The 'way that you say it' was very important to Henry Reed, always keen to the subtlest hues of sound and syntax. So it is to a sergeant as he reminds his charges 'Not only how far away, but the way that you say it/ Is very important' in the opening lines of 'Judging Distances', the second *Lesson* in number and merit. It would have been almost impossible for Reed to surpass 'Naming of Parts'; perhaps like Ralph Ellison and Harper Lee he made the unwise career move of writing his great work first. The only serious defect of 'Judging Distances' is that it follows 'Naming of Parts', 'a work so original and fully achieved', in Vernon Scannell's words, 'that further poems adopting the same or similar form and strategy are almost certain to fall below the standard set by the original' (137). 'Judging Distances' does, I suppose, live dangerously by adopting the same basic stanza of five long lines and a short line. But, although it might be argued that Reed was writing himself into a corner by maintaining that distinctive stanza throughout the *Lessons*, certainly no undue pressure is exerted by that form on the content of 'Judging Distances', a poem of supreme accomplishment.

Scannell also recognizes the artistry of this second *Lesson*. In arguing that 'Judging Distances' suffers from some blurring of the two familiar voices, however, that they are 'not nearly so distinctly variegated as in ["Naming of Parts"]' (137), Scannell seems to me to be scrutinizing the poem too microscopically. Unlike 'Naming of Parts', in 'Judging Distances' the sergeant's voice performs solo through the first three stanzas and most of the fourth; its distinctive features, especially the tortured syntax, are amusingly apparent certainly by early in the second stanza. When he thinks better of explaining why in the army 'maps are of time, not place', his almost-explanation comes out redundantly: 'the reason *being*,/ *Is* one which need not delay us' (*emphasis mine*). The lapse in grammar probably signals a larger failing. In a letter to his sister Gladys, 10 July 1941, Reed wrote of 'military lecturers who rarely manage to conceal their dubiety at what they are teaching' (Stallworthy xv). The lecturer of 'Judging Distances' might also be bluffing, as his syntactic double-clutch hints; Reed implies that he is a functionary unable or unwilling to offer his men a clear rationale for the military's way of doing things.

Reed takes further pains to distance the language of the sergeant from that of the recruit, even inserting the vulgarism *bleeders* into the sergeant's script. And though Scannell finds in at least three of the sergeant's phrasings a 'distinctly artificial, literary, even a quasi-philosophical note' (137), Liz Gunter and

Jim Linebarger rightly observe in these stanzas 'no insoluble problems of voice or tone' (9). In fact, the sergeant's statement that 'maps are of time, not place' is, on one level, a realistically clumsy way of explaining the military practice of designating position or 'place' according to the numbers on a clockface. And 'things only seem to be things' is no profound statement such as Hamlet would utter on the great discrepancies in this world between appearance and reality. Rather, it is the sergeant's maladroit way of expressing the army's preference for intentional imprecision and simplification in identifying objects—for example, trees, not according to their Latin names or a John Muir field guide, but in a simple tripartite classification scheme according to their characteristic shape: 'bushy topped', conical ('fir'), or round but elongated ('poplar'). Whatever is 'literary' in the instructor's phrases was not put there for the instructor in a role poorly scripted by Reed, but *found* there by Reed as he found his anapestic trimeter in 'Naming of Parts'.

The sergeant is, then, the same kind of pedagogue we saw in 'Naming', and he uses the familiar teacher's trick of attempting to involve (or embarrass) an inattentive student by pointing a question directly at him:

> . . . suppose, for the sake of example,
> The one at the end, asleep, endeavours to tell us
> What he sees over there to the west, and how far away,
> After first having come to attention.

The inevitable shift in voice that we see in each *Lesson* except for 'Movement of Bodies' occurs after this challenge from the instructor. The shift to a second voice is relatively easy to follow in 'Naming' and 'Unarmed Combat', but in 'Judging Distances', as in 'Returning of Issue', the modulations are problematic. Gunter and Linebarger see the recruit's response at the end of stanza four and through stanza five as sub-vocal. The snoozing recruit, they believe, is a third character who stands and gives a reasonably by-the-manual reply while the 'sensitive' recruit internally voices his more poetic rendering of the scene. Gunter and Linebarger's contention that '[o]bviously' the instructor 'would have been driven to apoplexy' (10) by such an inappropriate response is appealing, but I believe the response *is* voiced aloud by the sensitive recruit. A teacher might refer to any inattentive student as 'asleep', and our sergeant particularly would not seem attuned to fine behavioural distinctions such as that between 'not listening to my lecture' and 'looking longingly at a gentle scene of romance against a lovely background of white, purple, and gold'. When the recruit first responds, having been caught off guard, his language conveys sincere appreciation of the beauty of the scene, organized by his artistic sensibilities to take in the broadest elements of the landscape—the season, the direction, the sun, the fields—before later tightening his focus on the houses, the elms, and the lovers. In these words at the end of stanza four, there is perhaps only a hint of mischievousness. However, he surely realizes he is getting himself into trouble by the time he speaks his lines at the beginning of stanza five: 'The still white dwellings are like a mirage in the heat,/ And under the swaying elms a man and a woman/ Lie gently together'. His description is filled with modifiers ('swaying', 'gently') which he knows are superfluous and unacceptable, from the point of view of an ordnance squad homing in on potential targets. Moreover, his use of 'mirage' to describe the distant scene, while literally apt to describe the houses wavering in the sun, is also an impish suggestion of how unreal and out-of-range a scene of romantic love must seem to the recruit from his vantage point among decidedly male, heavily clad, probably sweaty comrades. By this time he has got away with just about as much as he can and recognizes that 'west' must be corrected to 'left of arc' and 'elms' to 'poplars'. Remembering that 'things only appear to be things', he re-describes the lovers as 'a pair of what appear to be humans [,who]/ Appear to be loving'. This amended response—playfully unrepentant—completes stanza five.

Gunter and Linebarger's reading of stanza six as a combination of the sensitive recruit's musings and the instructor's words of correction to the second recruit is overly ingenious. The sensitive recruit's hastily recast description can easily be characterized as '[m]oderately satisfactory only', as the sergeant terms it, and indeed 'two things have been omitted' from it: the distance from himself to the 'human beings' and their direction (he has identified that of the houses but not the lovers). So it seems reasonable that stanza six is quite literally the sergeant's counter to the recruit's borderline insubordinate reply of stanzas four and five.

The seventh and final stanza is characteristic of the recruit's coda in three of the five *Lessons*: it mimics, yet reshapes and invests further meaning in the most mundane phrasings of the instructor. Adhering to the injunction of his mentor, that one 'must never be over-sure', the trainee admits he 'may not have got/ The knack of judging a distance' and heavily qualifies his final statement:

> . . . I will only venture
> A guess that perhaps between me and the apparent lovers
> (Who, incidentally, appear by now to have finished)
> At seven o'clock from the houses, is roughly a distance
> Of about one year and a half.

The pleonasm ('roughly . . . about') and excessive qualifications satirize the language of the instructor as well as his and the military's preference for tentative description of even the obvious. His estimate of the distance between himself and the lovers operates on several levels. Literally, the trainee is estimating the time from his conscription and/or to his release. A year and a half must seem an almost hopelessly large number of revolutions around a clock. If distance can be measured in terms of time, then indeed he feels, to put it more tritely, 'light years' away from his home, civilian life and romantic love. Reed's wit forces us to think of that 'distance' as not just linear, but temporal and emotional.

In 'Judging Distances', which certainly approaches the 'inevitability and unassailable perfection' (137) that Scannell ascribes to 'Naming of Parts', we might be only slightly less inclined to forgive a certain hint of what A. T. Tolley calls 'precious' in both poems' more lyrical passages. By this he means, according to one dictionary, 'affectedly dainty or overrefined'. Perhaps we overlook this relative shortcoming because the lines provide such sharp counterpoint to the vague and verbose cant of the sergeant's voice. But truly, taken out of context, lines like 'the sun and the shadows bestow/ Vestments of purple and gold', as with the glistening coral of the first poem, may not hold up to close scrutiny as mature and moving lyric poetry. Rather than genuinely poetic lines, they sound a bit like mannerism from young poetic types trying to be poetic. It is possible, though unlikely, that this effect was Reed's intent. Regardless, no minor lapses in the most lyrical portions seriously mar either 'Naming' or 'Judging', which rise far above Tolley's faint praise of them as 'congenial but minor poems' (49).

Like most commentators, Tolley does not critique 'Movement of Bodies' and 'Returning of Issue', the two poems Reed added for the 1970 edition of *Lessons of the War*. Ironically, though, his contention that '[t]he life of the poems is in the imitation of the instructor', as opposed to 'the counterpoised poetic response' (210), applies more closely to the two added poems than to the original three. In fact, in 'Movement of Bodies' only the voice of the instructor is represented; the response of any intelligent and sensitive recruits is seen—as laughing, sniveling, and becoming faint—only from the perspective of the instructor. His heroic but losing battle with English sentence structure helps make 'Movement' more broadly humorous than 'Naming' and 'Judging'. His topic is 'tactics', and he has a devil of a time with subject-verb agreement: 'But that is what tactics is./ Or I should say: are'. In his definition of the term, the problem of number has also defeated him: 'Tactics is merely/ The mechanical movement of bodies, and that is what we mean by it./ Or perhaps I should say: by them'.

The content of the instructor's thirteen-stanza lecture can probably be summed up as simply 'One must be prepared for all possibilities when one fights', so the comic effect of his prolixity is cumulative: every tangled word makes the poem funnier. Stanza three, in which he introduces his 'brown clay model' presumably set on a metal tray, will serve as a characteristic stanza of a simple and typical kind. My phrasing is actually that of Reed's speaker, describing the model itself in his redundant militarese. The character of the terrain modeled on the tray, he says, '[s]hould be taken in at a glance, and its general character/ You can see at a glance it is somewhat hilly by nature'—as opposed to just 'somewhat hilly', we must assume—'[w]ith a fair amount of typical vegetation/ Disposed at certain parts'. The wordiness, redundancy, and vagueness remind the reader of those qualities found in 'Judging Distances',[10] and one appreciates Reed's rationale for inserting this poem after 'Judging' and before 'Unarmed Combat' in the 1970 *Lessons*. 'Movement' also echoes 'Judging' more specifically in 'the bushy-topped trees' and the idea that one must never be over-sure in identifying, for instance, 'what appear to be bushes'. Military people and astute readers in general will recognize the necessity of such cautious labeling and simplified categorization schemes during battle situations in which time is paramount, but both poems also point up the deadness of this kind of language and its potential for obscuring the truth.

The military lecturers in 'Movement' and, later, 'Returning of Issue' speak more conversationally, even more intimately than those in Reed's original three *Lessons*. They are more fully drawn, in fact more sympathetic characters, perhaps in concession to the poet's advancing years and tempering political position.[11] They are well-intentioned men, but those good intentions often backfire. In 'Movement', the speaker genuinely seeks to impress upon his trainees that real warfare evokes harrowing situations for which classrooms and clay models cannot fully prepare one. But his repeated variations on the caution that 'it will not be a tray you will fight on' conjure an image that becomes progressively more absurd and may evoke some of the nervous laughter the instructor finds so baffling and frustrating. Moreover, he warns that in the course of action, his young charges may pass 'a recently dead friend', and his verbal clumsiness is compounded by the unintentionally offhanded modifier describing the body as '[l]ying about somewhere'. The tactical jargon that dehumanizes 'movement of humans' or even 'movement of soldiers' into 'movement of bodies' has also backfired, implanting an image of corpses into impressionable minds, an image which becomes increasingly concrete with the reference to the dead friend and initiates the snivelling and nausea. It is further likely that the word *feint* in stanza nine has some power of suggestion for the five men who later feel 'faint' and are asked to fall out to the back of the room. In fact, originally the line in stanza eleven read 'Yesterday a man was sick'. Stallworthy follows Reed's typescript emendation, a change that foregrounds Reed's intended emphasis on the first *feint*.

And, though perhaps not as densely packed as 'Naming of Parts' or 'Judging Distances',[12] the language of the third *Lesson* sometimes takes the reader outside the circumstance of a well-meaning but dull instructor's droning. When the noncom is attempting to distinguish tactics and strategy in stanza two, his words hint at the mysterious, even sinister nature of the war machine, and the helplessness of the individual will to influence that machine: 'Strategy, to be quite frank, you will have no hand in./ It is done by those up above, and it merely refers to/ The larger movements over which we have no control'. Taken a step higher, the phrase 'those up above' hints at the malign forces guiding the destiny of ignorant humans, as in Leopardi's poem 'the harsh nurse covers her children's eyes' (in Stallworthy 113).

Lest we ascribe too much high seriousness to this *Lesson*, a letter to Herbert Read from J. R. Ackerley, Reed's friend and the longtime literary editor of the *Listener*, suggests still another, more risqué level of meaning to 'Movement'. In the letter, dated

10 March 1950, Ackerley writes, 'Soon, I hope, you will find an exceedingly improper poem by Henry Reed in *The Listener*' (84). That poem, 'Movement of Bodies', did appear in the BBC organ less than a month later. Not until the last two words of the poem—'two hills'—is the major hint of the poem's bawdiness evident. These two hills on the sergeant's 'brown clay model' may appear to hormonal young soldiers as any number of possible pudenda, but testicles is most likely. A 'headland' is a point of land jutting into the seas, usually high and with a sheer drop; its particularly three-dimensional appearance on the model would augment its phallic suggestions in the atmosphere of 'sexual longing and deprivation' of which Scannell spoke, and the 'crown of bushy-topped trees' easily becomes pubic hair, especially when we examine the eighth stanza. Here, 'what appear to be bushes' are concealing and protecting the object of capture. To obtain such a sexual goal, of course, often requires the tactical 'movement of bodies': 'a thoughtful deception' or 'a strong feint'.

As with Coleridge's 'Kubla Khan', the exact layout of the terrain, geographically—and in Reed's poem, anatomically—is very difficult and perhaps fruitless to try to ascertain precisely. The anatomy described could easily be female, in fact. What is important is that in this poem, as in 'Naming of Parts', a sexual undercurrent flows, one that is absorbed by otherwise innocent lines like 'I cannot think where such emotional privates come from'. In fact, the emotion some of the privates are displaying may be hilarity, barely held in check by sniffling noses and watering eyes, and interpreted by our dense sergeant as necessarily fear and squeamishness. Finally, perhaps 'Movement of Bodies' exemplifies better even than 'Naming of Parts' that quality of Reed which Kermode and others saw as funny and sad at the same time. As one reviewer of *A Map of Verona* observed, with some mixing of metaphor, in the first three published *Lessons* 'a theme is constantly being shifted from the comic to the serious key, with such tact that sentiment and satire never come to blows' (*Listener* 13 May 1946, 690). Only in 'Movement', however, do the tones, instead of modulating back and forth, run parallel to each other. In a different kind of virtuosity than displayed in the first two Lessons, Henry Reed has succeeded in playing his piece in a minor and major key at the same time.

Unfortunately, the last two poems of the sequence as Reed published it in 1970 are the weakest of the group. Again, it must be stressed that these are very good pieces: at least worthy of the 'solid' evaluation they receive, along with Reed's other four poems of the war, in the *Virginia Quarterly Review*'s notice on *Collected Poems* (102). The long shadow of 'Naming of Parts' does loom over both poems, just as Reed's detractors felt the imposing shadow of Eliot coloured all the poet's work. But lessons four and five reveal the poet not as a bad T. S. Eliot but as a very good Henry Reed. 'Returning of Issue', especially, succeeds fully in its evocation of the crude, yet somehow pitiable sergeant, if not as elegantly as 'Naming of Parts' in counterpointing that voice with the recruit's. While the modulations of the two voices in that poem are even more complex than in 'Naming', the dramatic interplay between the voices in 'Unarmed Combat' is the least interesting in the *Lessons*: the sergeant speaks the first four stanzas and the recruit muses the last four. The meditations in lesson four thus seem more pre-processed, as opposed to those in 'Naming' and 'Judging', in which the cumulative ironies and absurdities seem to grow on the recruit, gradually, yet inevitably.

'Unarmed Combat' begins with the instructor's admission that, as for the first lesson, his charges have not got something; they are in some way not fully equipped. Into that simple line and a half, Reed somehow squeezes two repetitions: 'In due course of course you will be issued with/ Your proper issue'. In the meantime the sergeant will teach 'various holds and rolls and throws and breakfalls'. Most of this line falls neatly into iambic feet: once again Reed's ear has caught music where one would not expect to find it. In fact, the sergeant's half of 'Unarmed

Combat' is rich in rhythm: all of the stanza-ending lines, for example, can be scanned as three tidy iambs. In substance, however, the sergeant's lesson, like that in 'Movement', is extremely thin. In fact, only one bit of concrete instruction is dispensed: to 'tackle from behind . . . may not be clean' but in 'global war' may be necessary; and only one other is promised: how to 'tie a Jerry/ Up without a rope'.

It is phrases such as these that, as in lessons one and two, appeal to the wry sensibilities of one of the recruits. Yet despite a good deal of authentic language from the sergeant, the blurring of his language with the recruit's that concerned Scannell in 'Judging Distances' is even more pronounced in 'Unarmed Combat', where the 'voice of the instructor . . . is still less differentiated in tone and syntax from the soliloquising voice of the recruit' (Scannell 138). In fact, when soon after such a distinctively clumsy opening the sergeant announces that the day's lesson will revolve around the 'ever-important question of human balance/ And the ever-important need to be in a strong/ Position at the start', we are already halfway to the characteristic tone and syntax of the recruit. The phrasing *is* 'quasi-philosophical' and how the recruit will commandeer it much more predictable: we anticipate none of the wonderful surprise we got in meeting phrases like 'easing the spring' in their new contexts.

'Naming of Parts' had no first person in the recruit's voice, and in 'Judging Distances' it appears unobtrusively just twice, and then only in self-deprecating phrases: 'I may not have got/ The knack of judging a distance; I will only venture/ A guess …'. But the pervasive use of it in the recruit's half of 'Unarmed' leaves the poem open to the charge that it strikes 'a note of self-pity and one almost of self-parody' (Scannell 139).[13] The phrases the recruit appropriates suggest only generic shortcomings, problems, even neuroses. He seems to say: in the previous confrontations of *my* life (whatever they were), 'I was the tied-up one'; 'I have given them [whoever they are] all I had,/ Which was never as good as I got, and it [whatever it was] got me nowhere'; my attempts to combat my difficulties, whatever they were, 'Somehow or other I always seemed to put/ In the wrong place'; indeed, he implies, my problems have been plenty as bad as fighting a Jerry without a weapon, thank you very much. And the upper-crust British version of that most self-absorbed phrase 'I'm the kind of guy who . . '. intrudes: 'I was always the sort of person/ Who threw the rope aside'.

Even the phrase which is most artfully transformed by the recruit seems the most self-pitying: 'my wars/ Were global from the start'. Since we cannot freely sympathize with the recruit, in part because we do not know the nature of his sufferings,[14] his decision to carry on and fight the best he can does not evoke the shared emotion I believe the poet intended.[15] There is no way, of course, a poet like Reed could trumpet a call to arms in the manner of Richard Lovelace's 'To Lucasta' without blushing on the page. The 'muted clarion call' (Scannell's phrase) of the last stanza is more Reedian:

> . . . we must fight
> Not in the hope of winning but rather of keeping
> Something alive: so that when we meet our end,
> It may be said that we tackled wherever we could,
> That battle-fit we lived, and though defeated,
> Not without glory fought.

Perhaps the abstracts for which English soldiers have fought over the centuries—'freedom' or 'democracy', Lovelace's 'honour' or Rupert Brooke's 'England' itself—are hollow and impossible to maintain or protect through armed conflict. But the values which Reed's recruit determines to fight for seem equally abstract: to 'learn the lesson/ Of the ever-important question of human balance', to keep '[s]omething alive'; to fight '[n]ot without glory', even though 'defeated'. Though it is the most musical of the *Lessons*, 'Unarmed Combat' has its disappointing ambivalences, rather than the challenging ambiguities of the earlier *Lessons*. But if, as F. Scott Fitzgerald wrote, 'The test of a first-rate intelligence is the ability to hold two opposed ideas in the mind at the same time, and still retain the ability to function' (69), then 'Unarmed Combat' is another worthy contributor to Reed's evocation of the almost unbearable tension which must sorely test the ability of intelligent fighting men to function: a tension between questioning of authority or submission to it; between collective and individual will; between action and contemplation.

The delicate 'point of balance' that is so exquisitely maintained in the earlier *Lessons* is most severely challenged in 'Returning of Issue'; in none of the poems is the distance of the serious and the comic elements from the fulcrum so great. Neither is the sergeant in any other poem given such a fully sketched character: so dominating, quick tempered and prone to profanity, yet so paternal, even likable in some ways, and so inept with the English language. Juxtaposed against the comic bumblings of the sergeant is a theme of higher seriousness than in any of the other four *Lessons*. No longer is the younger man (now a full-fledged soldier at war's end) suffering from an attack of the sillies as in 'Movement' or mere sexual longing as in 'Naming' and 'Judging', but instead wrenching guilt at his failure to have reconciled with his now-dead father. Direct quotations from Jesus's parable of the Prodigal Son and fainter, yet distinctive echoes from that passage in Luke invest the son's anguish with even profounder secondary vibrations of meaning. Subjected to the tension of such riotously disparate elements, the poem coheres, though at times it threatens to break all its bonds.

The tension is beautifully anticipated in the fine pun of the poem's title. The 'lesson' of the day concerns the soldiers' turning in their equipment, or 'issue'. But the second 'returning' implied is the one which cannot now be enacted, the reunion of the 'issue', or offspring, with his father. The soldier's deeper musings on this theme are prompted by the fatherly aura the sergeant at first emanates in delivering a farewell address of sorts to his troops. Granted, the paternal veneer is a thin one, as attested by his lightning transformation to a belittling, profane,[16] almost abusive persona later in the poem. Nevertheless, the early lines in the sergeant's speech—'Tomorrow will be/ Your last day here,// But we hope not for always'; 'We hope that many of you/ Will be coming back for good'; 'How sorry we are to lose you'—arouse deep and genuine pity in the heart of the soldier. Yet Reed's portrait of this sergeant is also his broadest and most satirical in all the *Lessons*. As a staunch conservator of the purity and precision of English, Reed would have found the voguish *finalize*, used by the sergeant in stanza six, particularly galling and possibly indicative of laziness of mind. In an earlier letter to Robert Heilman, Reed playfully showcased his scorn of such formations by adding *-ize* to form no fewer than nine verbs, including *scribalized*, *ironizing*, *Londonized,* and *rememberize*.

Putting such classic bureaucratese into the mouth of the sergeant in this early stanza is an isolated bit of satire. Stanzas eight and eleven are true comic cadenzas. In the first of these two, the poet brilliantly scripts at least five repetitions into the sergeant's instructions for returning military gear to storage:

> The first thing you do, after first thing tomorrow morning,
> Is, those that have not been previously detailed to do so,
> Which I think is the case in most cases, is a systematic
> Returning of issue. It is all-important
> You should restore to store one of every store issued.
> And in the event of two, two.

Reed's ear is also alert to the tendency of basic writers—and basic speakers—to get lost in their own syntax after inserting a parenthetical and thus inadvertently repeating a word, as the sergeant does with *is*. And in a setting of males in fatigues and combat boots, 'two, two' might in more playful minds evoke the incongruous image of a ballerina's skirt.

Like the sergeant in 'Movement', this speaker is also overmatched by the grammatical concept of number, misusing *personnel* as a singular countable noun ('each personnel') in stanza eleven and adding *-s* to the already plural *impedimenta*. And, with great malapropian firmness, he warns soldiers that, on the point of stealing military property for souvenirs, he must 'be quite implicit'.

In and out amongst this kind of language thread a few direct responses from the soldier but mostly bitter and guilty introspection on his broken relationship with his own father. The young soldier is the prodigal who never came home, and his evocation of the family property, now 'sold and built on', and his imaginings of how the reunion that never took place with a loving father might have been, are profoundly moving. The setting of the poem, as we are told in an early parenthetical 'stage direction', is autumn (thus, following the progression established by the spring of 'Naming' and the summer of 'Judging'): the reconciliation should have taken place in that season, at the bountiful harvest time. As the father approached his son, he would still have been practising

> ...his speeches of sorrow,
> Not less of truth for being long rehearsed
> The last distilment from a long and inward
> Discourse of heartbreak.

Not much is known about Reed's relationship with his own father, but he did have a history of disappointing his most beloved friends—Walter Allen, Elizabeth Bishop, the Italian family memorialized in *Return to Naples*—with poor correspondence, non-arrivals, and late arrivals. In a letter written to Ruth Heilman on Thanksgiving Day 1966, he makes tentative plans for a return to Seattle around Christmas, admitting: 'I will write or cable at the very last practicable minute, as is my stricken and incompetent wont'. He had that romantic tendency of revelling in the melancholy of giving or receiving emotional hurt, of turning it inward and perhaps converting it into art rather than acting promptly to correct the hurt. Published first in 1970, 'Returning of Issue' seems in part an emotional purging for the poet and contains an autobiographical element of the great act imagined after the fact rather than performed. The young soldier, 'as ever late', regrets his lost opportunity to 'know that lifted fear' yet 'shout of compassion' coming from his long-suffering but forgiving father.

The young soldier's regret is part of a complex of factors that bring about his perhaps surprising decision to re-enlist after all. Further parenthetical stage directions seven times call attention to the 'silence' which greets the sergeant's repeated entreaties for men to rejoin the army. The silence is once labeled as 'embarrassed', and we all recognize the pressure which a silent group exerts and the sometimes blurted, soon-regretted responses it can elicit. The word *home*, used thrice by the sergeant, becomes a sort of talisman in the young man's mind: 'You can think of us here, as *home*', says the reassuring voice of the older man, 'a home we shall any of you welcome you back to'. The young soldier admits, 'I have nowhere else to go', and the chance for a place to be welcomed, a place to belong when he has lost his opportunity 'in time of famine, to seek/ His father's home', is compelling.

The comic has been fully subsumed by the dramatic and the lyrical by the time the silence is broken in the fourteenth and fifteenth stanzas; this emotional climax is mirrored by the rapid shifts in point of view. Reed's dramatic sense, as well as the reader's, is tested in stanza fifteen, where there are not two, but *four* voices to sort out: in addition to the familiar spoken voice of the sergeant and the meditations of the soldier, the soldier speaks aloud and a fourth voice supplies the stage directions. The first line of stanza fourteen is voiced only inwardly by the soldier: 'And am I to break it, father, to break this silence?' The second, fifth and sixth lines are the sergeant's—aggressive rhetorical questions about manhood of his listeners, satisfaction at the young man's decision, and an order: 'for Christ's sake, tell them all,/ Why you are doing this'. The middle two lines of this stanza suggest more convincing reasons than the firm, but humble response he gives orally in the next stanza. He feels he is doing his father's work, and in fact, addresses his thoughts to his father. His conflation of his own father with the paternal sergeant at the peak of his emotion is so complete, in fact, that all three sentences in these lines may be numbly spoken aloud: 'I will break the silence, father. Yes, sergeant, *I* will stay/ In a group of one. Father, be proud of me'. The poet may even intend that the young soldier believes he is serving a third 'father', a reading that the poem's echoes of Luke 15:11-32 do not discourage. That word's apparently random positioning in the poem's stanzas brings it occasionally to the beginning of a sentence or a line, necessitating capitalization. For at least a moment, when the soldier's heart cries out, 'Father, be proud of me', in his mind he may see his decision to serve as divinely commissioned. The sergeant's casual profanity 'for Christ's sake' is, of course, authentic given his string of *bloodys* in the previous stanza but also adds at least a hint of additional timbre to the poem's music.

The poem's final stanza takes a sharp turn in tone, seeming to undermine the trend towards acceptance of at least some degree of dignity in military service that is evidenced in Reed's final two lessons. The soldier's decision to 'remain a personnel' has been given a positive, if not triumphant spin when he speaks aloud his purported reasons in stanza fifteen: 'I hope to shame no one ... / ... I have been such a thing before./ It was good, and simple; and it was the best I could do'. In the last stanza the decision is seen as a shameful one, made in part simply for the 'relief' it provides. The Prodigal Son, having failed to make a peace with his father, will remain in the fields, as it were, with the pigs and husks. As a career soldier now, he will move up in the ranks, and he will speak *at* (that is the preposition, not *to*, which Reed uses in the poem's second line) his men the way he was spoken at. The values he will teach (albeit with 'dubiety') appear to be a sort of summation of the unfortunate lessons which Henry Reed felt would 'emerge' from the sergeant' voice in these poems, the lessons Reed's war training taught him and which his young man will now pass on to future young men:

> A rhetoric instead of words; instead of a love,
>   the use
> Of accoutrements, impedimenta, and fittings, and
>   military garments,
>         And harlots, and riotous living.

Still, such a noisy outward existence will never be the true life of this soldier. In keeping with the romantic self-recrimination of Reed but more importantly the contemplative nature of his mouthpiece character throughout the *Lessons*, even clearer in his mind than that pivotal autumn scene—'the astonished faces of my fellows,/ The sergeant's uneasy smile, the trees'—and the future life it implies, will always be the 'reconcilement, never enacted between [my father and me],/ Which should have been ours, under the autumn sun'.

Like so much of the work of Reed's literary idols, Joyce and Eliot, 'Returning of Issue' and the other *Lessons* thus privilege the act that is imagined—or remembered or meditated upon or almost performed—over the deed actually performed. We are reminded of 'The Love Song of J. Alfred Prufrock', for example, which is rife with almosts: the hero nearly asks his question as his kindred spirit, the cat/fog, almost makes its leap but decides to curl up and go to sleep. Or the final scene in 'The Dead', in which the true life of Greta Conroy is taking place in her memory of the love of Michael Furey. Her husband's gentle, but ineffectual touches do not move her; his mundane disrobing is mere static; his heartfelt, but inarticulate words become a drone.

Much the same is true in *Lessons of the War*. The only *act* in all the *Lessons* is the reenlistment in 'Returning' and even that, as we have seen, is a highly ambivalent act. Although for the reader much of the fun is in the voice of the man of action, the sergeant, Reed wants us to see the *life* of the poems in the man of introspection: in the intelligence, wit, and emotions of the recruit. He wants us to live, for a time, alongside him at an ironic distance from his military superiors. He wants us to share in the trainee/soldier's pangs of regret for unfulfilled relationships, his longings for romance, his contemplation of natural beauty. Even in the *Lesson* in which the recruits have no voice, we sense their nervous youthfulness as some laugh, some cry in their unique reactions to the 'movement of bodies' lecture.

Henry Reed was not a vigorous man. He was no Ernest Hemingway or even Rex Warner, and his verses, as one reviewer maintained in an otherwise highly complimentary review of *Map*, were not 'robust'. He did some training, was released, and wrote what he knew. Thus, his war poems contain nothing like soldiers rasping through lungs ravaged by chlorine gas, no fliers splattered inside plexiglass gun-turrets, nor even a 'queer sardonic rat' scurrying across battle lines. Yet, as John Lehmann saw, they are, without being propagandistic, potent 'rejection-of-war' poems in their own way (168). In them, we find out what kinds of bright young minds and hearts might be sacrificed to war. We see the ignorance—or 'dubiety'—of instructors numbing the sensibilities of their charges, young men who may soon find themselves, almost willy nilly, on the other side of the lectern, and like new parents, mouthing the platitudes they heard from their parents and swore they would never utter. And, though *Lessons of the War* never carries placards, it can be chilling, almost Orwellian, when 'it refers/ To the larger movements over which we have no control'.

A statement Roger Savage made about Reed the playwright, that his radio drama 'was content to leave the medium technically much as it found it' (189), does not seem to apply to Reed in his 'medium' of war poetry. Reed created a unique and pliable stanza to serve the sound and sense of his *Lessons*. In each, the long, prose-like lines vary from ten to sixteen syllables, from four to eight accents. The foreshortened sixth line uses the opposite approach to serve the same function of an Alexandrine at the end of a Spenserian stanza, slowing reading down and forcing close attention.[17] Except in 'Returning of Issue', the most vernacular of the *Lessons*, these lines do not enjamb into the next stanza. Rather they house some well-packaged clauses or self-contained phrases, usually in a more regular metre: 'Which in our case we have not got'; 'It isn't always a tray'; 'Well, some of us live'; 'But this is global war'; 'It is courage that counts'. In fact, the last two lines cited are prosodist's dreams: perfect iambic trimeter and anapestic dimeter, respectively. The poet Milton Kessler once praised a student by saying, 'Your poem hears well'. This I take as something more than just a pretentious way of saying 'sounds good'. Rather, as Kessler might have remarked and as John Lehmann did observe, *Lessons* (along with Reed's dramatic monologues from *Map*) bears oral presentation better than most poems because it 'hears well'.

*Lessons* makes another contribution for which Reed is never given acknowledgment. Though certainly he would be embarrassed by the pretentious silliness of some of its practitioners, Reed was really producing, as early as 1942, 'found poetry'. The manual-style jargon in 'Unarmed Combat' and 'Naming of Parts' seems somewhat more crafted than the language of, say, Ronald Gross's 'Yield', but most of the sergeant's words in the *Lessons* appear to have simply been 'found' and transcribed by a man with a gifted ear, an ear which troubled to find the perfect anapests of 'Today we have naming of parts' and the internal rhyme of 'have not got'. Enormous skill, not to mention a profound sense of one's security as a poet, is required to turn so much 'bad' language to such good effect. In fact, the final lesson of *Lessons*, I believe, is the power of words to move men, though perhaps in a direction, ironically, over which the speaker has no control. In this way, Reed also prefigures Absurdists like Pinter and Ionesco, who more than incidentally came first to British audiences through the wireless.

In 'Movement of Bodies', while the sergeant tries in all sincerity to temper his men for battle, chance words and phrases accrue and the result is not a steely group of fighting men, but rather snivelling, snickering, and nauseous boys. If Reed was not exactly avant-garde, he was, like Ionesco, Pinter and later David Mamet, exploring the most modern of issues: the desperate struggles of human beings to communicate while tuned to different frequencies.

1 The first offence was committed by John Lehmann, A. T. Tolley and Michael O'Toole; the second offence by Linda M. Shires, Robert Hewison, and the writer of the Reed entry in *World Authors*.

2 I suppose it is Stallworthy's work. His 'rough' translation is exactly the same as that given by the *Norton Anthology of English Literature*. In fact, Scannell, Stallworthy and the *Norton* form a sort of mutual plagiarism society. Their words on the metamorphosis from Reed's comic impressions of a sergeant to the artistry found in *Lessons* are also exact copies of one another.

Many, of course, have assayed verse translations of Horace's lines. One that I think Reed would have appreciated is James Michie's (1963):

> In love's wars I have long maintained
> Good fighting trim and even gained
> Some glory.

3 Whether this is to exonerate or further condemn Kermode I do not know, but he does credit the innocent Stallworthy for first observing Reed's remarkable literary trickery.

4 Thomas and Reed were born in the same year, but their lives and careers markedly diverged. While Reed's career path rose gently and levelled off at a modest height during his BBC days of the fifties and sixties, Thomas's shot up nearly vertical before his famed flame-out in 1953.

5 In his 'Radio Notes' for The *New Statesman* and *Nation*, 6 December 1947, Reed's hilarious review pans an 'inauscultable' ('unlistenable-to') production of *Paradise Lost* which featured 'the voice of Mr. Dylan Thomas coming up like thunder on the road to Mandalay; rarely can such gusty intakes of breath have passed across the ether' (449).

6 Plomer was a respected writer of poetry and fiction in his day. Reed discusses Plomer's novels in *The Novel since 1939*.

7 To borrow from popular psychology, the recruit seeks his identification as a human *being*, where the sergeant is training him to be a human *doing*. Reed and the recruit admire the same qualities in this landscape—its silence, stillness, cleanness, and intelligence—that Reed and the young lovers of *The Streets of Pompeii* admired in the older couple.

8 See also Richard A. Condon in the *Explicator Cyclopedia*, vol.1, 244-5.

9 Cavilers may find other imperfections in 'Naming of Parts'. (Slow motion replay reveals flaws in Nadia Comaneci's '10'.) Perhaps the last stanza doesn't fully satisfy; perhaps the capitalized *S* does 'foreground' the pun in 'easing the Spring' a little too obviously, as O'Toole suggests; perhaps the lyrical passages are a little 'precious' or suffer from a certain emptiness, as Tolley contends.

10 Other examples indicating the speaker's lack of grammatical and rhetorical control include a split infinitive (ll. 1-2): 'I am going to rapidly/ Devote'; a usage error: 'even this tray is different to what I had thought'; and numerous additional instances of wordiness: 'somehow never always' and the phrase 'in this connection' (stanza 9), for example.

11 Scannell sees a similar pattern even in the original three 'Lessons': 'a development towards a more affirmative stance or, at least, towards a greater measure of acceptance' (137) of the recruit's predicament.

12 In fact, it is striking that each successively written Lesson, though maintaining the characteristic form of five long lines and one short per stanza, contains a greater number of stanzas: 'Naming of Parts' was first published in 1942 and contains five stanzas; 'Judging Distances' (1943) contains seven; 'Unarmed Combat' (1945), eight stanzas; 'Movement of Bodies' (1950), thirteen stanzas; and 'Returning of Issue' (1970), eighteen stanzas. (That makes it 108 lines, exactly as many as 'The Raven'.) The effect as we proceed through the Lessons is somewhat less elegance but fuller characterization.

13 I am not sure that a writer without a large body of work or great familiarity *can* parody himself, but Strickland makes a similar charge regarding 'Returning of Issue': Reed's 'gifts for parody and self-parody are here an obstacle to the expression of strong poignant feeling' (79).

14 We might assume he's a sensitive poet-guy with sensitive poet-guy problems, like getting beat up by rugby players.

15 We can 'only venture/ A guess that perhaps' the young speaker is fighting 'the poet's struggle to preserve his individuality and humanity against the depersonalising and mindless processes of army training and the enervating boredom of routine' (Scannell 141).

16 Or perhaps as profane as Chilmark Press would allow in 1970. The use of *arse* seems particularly quaint.

17 Regrettably, Reed used this serviceable 'anti-Alexandrine' in only two other poems, 'South' and 'The River'.

# NO HAPPY ENDINGS: LATE POETRY

Frank Kermode, in his review of *Collected Poems*, described Henry Reed as 'a sad man but a funny man' whose 'poems are funny or sad' (17). These quick brushstrokes of course cannot capture all the complexities of Reed's character as a man and as a poet. But, at least after 1950, the exact mid-point of Reed's life, Kermode's minimalist adjectives seemed more and more apt, and eventually even one of these peeled away, leaving only 'sad' as a remarkably accurate and complete description of Reed's later life and especially of his later poetry.

Although Reed always had a sense of 'the infinite vanity of all our days', it had never been his way to react to life's frustrations and injustices with angry fist-shaking. He was not one to rail like Leopardi, to 'curse the ways/ Of that hidden ugly Power who orders our common ill', which is why Kermode rightfully takes issue with Jon Stallworthy's choice of these lines from 'To Himself' as an epigraph to Reed's collection. In his association with Reed in his later years, Kermode got from the poet 'a sense that his life, though marked by a great deal of idiosyncratic achievement, was radically disappointing' (17). Reed's typical response to the often profound discrepancy between a man's desires and his realization of those desires was to be funny, to sigh, or to drink, as he did on many occasions with Kermode in London, to then be 'poured into a taxi' (17) after eleven and driven home to 9 Upper Montagu Street. Reed's later poems do not drink, and they are funny in lesser proportion even than his pre-1950 poetry; with the exceptions only of 'Aubade'[1] and 'Psychological Warfare', they sigh.

Stubbornly, in his later work, at least the individual poems both published and left in manuscript, Reed appears to have tried to relive the literary aspirations of his youth; he all but repudiated the dramatic and comic strands of his poetic nature that had made him such a successful playwright in the late forties and early fifties. The comic and dramatic come together in his excellent, never published 'Psychological Warfare', but make only the most timid appearances elsewhere. He seemed wisely to have confined his aphorisms to his critical work and a few judicious instances in the poems, but his earlier dreams of being a great novelist assert themselves through a stronger narrative element in his poetry, most notably his best late poem 'The Auction Sale', and even in a sort of peace-making with allegory. But it is of course the Lyrical strand which he had always sought most assiduously to develop. Though melancholy is very nearly the only emotional note he strikes, the late verse shows his marked maturity as a lyric poet.[2] His varied music and forms are more consonant with his subject matter, the emotions less manipulative, and the meanings less obscure (or at least the obscurity rewards one's sounding efforts).

The theme that nearly every late poem of Reed's elaborates is that of exile or intrusion; his characters are outsiders, separated from others or from places of comfort and peace. One of the causes of what Kermode sees as 'the characteristic exclusion from delight' (17) in these poems is blocked communication. In these pieces, so many of which contain a strong autobiographical element, poets cannot revive their long abandoned poems (or are embarrassed by earlier work they 'wish to efface'); obviously lonely people cannot connect with each other; a sergeant once again blathers his inarticulate message to an inattentive audience whose values find no apparent intersection with his. Reed had evidently rehearsed the theme of inarticulateness in a manuscript poem called '*De Arte Poetica*', which Stallworthy positions early in the poet's career based on 'numerous (? provisional) autograph revisions in the author's earliest—i.e. 1940s—hand' (163). 'The words stream out', says the frustrated speaker, 'are fashioned into sense,/ But not in the song I wished, this gross pretence,// Strange to my ear, false to my watchful eye . . '. (130). But the poem also seems to speak of how a poet may be haunted by the ghosts of earlier unfinished poems, as notebook entries tell us Reed was in the 1980s by 'the three or four poems from the 50s' he still sought to finish: 'Shall these bones live again? And if they do,/ How can they love this flesh they never knew?' For Reed the recollection was not in tranquility but in vexation: 'I betray// Even the wounds I have bled from' (130), suggesting not joy and revelation at the new flesh on old bones but rather frustration at his inability to capture with precision his former thoughts.

Reed's only consistently comic realization of the theme of inarticulateness is 'Psychological Warfare', a piece which Reed seems at one point to have considered including as one of his *Lessons of the War*. Its comedy is broader than that of the other *Lessons*: the sergeant (who speaks all but one line in the poem) exhibits greater intellectual and verbal clumsiness even than the NCO in 'Returning of Issue', the poem Reed did select to complete his sequence. We can assume, therefore, that if there are figures in the sergeant's audience even remotely as intelligent and sensitive as the second voice in 'Naming of Parts' and 'Judging Distances' especially, then the sergeant's message is not being received on the same wavelength as its transmission.

Like Reed's shorter dramatic, comic, and narrative pieces of the late thirties, among them 'Dull Sonnet' and 'Falange', 'Psychological Warfare' is a worthy poem which Reed may nonetheless have consciously kept out of print. Part of its comedy arises from its dramatic situation: though 245 of its 246 lines are spoken by the sergeant, the reader is intermittently made aware of his audience of young men 'that have not seen service overseas', including 'four excellent West Nigerians . . .,/ As black as your boot' (137). Much like the trainees in 'Movement of Bodies', these listeners snigger at the NCO's often unintentionally sexual language; they also smoke, one speaks, and one attempts to masturbate during the lecture.

As with many songs and other comic bits from Reed's radio plays, the humour is sharpened by its serious framing. The great issue which the sergeant has failed to treat coherently in his long, sermon-like discourse is nevertheless delineated quite gracefully in his last few lines. Taken by themselves, and lent extra gravity by their placement on the page, they pose to the men the profound problem

> Of how on God's earth we shall ever learn to attain some sort
> Of dignity.
> And due respect.
> One man.
> For another. (142)

But the broad humour of 'Psychological Warfare' prevents the speaker of these weighty lines from attaining the dignity of Reed's otherwise most sympathetic military voice, the sergeant in 'Returning of Issue'. Aside from his dealings with the onanist 'at the end of row three' (who is advised: 'Don't stand up, for God's sake, man,/ . . . Just tuck it away,/ And . . . Report to me/ At eighteen hundred hours'.), the sergeant is at the centre of several other ribald situations. After he has with absurd primness described the act as what in the Bible 'begins with an O,/ Though in modern parlance it usually begins with an M', he intends to advise his charges to discourage, in a kind and manly way, any comrade from masturbation. His unfortunate words are 'Give him all the help you can' (138). The sergeant's own sexual inclinations are revealed in his exceptionally detailed description of typical German fighting men:

> They are usually blond, and often extremely well-made,
> With large blue eyes and very white teeth,
> And as a rule hairless chests, and very smooth,
> muscular thighs,
> And extremely healthy complexions, especially when
> slightly sunburnt. (138)

Later he relates the story of a 'ballet-dancer/ In the last mob but three' who had been ridiculed 'until he was seen in the gym./ And then, my goodness me!' (140) Shortly after reporting that the attractive young ballet-dancer was 'demobilized' despite his own 'strong pressure on the poor lad's behalf' (140), the sergeant proceeds to 'point nine' of his ten-point lecture, completing another low joke that has run through the poem. Point nine in fact follows point seven, which actually precedes the second instance of point six, whose first occurrence precedes point five and immediately follows point four.

The sergeant's numerical crimes, however, are outstripped by his subtler linguistic abuses. After giving a bogus etymology of the first morpheme in *psychological* near the opening of his lecture, he waves away his analysis of the second part of the word because 'logical, of course, you all know' (136). But the sergeant himself does not know 'logical', dismissing, for example, the notion that the intent of the Germans is to rape the soldiers' sisters as 'a patent absurdity for two simple reasons: (a)/ They cannot know in advance what your sisters are like:/ And (b) some of you have no sisters. Let that be the end of that' (139). The sergeant rivals Flannery O'Connor's characters in his equally peremptory delivery of platitude: 'People say: "We are all as God made us"./ And so they are. So are the enemy. And so are some of you./ This I in fact observed . . '. (136). He mistakenly attributes Polonius' words to St. Paul in admonishing his men, 'This above all, to thine own self be true' (140). He is also prone to the kind of redundancies we have seen from similar characters, labelling part of his message, for example, 'basically fundamental' (135) and asking the men to counsel any 'fellow-comrades' caught masturbating. He also has the gift of malapropism, referring for instance to 'homosensualists' (who are 'easily detected by the way they lace up their boots' [137]) and to that deep recess of everyone's mind, the 'self-conscious', whence the strangest things are likely to 'ebb up' (139).

In good comedy, Henri Bergson determined, our hearts must undergo 'a momentary anesthesia'. 'Psychological Warfare' certainly numbs our sense of pathos, never quite allowing us to pity the sergeant or even the ballet-dancer who spends all but a few days of his 'three weeks' service' in prison before being discharged. Despite some hints of comedy in 'The Château' and 'The Auction Sale', no anesthesia is offered by any other of Reed's late poems. They may be an unintended kind of deadening, as in '*Bocca di Magra*', an abortive love poem which smothers emotion in a blanket of abstracts:

> Your voice and mine will leave our joyful echoes . . .
> And emerge, us gone, as the fretful mouthings of winter,
> Hoarse in the caverns, or simply muttering
> In the damp and rotting constructions mouldering here.
> And if from their grovelling slumber
> A murmur swells, it will swell not with our warm voices,
> But rise and shriek in a whirlwind of blinded crying,
> Screaming along the river's bank to greet its companion,
> The great impassive cold that already seems to chide us
> From the bluffs of Carrara, gashed by the great
> into greatness. (85)

The pointless wordplay and alliteration of the last line, like the stretching-thin of the abstracts, are characteristic of the worst poems in *A Map*. For the most part in Reed's late poems, though, the lyricism is less contrived, the music and emotions truer.

Some of these poems offer faintly affirmative glimmers, but in most the speaker or one or more chief characters remain apart from their birthright of love, artistic fulfillment, companionship, security. All the poems can be seen at some level as autobiographical. One poignantly characterizes two lonely people, an old woman and a young man, who daily pass each other 'without salutation'. The pity is that neither the narrator nor his friend Pierfrancesco (the third and fourth of the poem's 'Four People') gets to know either beyond Pierfrancesco's 'instituted inquiries' about the woman and his purchase of postcards he does not want from the young man. More sad is that the old woman, 'a former aristocrat' whose only devotees now are 'the cats and dogs who dawdle along behind her', and who clings so tightly to 'a ten-page letter,/ A plaintive fragment perhaps from her still insistent past', can make no connection with the young man. He is kindly but very ill (possibly in Italy for his health); both he and the woman are thus 'at the thinning end of their time'. The portraits of these two are so movingly wrought that Reed, in a poem of just over two pages, has earned a rare aphorism: 'Is that why they never dare to acknowledge each other,/ Having so little in common, and so much?' He has also earned tears, though he will not allow them. With the recent epiphany that his impending death is known, the young man looks toward Pierfrancesco, but Pierfrancesco 'looks hard at the sea, and bites hard on his nether lip'.

Reed does admit tears at the end of 'The Auction Sale', his most original of these poems about outsiders. It is also Reed's most consistently narrative poem, his most exquisitely rhymed poem, his longest published poem; it is in truth his finest poem apart from his great war sequence. 'The Auction Sale' is also the only late poem to juxtapose sharply contrasting characters, tones, mood, and language in the manner of *Pytheas*, *The Streets of Pompeii*, and of course *Lessons of the War*. It speaks, in fact, in three voices. One is the voice of the auctioneer, a man of limited sensibility whose pecuniary motives and corruptions of English diction and syntax make him a fair target of Reed's satire. The tones of the other two idioms are identified by Alan Jenk: the narrator's 'flat, understated English matter-of-factness' which relates the story of a young country bidder who competes mightily but fails to take home a painting of Mars and Venus that has so stirred him; and the 'richly romantic-erotic-Italian' quality of the third voice and that which it describes: the painting itself (46).

The narrator begins the poem, says Stallworthy, 'in a voice as flat as if the speaker were reading from a country newspaper' (xx). And indeed, he takes great pains to keep matters low-key, stressing that the locals 'in shillings genially strove' over small items—a chair, 'mirror, vase, or vinaigrette'—and though the loser might shake his fist, 'there was nothing meant./ Little gained was little missed,/ And there was smiling in the tent' (66). In his uniquely charming tone, the speaker faithfully records dull facts, remarking for example that 'some came in, and some went out'; he seems a strict and objective observer, learning things about the scene just when we do and setting down even the process of discovery: in the third verse paragraph he notes two attendants carrying something 'which might have been some sort of frame,/ And was a picture frame in fact' (67). But as one reviewer remarked on the best of Reed's verse in *A Map of Verona*, 'the flatness and tiredness are deceptive' (Breit 8); so it is with the narrative verse of 'The Auction Sale'. The speaker's off-hand observation that 'often, after certain sales,/ Some looked relieved that they had lost,/ Others, at having won, upset' (66) prefigures the later and sharper irony among the winners and losers when the bids exceed two hundred pounds. And two of the chief out-of-town combatants are lightly but significantly introduced in the first verse paragraph, 'apart,/ Both from the rest and each from each', gazing 'intent upon the floor' and ignoring 'the endless stream/ Of bed and bedside cabinet' (66). The everyday language of the first three unabashedly straightforward narrative stanzas masks their technical virtuosity. Elizabeth Jennings' praise, directed at *A Map of Verona*, nevertheless applies: 'Henry Reed writes with a skill which conceals itself' (1253). In the manner of Auden (in 'Musée des Beaux Arts', for example), he sprinkles his rhymes lightly throughout, the tension of the rhyme sometimes resolved in a neighboring line—the two local boys 'steadied [the frame] gently and with care,/ And held it covered, standing there'—more often two lines later, and sometimes as many as six lines later. Of the first forty-eight lines, all but ten are perfect iambic tetrameter, which even neatly accommodates multi-syllabic words such as *auctioneer*, *colloquy*, *vinaigrette*, *ministrants* and, remarkably, *unacquiescent*. Departures from the steady rhythm sometimes house the most colloquial language, as when the speaker begins line seven tersely with 'It was getting on'.

Stallworthy sees the narrative as a 'Forsterian or Hardyesque short story' (xx), but the voice we hear is much more like Robert Frost's.

Although the ugliness of the auctioneer's first words in stanza four admit even a triplet rhyme, perhaps to convey his attempt to elevate his language to suit the superiority of the painting to his other wares, the tetrameter falls apart, as does the precision of the poem's language:

> . . . Well, friends, I have to say
> Something I have not said today:
> *There's a reserve upon this number.*
> It is a picture which though unsigned
> Is thought to be of the superior kind,
> So I'm sure you gentlemen will not mind
> If I tell you at once, before we start,
> That what I have been asked to say
> Is, as I have said, to say:
> *There's a reserve upon this number.* (67)

Unable to articulate himself the beauty and innate worth of the painting, he can only mouth the tastes of others and report the tangible monetary value assigned to the painting by him who put in an advance bid on 'the number'. Even that word carries two shades of meaning which fit the character of the auctioneer. As well as identifying the painting with the colloquial 'number' as one might designate a woman perceived in basest terms as a 'hot number', his is a mentality that seeks to quantify in very discrete, numerical terms the worth of art. The auctioneer's words are thereafter devoted strictly to the function of conducting the bidding except for one other speech which in similarly wordy, redundant language further satirizes his one-dimensional worldview:

> . . . I am sure I'm right in feeling
> You will not feel it at all unfair

> For what when all is said and done
> Is a work of very artistic painting
> And not to be classed with common lumber,
> And anyway extremely rare . . . (68-9)

After the fifth verse paragraph we finally hear the poem's third voice, whose neoclassical verbiage, italicized and indented, invokes a scene which could not be more at variance with that being enacted in and around 'the great grey flapping tent' (66). The scene within the smaller compass of the picture frame is one of great vitality: Mars's mouth and hands are poised at Venus's lips, hair, and breasts; nearby, Cupids 'leaped and sported' and 'played with horns and pikes';[3] 'the sunwarmed earth' of summer gives forth flowers which around the lovers 'sprang and twined' (68). Contrast the 'moist November air' surrounding the grey tent wherein hangs a 'leaden air' and where a more mundane vying proceeds. 'The azure day' depicted in the Paduan painting, backdrop to the replendent *bronze* of Venus's hair and the 'blue and scarlet sails' must seem nearly blinding to the men in *brown* and *grey* in a grey tent on a grey day. Once again, however, when Reed's language most aspires to be lyrical, though it sets off his other language registers, it is not by itself entirely convincing. The diction in these passages is by no means more artful than that Reed scripts for his auctioneer or his narrator. It is more emotive—seven consecutive lines beginning with 'Oh' in one section—but its words are not necessarily more beautiful, pleasing, or well chosen: rather they are simply more Latinate (*Effulgent*, *ardent*, *aureate*, *azure*), affected (*enlaced*, *burnished*), even archaic (*deposed* in the sense of 'put' or 'laid down').

Into this world of contention—among differing values and language registers, among the locals and the two London dealers; between the lustful Mars and the coy Venus, between bright Italy and grey England, between the two Londoners—Reed injects another figure. This young man from 'out Stalbridge way' possesses the great Reedian virtue of silence.

The narrator in fact makes a superfluous observation that he is '*quiet*, as anyone would tell you', for we hear him uttering only one word, 'Yes', as he joins the bidding at two thousand shillings. He is an outsider in two ways. He is 'not from round here in any case', says the narrator, nor is he adapted to the high-powered world of London art dealers. Shortly before the young man is forced to drop out of the bidding, Reed gives us the most ambitious attempt in all of his work to interlace voices. It nearly works. In the 'tightening atmosphere' (there had once been 'smiling', 'silence', and 'laughter in that place') the 'grey voice and the golden contrapuntally compete' (Stallworthy xxi):

> *Naked upon the sunwarmed earth*
> Pauses were made and eyebrows raised,
> Answered at last by further nods,
> *Ardent to yield* the nods resumed
> *Venus upon the sunwarmed* nods
> *Abandoned Cupids danced* and nodded . . . (72)

Perhaps my expectations are too high, but especially with the rather arbitrary and unhelpful punctuation, most of the passage's syntax does not quite succeed, whether we look at each voice separately or take them together. '*Venus upon the sunwarmed* nods', for example; what does that mean? The last four lines do cleverly mesh the voices:

> *His mouth towards her* bid four thousand
> Four thousand, any advance upon,
> *And still beyond* four thousand fifty
> *Unrolled towards the* nodding *sun*. (72)

Here Reed's unique lines exquisitely conflate the nodding heads of the bidders and the nodding sun (as it droops towards dusk) and acknowledge the irony of the mouth as an instrument of both passion and business.

The poem's dénouement is then 'seen, and very quickly' (72) as the young man, who has been observed to blanch and sweat, fails to respond when the bids exceed two hundred pounds. Sad ironies accrue as all three bidders are seen to have lost in some way. Ironically, the only triumph, a mean-spirited one, is in the aspect of the 'man in grey', the Londoner who does not take home the Mars and Venus. Anyone 'practised to read the human face/ Might on his losing mouth descry/ What could no doubt be termed a smile' (72-73), for he has presumably left his competitor with a white elephant, a 'number' he neither understands nor, apparently, can afford. The Stalbridge farmer, the reader has been led to believe, is the one who can most appreciate the painting; he is sighted by a young girl an hour later and, in the Biblical language Reed employed more and more in the later poetry, his narrator leaves us with a vision not unlike that of Peter after his denial of Jesus, a young man trudging

> . . . through the soaking grass,
> Crying. That was what she said.
>
> Bitterly, she later added.
>
> Crying bitterly, she said. (73)

'The Auction Sale' is peopled by some of the poet's most original characters, yet there is still much of Henry Reed himself in the way the poem 'juxtaposes hard cash and high art' (Savage 171) and, of course, in the figure of the sensitive hero. Although 'The Interval' and 'The River' both draw from Greek myth and literature, they too can be seen as indirect autobiography, in the same way that John Lehmann saw 'Chrysothemis' and 'Philoctetes' as parables of artists who cannot find their place in a world uncongenial to their sensibilities. Regardless of whether readers choose to consider that level of meaning, 'The Interval' and 'The River' (published in 1969 and 1970, just a year or two removed from Reed's experience in Seattle, the last 'Great Good

Place' he would ever know) present haunting images of wanderers and exiles.

The principal figures of each poem have made a grim peace with their condition, indeed even seek it out. 'The River' is spoken from the point of view of one who has attained the highly qualified peace of Hades and directed to one who still wanders on the other side of Acheron, 'the black, slow river'. In 'this dark place' the speaker yearns 'for one yet darker'. He desires an isolation even more profound than the isolation of the damned, bending 'in a separate silence' from his fellows, praying to be the one chosen to conduct his beloved over. 'Oedipus cried for his exile', says the speaker of 'The Interval'. Much as Reed seemed at times to revel in his differentness and suffering, his detachment from the conventional relationships, politics, and economics of the bourgeois world, Oedipus, because the order is not immediately given for his banishment, chooses 'to sleep on a bed of stone,/ Unpillowed, and never indoors'. Perhaps there is a hint of the autobiographical, the notion of forbidden love, as Oedipus is wrenched from a dream by his own voice, 'cleaving/ The remnants of sleep, saying: *Love is love,/ Whoever has felt it, for whom. . .* '. Deprived of the power of tears, Oedipus 'learned to weep elsewhere a grotesque new weeping/ That cut like salted swords'. In 'a deeper dream' the image and voice of the dying Laios shame him 'beyond reach of tears'. Cruelly, after Oedipus has become accustomed to the voices of his sons and daughters, when 'the sun and the air around [him]/ And [his] wish for exile vanished', the guards at his shoulder relay God's message:

> *. . . The roads are empty, the ways of the desert*
> *Should be cruel enough by now. On the cooling winds from Athens,*
> *The eagles are wintrily swinging, and the caves will offer no solace.*
> *It is time, oh men. I am ready. You may open the gates for him now.*

Several other poems more directly than these seem to deal with Reed's lifelong yearning to find that place where he could feel needed, appreciated, and loved. In that 'house of peace', such as was denied Giacomo Leopardi as it had been his Italian literary forebears, Reed had always felt himself to be 'The Intruder'. The speaker of the manuscript poem of that name mounts a 'sunlit hill' but it is, as he says to his companion, 'Your hill, and almost mine. . . '. The Reed figure speaks rapturously of the sea, with

> . . . porpoises leaping over
> And deeply the red reefs under
> With their green scarves sombrely always
> Swaying in the long blue swell . . .

but again, he confesses, 'that sea [is] yours, not mine'. Even Reed's ever-faithful Verona, addressed in the title poem of his first collection and as 'my darling' in 'The Town Itself', rejects him. In this poem published in 1974, the 'courteous banners of welcome have been folded away', but worse is the chilling prospect of unstable governments, of capriciously shifting allegiances, of revolutions which may render obsolete one's papers which were valid just the day before. The atmosphere of the poem is like that of *The Queen and the Rebels*, a pre-absurdist play of Ugo Betti, translated by Reed and published in 1956. In Betti's play, menace is in the air always, but from what quarter no one can be sure: characters refer vaguely to 'the trouble', kangaroo courts are convened, authorizations are required, papers and permits are scrutinized, as are one's religion, one's accent, and one's hands (to see if one is truly a labourer aligned with the Cause). Democracy has subtly crossed over into bureaucracy and then again into totalitarianism and the police-state; this was perhaps the only political issue that consistently interested Reed, from early poems like 'Hiding Beneath the Furze' and on through some of the plays: *Leopardi*, *The Great Desire I Had* and, most notably, *Return to Naples*. In 'The Town Itself' the speaker confesses, 'I am apprehensive . . ./ That my sojourn-permit, before it has expired,/ May yet be taken from me, on some unprepared-for day'. 'I had not known', he continues, 'that the weather' (political climate?) 'could be so variable'. There may be 'strikes', 'martial law' and a 'curfew'. The speaker's greatest fear is that 'on some day, not long to be postponed,/ The police will knock at the door, and I shall be told to go' (78).

'The Blissful Land' presents the case in more general terms. This poem and 'The Changeling' show the influence of Hardy, setting up the reader almost as skillfully as the master for the devastating irony at the end.[4] Despite some strange and pretentious use of repetition, 'The Blissful Land' proceeds effectively through its agonizing build-up as the speaker, like 'The Intruder', first climbs a 'well-known hill'. He hears behind him 'that beloved rustling smile/ Of tree and bush and flower and flower and bush and tree', confessing later that he has 'come in this last hour to believe that everything/ Inside this land still loved and would love me always'. But the speaker senses something amiss when the elements of this idyllic seaside refuge—'Trees, stone, and broken headland,/ Stone, archway, earth, stone, grass, stone ...'—pause and stare at him. The rejection he faces is even more emphatic than Prufrock's after he has 'squeezed the universe into a ball/ To roll it toward some overwhelming question', only to be greeted with boredom and disdain by a woman, 'settling a pillow by her head'. In Reed's poem, the stone and company assess him, 'choose a spokesman' and ultimately scream 'in rancour, contempt, and disappointment:/ 'It was not *you* that we wanted! How dared you to come here alone?''

Though written in third person, 'The Changeling' is probably Reed's most directly personal poem. Reed adopts an even more rigorous form than he would for 'The Auction Sale' as a medium for what Stallworthy calls 'a brilliantly condensed autobiography' (xix). In both narrative poems the rhymes are idiosyncratically dispersed, but in 'The Changeling' even shorter, six- and seven-syllable lines present a greater challenge to Reed's clarity and sincerity. The poem as a whole succeeds on both counts.

In the first stanza the young scholar 'turns to the darkening room,/ The garret grate, the books' and asserts that he was switched at birth. In something like the predicament of E. A. Robinson's Miniver Cheevy, he is

> . . . of another age,
> A changeling whisked from the grace
> And the ceremonious kiss
> Of a noble time and place. (63)

Stallworthy sees this stanza as melding the changeling figure, a staple of the fairy-stories told by Reed's mother, with the family legend 'that the Reeds were descended from a bastard son of an eighteenth- or nineteenth-century Earl of Dudley' (xi). A relatively weak second stanza is an allegory of Reed's early graspings at love, and the third tells of 'a still later day' when as a young soldier he sends a silent lament from his post

> Into the still-born day:
> 'My life, my life, my life,
> Beyond the barrack-wall,
> Where are you drifting away?' (64)

From the vicissitudes of low upbringing, failed love, and soldierhood, 'his days at least relent', and he finally and justly returns to his proper home. It is much like that sanctuary Leopardi had hoped for, 'the servants docile and good' (*Monument* 116), and much like Gable Court, the estate he and the much more privileged Michael Ramsbotham had shared until February 1950, one month before 'The Changeling' was published. From 'his scented evening lawn' he looks up and sees not the gloom of the garret nor the gleam of the tawdry street lamp under which he had waited in vain for love: there in his mansion,

. . . proudly set,
. . . the single light burns
In the room where his sweet young wife
Waits in his ancient bed.

Of course, as the Macerata bell had chimed to end Leopardi's transcendent day with Pietro Giordani, a bell tolls for the hero of this poem. Significantly, it is the clock from the lowly stable. Under the 'pale stars' the 'changeling' bitterly concludes: 'All this is false. And I/ Am an interloper here' (64).

In five of the late poems, Reed offers some affirmation (though the affirmation is always equivocal). The door to the mansion may be left slightly ajar; the poet may slide cafe tables inches closer together so that the minds of two people can commune for at least a few beatific moments; one's dreams may not be racked with guilt and pain like those of Oedipus—one may in fact have 'A Good Dream'. Significantly, all five of these poems remained unpublished during Reed's lifetime. Whereas in 'The Changeling', 'The Blissful Land', and 'The Town Itself' the Reed figure remains unwelcome, in 'The Château' he gains at least a highly qualified entry to the house of peace. In the speaker's imaginative vision (the end of which Stallworthy believes 'will stand comparison with the close of "Little Gidding"' [xxii]), his life is being lived 'beyond that great facade'. While he appears to be skulking outside his 'own and veritable door', occupying himself by 'counting the flagstones', he feels certain that inside the great chateau his life is being lived, as it were, without him. Filled with 'gaiety and ardour', that life

. . . dances
Nightly the length of the lighted hall to the starry
  feast,
Stoops in the dawn to the kindly fountain, rests and,
  rested,
Breathes on a single breath its anthem of love and
  praise.

But even the alloyed joy that one is living somehow outside of oneself a full and rich life is too optimistic for Reed. The speaker doubts the presence (or at least the approachability) of 'some great Someone here,/ For whom these pennants hang ...'. Comically, he muses on the assurance such a someone could provide that he is free to cross the threshold into his vicarious life:

> Surely there will be a signal? Inconspicuously,
> One of the giant roses in the gardens around us
> Will perhaps explode on to the autumn grass:
> Something like that, perhaps. I know I shall know the
>   moment.

And as in 'The Changeling', the speaker's protestations inject a tone of desperation. The last section of the poem, though ironically echoing a great psalm of assurance, is introduced by the speaker's fourth attempt to convince himself with the word *surely*. 'And surely (and almost now) it will happen', he avers,

> and tell me
> That now I must rise and with firm footsteps tread
> Across the enormous flagstones, reach, find and know
> My own and veritable door;
> I shall open it, enter, and learn
> That in all this hungry time I have never wanted,
> But have, elsewhere, on milk and honey been fed,
> Have in green pastures somewhere lain, and in the
>   mornings,
> Somewhere beside still waters have
> Mysteriously, ecstatically, been led.

Roger Savage remarked the 'mingled triumph and defeat' (177) which raised a lump in the throat of those who heard the final scene of *The Monument*; he might have said the same of the last stanzas of 'Returning of Issue' (and hence, of *Lessons of the War*). Something like that almost unbearable tension is achieved in the uniquely Reedian ambivalence of these lines from 'The Château'.

Stallworthy speculates that 'A Good Dream', like 'The Château', was composed in the fifties. This little piece's simple charm is a refreshing contrast to the complexity of its contemporary. The dreamer finds himself in a similarly pastoral setting, in which 'a flight of birds from a Roman portico/ Flew out' in a 'park or garden, hilly and green'. And even though 'a duty nagged at [his] forehead', the speaker discovers he is 'free of something' and need not be burdened by the obligation: 'I said, "Why should I go?" or "I need not go".' Any regrets are not expressed by the speaker: 'I forget if I wept as I said it, but if so,/ It was the duty weeping, not I . . . '. As we might expect, a good dream for Reed does not involve winning the lottery or even completing the perfect poem. It is merely a point, as in 'The Changeling', when his days 'relent' and he finds a node in place and time where peace is his.

Such a node is found by the two characters of his unfinished poem, 'The Sound of Horses' Hooves'. At times the poem puts its author in a class of poets Reed himself had deemed unworthy of discussion in his critical essay 'Poetry in War Time'. Its long unmetered lines leave it open to the classification as 'arbitrarily divided prose' which sidesteps 'technical difficulties'; and much of it, like the work of the younger poets Reed dismissed, is 'merely the undirected, casual annotation of daily experiences' (II—'The Younger Poets' 100). Some of the experiences are chronicled as dully as were the 'daily tasks' of the seamen in 'Sailours' Harbor'. But the experience which is not 'daily' is one of two intellectuals at a cafe, at first scouting each other in silence, then discovering they are reading the same book and opening a discussion on the book and its author, on a local production of *Romeo and Juliet*, and on 'the contentment/ Of speaking another language, the charms of another grammar' (152). The poem cross-references 'Four People', with its cafe tables, beach, and 'gentle, eager' young seller of postcards. But whereas that poem laments the failure of two needy people to bond emotionally, this one celebrates the meeting of two kindred souls. Their second topic of discussion is pure Reed. It concerns the hairline distinctions in sound and meaning between *scalpiccìo*, translated by the speaker's friend as 'the sound of horses' hooves, trampling or stamping' and *scalpitìo*, 'the pawing of horses' hooves on the ground'. A typical reader might not share the delight of the characters in such linguistic arcana but may appreciate the ineffable transcendence of one's own such moments. 'Oh, how to express/ The ecstatic peace that began to invade my heart', one might say, 'As you spoke, as you smiled and spoke'. The poem also cross-references Reed's second-to-last published poem, 'Three Words', though not as elegantly as that poem does it juxtapose mysterious oppositions: words and silence; permanence and evanescence. Characteristically, even as the speaker is savouring his node of ecstasy, he is looking anxiously toward another moment one second in the future:

> . . . in my first long look, I had known I could put
>   The thought of all my days and nights around you[.]
> How could you further guess that in a second
>   I could feel all that, and in another second
> Could forget you and lose you forever. (150-51)

'The Future' looks much farther ahead to times when the speaker imagines he has lost his sight and hearing, his passions, and his mind. The poem cannot be accused of avoiding 'technical difficulties': its three-stress lines fall into eight tightly rhymed stanzas. The first establishes the challenging pattern of two trios of rhymes per stanza and introduces a conceit reminiscent of Hardy's 'I Look into My Glass':

> How shall I one day be,
>         Having no longer youth,
> Nor power of ecstasy,
>         Nor passion for truth,
>         Nor even for uncouth
> Pleasures of flesh and sense
>         To drown me utterly?

More so than any other Reed poem, 'The Future' presents an argument, in vivid and memorable language. 'Shall I wander along,/ The streets with eccentric tread', asks the second stanza, 'Muttering a vile song?' Or will I be deaf and blind and 'all my sense reduced/ To fears of heat and cold', a madman

> [r]aving anonymously
> From a broken mind as he
> Menaces the passing whores,
> Like Timon or Lear. (133)

An equally great fear, though, is settling into a comfortable wealth in a 'bedizened living tomb' where there is not even a 'disturbing thought', much less passions or desires. 'Then' introduces the rhetorical conclusion of the last two stanzas as logically as it might in a poem by Donne or Marvell. Undoubtedly Stallworthy was chary of tampering with Reed's manuscript work, but sparse punctuation, in part, leaves the ending ambiguous. Might the 'single profound/ Image', asks the speaker,

> . . . be the good thing
> That teaches me to sing
> And may in the end be that
> Which keeps me sound?

The image may be that of a beloved, but more likely it is the speaker's pessimistic view of the future, like that of Terence in Housman's poem, which keeps him sound.

In another of these poems which peek through a crack in the mansion door, Reed's speaker takes a vow, one that sounds suspiciously aphoristic: 'Never weep'. If Reed had complete say in the poem's remaining in manuscript, again he seems to have misjudged its worth, possibly because of its hint of didacticism, its faintly optimistic conclusion, or that in his view it used the tools of a lyric poet too conventionally. It is written in iambic tetrameter, with quite liberal rhyming and even two instances of triplets, including the ending lines. The speaker recognizes the sententiousness of the vow, so he does not word it; rather, it admonishes him '[i]n sleep, or on the ledge of sleep'. Again, as it is embarrassing to have to articulate such a vow, the seeming paradox of an oath he 'will not take, but shall not break' is easily resolvable. 'You are the only vow I keep', the speaker says twice, 'though the clouds of faithlessness/ Sprawl over the brief, unyielding day'. Lines 19-26 give the reason that the speaker will keep his vow (the full stop ending line twenty-two should probably be read as a comma):

> You are the only vow I keep,
> And still in some untarnished place,
> Like a small echo in my soul,
> As I awake from threatening dreams.
> Are always there, that I may catch,
> Even through days of destined hell,
> The five notes of its distant bell,
> Telling me: 'All may yet be well'.

Again, we see that the vow speaks to him only in that limbo between sleeping and waking. 'The Vow', in sum, is something like *Henry Reed Meets Henry Wadsworth Longfellow*. Reed's 'psalm of life', though similarly written in rhymed tetrameter, includes none of Longfellow's cloying imperatives garnished with exclamation points:

> Be not like dumb, driven cattle!
>         Be a hero in the strife!
>
> . . .
>
> Act—act in the glorious present!
>         Heart within, and God o'er head!

Significantly, too, Reed's bell echoes Eliot's at the end of 'Little Gidding': 'And all shall be well and/ All manner of thing shall be well'. But as the sounds of the *distant* bell waft over the hill, Eliot's confident *shall* becomes Reed's diffident *may*.

Two of Reed's late poems touch resignedly on the frustrations and disappointments of his literary career. 'Three Words' (1970) is unique in its yoking of autobiography and literary autobiography. The three words, 'suddenly', 'forever', and 'silent', having weaved their way through each of the first five stanzas, are brought together and cinched tightly in the autobiographical part of the poem, its final stanza.[5] Kermode probably has this pay-off stanza chiefly in mind in calling the poem 'highly wrought', though he oversteps in crediting it with 'the lexical agility of "Naming of Parts"' (17). As in 'The Sound of Horses' Hooves', the speaker 'suddenly' realizes that, even though his love for another will last 'forever', he has lost that loved one 'forever'. 'And there will be two occasions', he concludes, 'and those not together,/ When you and I will be suddenly silent forever'.

The bulk of the poem, like '*De Arte Poetica*', is concerned with trials of poetic composition. Reed's speaker has days of 'nothing to say, the damnation of nothing to say', but, as in the earlier piece, he is haunted by what he has had to say before. These three favoured words 'would perhaps pursue me forever', he fears, 'Inescapable, watchful, loitering at a steady distance'. And partly because of the 'humiliation' of having relied on them so heavily, he comes to realize he will 'never easily use these words again', perhaps further damning him to wordlessness.

In 'Three Words', Reed has looked back on his body of work twenty years after 'The Changeling' and, ever the self-conscious literary man, compiled his own three-word concordance. Putting aside his recognizably characteristic *silent*, it must be observed that Reed's *suddenly*s and *forever*s do not possess the same dynamism and scope as they might in the lexicon of most writers. *Forever* for Reed does not usually touch on matters of heaven and hell, belief and unbelief,[6] nor, except by way of Leopardi and Melville, any matters of existence and the cosmos; and nothing like 'Suddenly a shot rang out' was in his repertoire. One of his *forever*s is an earthly one, a literary one in fact, much like that in certain Shakespeare sonnets: ' . . . every poem/ That is ever spelt must face the future forever,/ And perhaps forever in silence' (77). The *suddenly*s are almost always intellectual epiphanies, as when the speaker of 'A Good Dream' '[s]uddenly' knows that he does not care about the duty which nags at him. In 'Three Words' he thrice comes to know something 'suddenly'; furthermore, a poem (as a kind of birth, he says) may, like a life, come into being 'suddenly'.

Reed's second poem of literary autobiography addresses allegorically a similar problem of a writer in a rut.[7] The vehicle of '[*L'Envoi*]', a manuscript poem which Stallworthy places in the 1970s or 1980s, is a writer's notebook; the tenor is Reed's literary career though, as with another personal allegory, 'The Changeling', third person is used. The protagonist is told in the first line, 'You must turn over a new leaf'. The last leaves in the notebook, like Reed's output in the late years, are 'thin', already exposing the 'earlier words that a week ago were me'. But even more mortifying would be tearing out the last page to

> . . . show, naked, the pages before
> Which he would most wish to efface,
> To forget even more
> Than this latest, dreadful page, as it seemed to him,
> of disgrace.

Perhaps representing Reed's literary friends, men like John Lehmann, Douglas Cleverdon, and J. R. Ackerley who had always tried to buoy Reed during his personal and literary funks, 'they' enthusiastically suggest that he burn the old book and buy a new one.

But like many of Reed's later poems, this one protests too much. In the next eleven lines we find two instances of the word *glad*, one *gladly*, one *cheerful*, and one *happy* as the speaker's friends all congratulate each other on the impending rebirth of a career, watching the fire 'consume the crowded sheets' and advising the writer, again more times than necessary, to purchase a new book. The Henry Reed figure, always seeing the glass as half-empty, reminds them that the shops are closed on Sundays and, besides, it is 'snowing like hell'. When Monday is suggested, he seems to brighten, adding Tuesday and Wednesday as promising days to get started, but trailing off upon considering that 'Thursday is half-day closing'. A shiver runs through the reader as it does through those in the room as 'some of them guessed/ The last page had been the last and on Friday/ Or possibly Saturday he would be dying'.

Jon Stallworthy chose '[*L'Envoi*]' as the last piece in *Collected Poems*, not based on the probable date of its composition, but rather on its content (164). Stallworthy presumably titled the poem as well, emphasizing its function, like 'Envoy' in 'The Desert' of Reed's first collection, as a summary of what has gone before. The poem's last six lines most resoundingly justify his decisions, showing Reed in characteristic form.[8] The lines are long and uninsistent in both language (the qualifiers *indulgently* and *possibly*) and literary devices. Reed has used paradox effectively earlier in the poem, referring to the book-burning's concomitant effect of keeping out the cold from the 'pitiful, pitiless streets', but these last lines contain no intricate wordplay. The diction is decidedly homely: *possibly*, 'half-day closing', *Monday*, *Tuesday* and four other days of the week.[9] The poet uses a light rein on his metrics, with lines as long as eighteen and twenty-one syllables, tightening to eleven and twelve in the last two lines. The rhymes are gentle and unobtrusive, *guessed* following *rest* by three lines and *dying* completing the poem three lines after *sighing*.

The lines of '[*L'Envoi*]' are characteristic in mood, too. The only smile is given 'indulgently'. The *shiver*, be it physical or emotional, is a staple of numerous Reed pieces, from early lyrics like 'The Forest' and 'The Return' to the 'northern' radio plays like *Pytheas*. Along with the words highlighted by the rhyme are modest, unemphatic, wholly Reedian verbs: *beckoned*, *returned*, *sat down*, *said*, *added*, and *murmured*. Indeed, the key words at the last of the last poem in his last collection make a rather complete concordance of Henry Reed's life and work.

1 'Aubade' is one of a group of modern madrigals set by Sir Arthur Bliss for the Coronation of Elizabeth II in 1953. Much like Yeats, Reed was a liberal who nonetheless harboured a great reverence for the ruling class. A socialist, he seemed to admire the people only in theory: though he did create many characters of the bourgeoisie, the very lowest orders made few appearances in his work or life. Perhaps he envied the 'Sir' that had been conferred upon his friend Bliss and his near-namesake Herbert Read, and that would attach to the name of his acquaintance Laurence Olivier. At any rate, 'Aubade' is exceptional among Reed's poems. As one might expect of such an occasional piece, it is effusive, almost cloying:

> And the first tree, *What is this sound*, he said, . . .
> *It is her day!* came the bright leaves' reply,
> In millions glittering under the singing sky. . . .
>
> May the whole morning of England sing her praise.
> Crown her with light, crown with delight her days.
>
> (Stallworthy 65)

2 He does not seem to have matured as a critic of his own work: though I do not know how aggressively he shopped some of the post-1950 poems that never found print, I can say that the published late poems are not necessarily the best ones.

3 Reed's use of the past tense in describing the painting is striking. It seems counter to his belief in the permanence and reality of art, as expressed in *The Streets of Pompeii* and elsewhere. Present tense would have caused some problems with some of the rhymes, *caressed/breast* and *inclined/twined* for example, but surely a resourceful poet like Reed could have overcome that inconvenience. Perhaps maintaining past tense in narrating both the English and Paduan scenes creates more of a sense of simultaneity and balance.

4 Readers who have come to know Reed's melancholia, like those familiar with Hardy's pessimism, will foresee the inevitable 'exclusion from delight', but its predictability somehow takes away little of its force.

5 It seems that the literary is privileged, for the last stanza is enclosed, almost as an afterthought, in parentheses.

6 One of Reed's rare forays into the territory of religious disputation is a

review in his 'Radio Notes' column, and though the agnosticism which he often took quite seriously is apparent later in the review, the opening is more characteristically flippant: 'The long-awaited free discussions on religion were inaugurated last week under the title of "Belief and Unbelief". I hope that Disbelief will not be ignored . . .' (8 November 1947, 368).

7 With syntax only a sergeant's mother could love, Kermode calls '[*L'Envoi*]' a 'resigned, elegantly executed signing-off little allegory' (17).

8 As 'The Vow', 'The Future', and the early sonnets demonstrate, Reed could wrap his verse in tight packages of elegance and wit, but his other best modality was the meandering lines, for example, of 'Outside and In', 'Chrysothemis', and *Lessons of the War*, verse whose seeming laziness is its greatest vigor. Notwithstanding its trace of rhyme, '[*L'Envoi*]' adopts this second modality.

9 Recall Paolina's three-digit numbers set into the verse of *The Unblest*.

# ENVOY

Henry Reed, born on a Sunday in 1914, spent all day Monday as it were in study, in travel and languages, preparing for the grand days of his literary career. On Tuesday, mid-morning, while he was still fresh and full of bright promise, he dashed off his two greatest works, 'Naming of Parts' and 'Judging Distances'. Wednesday followed in the workweek of his life, and it was a busy one. He sat at his modest desk and put much satisfactory work in his OUT box, including *Moby Dick*, and *Pytheas* a half hour later; that afternoon, before retiring to the club for drinks, he finished *The Streets of Pompeii*, some jolly good comedies, and a nice longish poem called 'The Auction Sale'. Thursday before half-day closing, he was able to get in some translations and a few more comedies, but with all the music in his head, he just couldn't get his lyric poems to work out before the noon whistle sounded. That afternoon in all candour was pretty much wasted: a couple of drinks, some adaptations and translations, a couple more drinks.

Despite the hangover, Friday began well with 'Returning of Issue'; but once it was returned, Henry Reed seemed to have little left. In due course of course he realized that as he got older he wasn't getting any younger. So that afternoon he pulled out some old files marked 'Leopardi—translations' and 'Poems from the 50s'. He pencilled through a few words and added some others, but Friday certainly was dragging; it seemed like it was taking fifteen years. There to the west he saw the sun nodding, so he packed up a few things and took one look back at his not yet tidied desk.

He might have raged against the dying of the light, but thinking of someone who had died on Wednesday, he went gentle across the black, slow river.

# Bibliography


## I. Primary Sources

### *A. Radio plays*

*Hilda Tablet and Others: Four Pieces for Radio* (London: British Broadcasting Corporation, 1971).

*A Hedge, Backwards.*

*The Primal Scene, As It Were. . . .*

*The Private Life of Hilda Tablet.*

*A Very Great Man Indeed.*

*Moby Dick: A Play for Radio from Herman Melville's Novel* (London: Jonathan Cape, 1947).

*Pytheas.* Unpublished script. Obtained from BBC Written Archives, Reading, England.

*The Streets of Pompeii and other plays for radio* (London: British Broadcasting Corporation, 1971).

*The Great Desire I Had.*

*Leopardi.*

*Part I: The Unblest.*

*Part II: The Monument.*

*Return to Naples.*

*The Streets of Pompeii.*

*Vincenzo.*

### *B. Critical introductions*

Dedicatory Letter to George D. Painter. In *Hilda Tablet* (London: BBC, 1971) n.p.

Preface. *Moby Dick* (London: Jonathan Cape, 1947) pp. 5-11.

Foreword. *The Streets of Pompeii* (London: BBC, 1970) n.p.

Foreword. *Three Plays by Ugo Betti* (London: Gollancz, 1956) pp. 5-8.

### C. Criticism

'The End of an Impulse'. *New Writing and Daylight* (Summer 1943) pp. 111-23.

*The Novel since 1939* (London: Longmans, 1946).

'Poetry in War Time: II—The Younger Poets'. The *Listener* (25 January 1945) pp. 100-1.

'Towards "The Cocktail Party"'. The *Listener* (10 May 1951) pp. 763-4.

'Towards "The Cocktail Party"' [Part II]. The *Listener* (17 May 1951) pp. 803-4.

### D. Reviews

'Books in General' [Rev. of Billy Budd]. The *New Statesman and Nation* (31 May 1947) p. 397.

'New Novels'. The *New Statesman and Nation* (2 February 1946) pp. 89-90.

'New Novels'. [Rev. of *At Heaven's Gate* among others]. The *New Statesman and Nation* (24 October 1946) p. 570.

'New Poetic Drama'. The *Listener* (16 April 1946) p. 486.

'New Short Stories' [Rev. of Welty's *The Wide Net* among others]. The *New Statesman and Nation* (21 July 1945) pp. 44-5.

[Rev. of Raymond Preston. *'Four Quartets' Rehearsed: A Commentary on T. S. Eliot's Cycle of Poems*.] The *New Statesman and Nation* (15 June 1946) p. 435.

'Radio Notes'.The *New Statesman and Nation* (25 October 1947) p. 329.

'Radio Notes'. The *New Statesman and Nation* (8 November 1947) 368-9.

'Radio Notes'. The *New Statesman and Nation* (6 December 1947) 429-30.

'Radio Notes'. The *New Statesman and Nation* (10 January 1948) 28-9.

'Radio Notes'. The *New Statesman and Nation* [Rev. of *Paradise Lost* production with Dylan Thomas, among others] pp. 449-50.

'Short Stories' [Rev. of Pritchett's *It May Never Happen* among others]. The *New Statesman and Nation* (5 January 1946) p. 12.

'Two Novels' [Rev. of *All Hallow's Eve* among others]. The *New Statesman and Nation* (16 March 1945) p. 160.

### E. Poetry Collections

*Collected Poems*. Ed. and with introd. by Jon Stallworthy (Oxford: Oxford UP, 1991).

*A Map of Verona* (1946. London: Jonathan Cape, 1970).

### F. Correspondence and Miscellaneous

Personal letters to Robert B. Heilman (6 June 1966; 16 June 1966; 1 December 1966; n.d. [1968?]).

Personal letters to Robert and Ruth Heilman (27 August 1966; n.d. [late 1967?]).

Personal letter to Ruth Heilman (24 November 1966).

University of Washington Biography (6 November 1963).

## II. Secondary Sources

Ackerley, J.R. *The Letters of J.R. Ackerley*. Ed. Neville Braybrooke (Chatham: Duckworth, 1975).

Allen, Walter. *As I Walked Down New Grub Street: Memories of a Writing Life* (London: Heinemann, 1981).

Allen, Walter. Personal letters to Robert B. Heilman (6 October 1973; 2 December 1980; 17 April 1981; 18 May 1982; 12 June 1985; 4 January 1986; 18 December 1988).

Allott, Kenneth (ed.). *The Penguin Book of Contemporary Verse* (Harmondsworth and Middlesex: Penguin, 1950).

Bishop, Elizabeth. Personal letter to Wesley Wehr (26 February 1967).

Bliss, Arthur. *As I Remember* (1970. London: Thames Publishing, 1989).

Bowie, Dorothee, and Taylor Bowie. Personal interview (5 August 1993).

Breit, Harvey. 'Verona, Under the Still Lamplight'. The *New York Times Book Review* (28 December 1947) p. 8.

Carey, John. 'The Tribulations of a Man of Letters' [Rev. of *Hilda Tablet* and *The Streets of Pompeii*]. The *Listener* (28 October 1971) pp. 577-8.

*Collected Poems* (review) *Virginia Quarterly Review* (Summer 1992) 101-2.

Condon, Richard A. [On 'Naming of Parts'.] *Explicator Cyclopedia*, Vol. 1, Ed. Charles Child Walcutt and J. Edwin Whitesell. (1966) 244-5.

Coulton, Barbara. *Louis MacNeice in the BBC* (London: Faber and Faber, 1980).

Drakakis, John. Introd. to *British Radio Drama* (Cambridge: Cambridge UP, 1981) pp. 1-36.

Fitzgerald, F. Scott. *The Crack-Up*, Ed. Edmund Wilson (New York: New Directions, 1956).

Fountain, Gary, and Peter Brazeau. *Elizabeth Bishop: An Oral Biography* (Amherst: U of Massachusetts P, 1994).

Gunter, Liz, and Jim Linebarger. 'Tone and Voice in Henry Reed's "Judging Distance [*sic*]"'. *Notes on Contemporary Literature* (March 1988) pp. 9-10.

Hardy, Thomas. *The Dynasts* (1904. New York: Macmillan, 1931).

Heilman, Robert B. Letter to James S. Beggs (9 July 1993).

Heilman, Robert B. Memorandum to Henry Reed. n.d.

Heilman, Robert B. Personal interview (5 August 1993).

Heilman, Robert B. Personal interview (7 August 1993).

Hope-Wallace, Philip. 'Laying a Ghost' [Rev. of *Leopardi* plays], The *Listener* (16 March 1950) p. 492.

Hope-Wallace, Philip. 'Live Whale and Dead Sprats' [Rev. of *Moby Dick*]. The *Listener* (30 January 1947).

Jenk, Alan. 'In Other Men's Shadows' [rev. of *Collected Poems*], *The Independent on Sunday* (3 November 1991) p. 46.

Jennings, Elizabeth. 'Reed, Henry'. In *Contemporary Poets* pp. 1250-4.

Kennedy, X. J. *Literature*, 5th ed. (New York: HarperCollins, 1990).

Kennedy, X. J., and Dorothy Kennedy. Instructor's manual to accompany *Literature*, 5th ed. (New York: HarperCollins, 1990).

Kermode, Frank. 'Part and Pasture [Rev. of *Collected Poems*]', *London Review of Books* (5 December 1991) p. 17.

Klingopulos, G. D. 'Eliot's Heir', *Scrutiny*, XIV (Dec. 1946) 141-5.

Kroupa, Sandra. Personal interview (6 August 1993).

Lass, Abraham H., David Kiremidjian, and Ruth M. Goldstein, *Dictionary of Classical, Biblical, and Literary Allusions* (New York: Facts on File, 1987).

Lehmann, John. *I Am My Brother: Autobiography II* (London: Longmans, 1960).

Leopardi, Giacomo. *Selected Prose and Poetry*, Ed. and trans. Iris Origo and John Heath-Stubbs (New York: Signet, 1966).

Lewis, Peter, ed. *Radio Drama* (New York: Longman, 1981).

MacDonald, Dwight, ed. *Parodies: An Anthology from Chaucer to Beerbohm—and After* (New York: Random House, 1960).

*A Map of Verona* (review) The *Listener* (23 May 1946) p. 690.

*A Map of Verona* (review) Dust jacket of *A Map of Verona* (originally in *Time and Tide*).

Melville, Herman. *Redburn, White-Jacket, and Moby-Dick* (New York: Library of America, 1983).

Millier, Brett C. *Elizabeth Bishop: Life and the Memory of It*. (Berkeley: U of California Press, 1993).

*Moby Dick* (review) *Times Literary Supplement* (6 December 1947) p. 32.

O'Toole, Michael. 'Henry Reed, and what follows the "Naming of Parts."' In *Functions of Style*, Eds. David Birch and Michael O'Toole (London: Pinter, 1988) 12-30.

Painter, George Duncan. *Marcel Proust: A Biography* (1959. London: Penguin, 1977).

Parker, Peter. *Ackerley: A Life of J. R. Ackerley* (London: Constable, 1989).

Pritchett, V. S. 'Balzac and the Human Appetite for Life'. The *Listener* (26 May 1949) pp. 898-9.

Pritchett, V. S. [Rev. of *Moby Dick*]. The *New Statesman and*

*Nation* (31 January 1948) pp. 101-2.

Rago, Henry. [Rev. of *A Map of Verona*]. *The Commonweal* (16 January 1948) pp. 353.

'Reed, Henry'. *Who's Who* (1978[-79]) p. 2036.

'Reed, Henry'. *World Authors*, Ed. John Wakeman (New York: H.W. Wilson, 1975) pp. 1198-9.

Reilly, Catherine W. *English Poetry of the Second World War: A Biobibliography* (London: Mansell, 1986).

Savage, Roger. 'The Radio Plays of Henry Reed'. *British Radio Drama*, Ed. John Drakakis (Cambridge: Cambridge UP, 1981). 158-90.

Scannell, Vernon. *Not Without Glory: Poets of the Second World War* (London: Woburn, 1976).

Shires, Linda M. *British Poetry of the Second World War* (London: Macmillan, 1985).

Stallworthy, Jon. Introduction, *Collected Poems* pp. xi-xxiii.

Stonier, G. W. [Introductory words to winning poems for Contest #585]. The *New Statesman and Nation* (10 May 1941) p. 494.

Strickland, Geoffrey. 'Dumb Insolence?' [Rev. of *Lessons of the War*]' *Encounter* (May 1971) pp. 78-9.

Thomas, Dylan. 'I Am Going to Read Aloud', The *London Magazine* (September 1956) pp. 13-17.

Tolley, A. T. *The Poetry of the Forties* (Manchester: Manchester UP, 1985).

Trewin, J. C. 'Alive and Dead [Rev. of *The Private Life of Hilda Tablet*]'. The *Listener* (3 June 1954) pp. 983-4.

Trewin, J. S. 'Just Imagine It' [Rev. of *The Great Desire I Had*] The *Listener* (30 October 1952) p. 701.

Trewin, J. S. 'Return Journeys' [Rev. of *The Streets of Pompeii*]' The *Listener* (20 March 1952) p. 487.

Wade, David. 'British Radio Drama Since 1960'. In Drakakis, pp. 218-44.

Walker, Roy. 'Overdose'. The *Listener* (27 February 1958) pp. 379-80.

Wehr, Wesley C. Personal interview (5 August 1993).

Wehr, Wesley C. Personal interview (7 August 1993).

## VITA

James S. Beggs completed his undergraduate work at the University of Georgia, majoring in English. His first full-time job was teaching mathematics at one high school in Atlanta, Georgia and coaching gymnastics at another. That experience drove him to graduate school. He received his Master's degree in English from Clemson (SC) University in 1982, then spent three years teaching composition at the University of North Carolina at Charlotte. In 1987, he began his doctoral work in English while in the second of his six years teaching composition and literature at Tennessee Technological University. The doctoral degree was awarded August 1995. He is currently an instructor in the division of Literature and Language Arts at Modesto Junior College in California. His scholarly interests include war poetry, the American 1920s, poetic theory, and the writings of T. Coraghessan Boyle.

# INDEX